Cmdr. Bruce McCandles sifted through the rubble in the shattered pilot house of *San Francisco*. But before he was able to fathom the sudden destruction to the ship and the sudden death of almost all brass on board, destroyers *Harusame* and *Asugumo* veered from their positions in the Japanese column and swiftly closed in on *San Francisco*.

McCandles looked at the wheel now turning erratically left and then right at the whim of the sea. He shifted steering control to Battle Two manual and took the wheel. Then he called Cmdr. Shonland, the damage control officer.

"You're the last surviving senior officer," Shonland explained. "You'll have t con this flagship. In fact, since we've lost all outside communication, the whole column is yours."

Cmdr. Bruce McCandles felt his body grow numb. He stared about the damaged pilot house. Never in a thousand dreams had he seen himself in command of an American ship column in the most bloody surface-to-surface ship engagement since the Battle of Jutland . . . .

# BLOODY FRIDAY OFF GUADALCANAL

### BY LAWRENCE CORTESI

**ZEBRA BOOKS**
**KENSINGTON PUBLISHING CORP.**

ZEBRA BOOKS

are published by

KENSINGTON PUBLISHING CORP.
475 Park Avenue South
New York, N.Y. 10016

# Introduction

Thousands of pages in dozens of books cover the six-month Guadalcanal campaign of World War II that began in August of 1942 and ended in February of 1943. Writers and historians of this campaign have held varied opinions as to which of the many sea and land battles in the struggle represented the turning point in the Solomons. However, all writers agreed on one point: The Solomon Islands were a terrible place to fight a war.

Few people had ever heard of King Solomon's Isles before August of 1942 because the few white men who came here found nothing of value in its hot, steaming, humid climate. Mynah birds, cockatoos, and other squealing fowl populated the tall, gnarled trees in the rain forests. Lizards and a few crocodiles moved through its murky, greenish swamps. A few wild boar scooted about the damp jungle floor and over the stretches of kunai plains where blades of tall grass, stiff and razor sharp, could slice a man's skin like a bolo knife. Hostile Melanesian peoples, living in clusters of odoriferous, primitive huts, represented the only human population. They drank the waters of the streams and rivers, contaminated water saturated with human and animal waste that brought dysentery and typhoid. They ate wild boar, grubs, and wild taro roots that often gave them diarrhea and trichinosis. They suffered from a multiple of fungus infections that left their bodies ugly with actinomycosis or dermatitis. And finally, they fell victim to dengue and malarial fever. The Solomon Islands' native who lived to forty years was fortunate indeed.

The white men who came to the Solomons saw little reason to stay there. The endless square miles of green, insect-infested swamps, the many stretches of sharp kunai grasses, the dense, impenetrable rain forests, and the gnarled, impassable jungle floor made exploration next to impossible. There were no pretty coral beaches, swaying palm trees, and balmy ocean breezes in the Solomons; only hot, stifling air, occasionally broken by heavy rains, especially from November to March when the trade winds blow in moisture continually from the western Pacific.

The mixture of wild kunai plains, flat swamps, winding rivers, and rising jungle to mountainous interiors give these islands a strange, leperous appearance. And indeed, the seemingly lush landscape infests the visitor with tropical ailments and languishing fatigue, in an especially humid climate where the temperature averages in the mid-eighties. The malaria mosquito often delivers the coup de grace; the *anopheles*, breeding in the swamps along the coastal lowlands, saps the strength of men who dare to challenge her abominable terrain.

Finally, the fortune hunters found no gold, no silver, or other precious metals to encourage settlement there.

The waters that surround the countless islands of the Solomons offer little encouragement to sailors. Hidden reefs abound below the surface of the many straits and bays and sounds. Tropical winds turn calm waters into maelstroms within minutes, and shallow waters often wreck a ship without warning.

The Solomon Islands chain, King Solomon's Isles, runs southwestward from Rabaul in two columns for six hundred miles, from latitude 5 degrees to 11 degrees, south of the Equator. The largest island, the violin shaped Bougainville, sits at the top of the chain like a parade leader. The southeasterly column of major islands includes the Shortlands, Vella Lavella, Kolombangara, New Georgia, the Russells, and Guadalcanal. The northeasterly column of major islands includes Choiseul, Santa Isabel, the Floridas, and Malaita. The island of San Cristobal anchors the two rows of islands. An elongated sea channel runs for some four hundred miles between the two columns of islands, beginning below Bougainville and ending northwest of San Cristobal. The Japanese simply called this lengthy, nameless body of water the Solomons Strait; the Americans would reverently call this long channel The Slot, because the Japanese would send their columns of warships, strings of reinforcement convoys, and squadrons of bombers down The Slot to harass the Americans on Guadalcanal.

Guadalcanal, one of the largest of the King Solomon's Isles, is an oval-shaped island some ninety miles long and about forty miles wide. Along its northeast coast numerous small rivers zigzag down from the interior Popomanasiu Mountain Range and cut through the long stretches of flat kunai plains to the sea. The level plains run inland to rising ridges and then into jungle rain forests that slope upward into the mountain range cutting through the center of the island. Larva-ridden swamps intersperse the terrain and numerous ravines lie between the lowlands and the mountains. Some of the coastal kunai plains sprout out of marshes, but others, like the plains at Cape Esperance, Lunga Point, Kili Point, and Taivu, sit on hard, sandy surfaces. In these areas, bulldozers could scrape out roads, campsites—and airfields.

The first white visitors came to the Solomons in 1567 when Spanish explorer Don Alvare Mendana landed there from Peru. He had been told that the island chain was King Solomon's

"Ophir," that unknown land that held riches in gold. Mendana found only hostile natives, treacherous reefs, and repugnant terrain. He left the islands, which he disparagingly called King Solomon's Isles, with less than half his crew and only one of his two ships. In 1767, two centuries later, French explorer Sieur de Bougainville reached the Solomons. He explored Guadalcanal and Bougainville, which he named after himself, but dengue fever and malaria claimed half his sailors. He left the islands in disgust, never to return. In 1778, an English naval officer, Lt. James Shortland, surveyed the Solomons, naming the island group south of Bougainville after himself. But he too failed to find King Solomon's "Ophir," so he also abandoned the sinister islands.

The English came back in the early nineteenth century to abduct Melanesians for slave labor on the sugar plantations in Queensland, Australia. However, the sly, will-of-the-wisp natives soon learned to escape into the jungle to avoid capture, or they drove off the slave seeking "Blackbirders" with ambush attacks from the dense forest.

In the late nineteenth century Germany acquired the Solomons along with the islands of the Bismarck Archipelago. After World War I, the Commonwealth of Australia took over the islands. They sent missionaries and settlers into the islands, establishing a colonial capital at Tulagi in the Florida Islands, starting coconut plantations, and building a palm leaf cathedral.

On Guadalcanal, they built another mission, more plantations, and a trading station. But most of the profit seekers and missionaries who arrived full of hope left a few years later sick with malaria.

The Solomons remained relatively remote until 1942 when Japanese and American troops clashed in and around the inhospitable Florida Islands and Guadalcanal. Dengue fever, fungus, a stifling climate, and heat would agonize the soldiers and sailors of both sides. Between the two jungle battlegrounds of Guadalcanal and the Floridas lay Sealark Channel, a twenty-mile-square area of water. American bluejackets would soon call this channel Ironbottom Sound, for nowhere in the seven seas would anyone see an ocean graveyard with the bones of so many men and ships. In the space of four months, the Americans and Japanese would engage in seven major naval battles that often included surface warships and aircraft. Hundreds of sailors and dozens of ships would end up on the bottom of Ironbottom. The first naval battle, the battle off Savo Island on 9 August 1942, ended in a disastrous American defeat. The last naval battle in Ironbottom, the battle off Rennell Island on 30 January 1943, ended in disaster for the Japanese.

The most vicious of all these sea battles in Ironbottom was the clash on the night of 12–13 November that broke the stalemate of the Guadalcanal campaign.

L. Cortesi

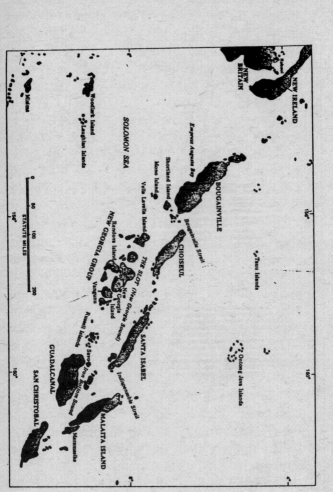

*The Solomon Islands*

NEW BRITAIN

NEW IRELAND

SOLOMON SEA

Woodlark Island

Laughlin Islands

Misima

Empress Augusta Bay

BOUGAINVILLE

Shortland Island

Mono Island

Vella Lavella Island

NEW GEORGIA GROUP

Rendova Island

New Georgia Island

Vangunu

THE SLOT (New Georgia Sound)

CHOISEUL

Bougainville Strait

Tauu Islands

Ontong Java Islands

SANTA ISABEL

Russell Islands

Savo

Iron Bottom Sound

Indispensable Strait

GUADALCANAL

SAN CHRISTOBAL

MALAITA ISLAND

Maramasike

0    50    100    200

STATUTE MILES

150°    156°    160°

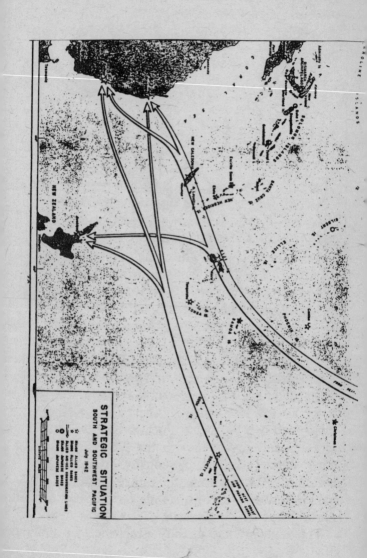

STRATEGIC SITUATION
SOUTH AND SOUTHWEST PACIFIC
July 1942

# Chapter One

In the Battle of the Coral Sea on 7 May 1942, Allied naval units thwarted a Japanese attempt to invade Port Moresby, New Guinea to gain a springboard for the invasion of Australia. When the Japanese lost the carrier *Shoho*, they withdrew their invasion fleet to Rabaul, the Japanese stronghold on the island of New Britain. Gen. Hitoshi Imamura, commander of Japan's Eighth Area Forces, then decided to move south through the Solomons. Such bases could give him two advantages. First of all he would be much closer to Port Moresby for land and sea incursions against this Allied base in New Guinea. Secondly, with airfields and naval bases in the Solomons, he could harass the supply convoys that came across the Pacific from the United States and passed through the Fiji Islands on the way to Australia and New Zealand.

The Japanese had already established an air

and sea base at Buin, Bougainville, in the upper Solomons, 300 miles southeast of Rabaul. In May of 1942, after Japanese air strikes forced the Australians to abandon Guadalcanal and Tulagi, the Third Kuri Landing Force disembarked from minesweeper *Okineshima* and occupied Tulagi. There, the Japanese immediately built a seaplane base.

At about the same time, the Allies occupied the island of Espiritu Sancto, 560 miles southeast of Tulagi. Here, the Allies built a long range bomber base. The Allies also occupied New Caledonia, 800 miles south of Tulagi, and established a naval base. Both operations were designed to protect the convoy routes from the United States to the Southwest Pacific. Adm. Chester Nimitz, the American CINCPAC,[1] appointed Vice Adm. Robert Ghormley as COMSOPAC[2], stationed at Noumea, New Caledonia. Ghormley's forces included the First Marine Division, two other combat battalions, a naval fleet that included the carriers USS *Wasp*, USS *Enterprise*, and USS *Saratoga*, and the Eleventh Bomb Group of Flying Fortresses at Espiritu Sancto.

General Imamura responded to the Allied occupation of Espiritu Sancto and New Caledonia by turning to Guadalcanal. He sent a construction battalion to Lunga Point at Guadalcanal to build an airfield. On 19 June 1942, coastwatchers in the Solomons reported

1. Commander in Chief Pacific
2. Commander of South Pacific

this airfield construction to COMSOPAC. The Japanese had already built wharves, light bridges, machine shops, camp buildings, and hangars. They had begun leveling a 3,600 foot runway. The coastwatchers' reports rattled Admiral Ghormley and he saw no choice but to invade Guadalcanal to stop the Japanese threat to the Allied supply line from the United States.

Like the explorers of earlier times, neither General Imamura nor Admiral Ghormley wanted any part of the Solomons. But, the abortive attempt to invade Port Morseby, the increasing American supply convoys to the Southwest Pacific, the building of an airfield on Guadalcanal, and the Allied occupation of the Fijis hastened a confrontation between the Americans and the Japanese on King Solomon's Isles.

Ghormley met with his COMSOPAC staff and they planned Operation Watchtower, the invasion of Tulagi and Guadalcanal. Ghormley formed Task Force Sixty-one, appointing Adm. Richmond Turner to lead the amphibious landing convoys and Gen. Alex Vandegrift to lead the invasion troops, the First Marine Division. Adm. Frank Fletcher commanded the supporting American warships that included the carriers *Wasp, Saratoga*, and *Enterprise*. The invasion fleet left Espiritu Sancto on 22 July 1942 for the 550-mile sail to Guadalcanal.

At 0200 hours, 7 August, Task Force Sixty-one entered Sealark Channel, which the

Americans would soon call Ironbottom Sound. Just before dawn, Eleventh Bomb Group B-17s softened the targets with several bombing raids. At 0800, the Second Marine Regiment landed at Tulagi where 500 Japanese troops resisted fanatically to almost the last man. Only three soldiers survived and surrendered. The Fifth Marine Regiment along with the First Defense Battalion and Third Pioneer Battalion landed on Guadalcanal. They met no opposition and they moved swiftly along the Tenaru River. By nightfall, they had advanced 3600 yards inland and established a defense perimeter. The next day, the marines crossed Alligator River and swarmed across the kunai coastal plains to occupy the unfinished Japanese airfield. The marines took a few prisoners, Japanese construction workers, and Korean laborers. A few Japanese fled into the Popomanasiu hills.

The Japanese responded to these American invasions with an air strike by twenty-four Betty bombers from Rabaul, with Zero escorts from Buin, on the afternoon of 7 August. However, American carrier planes shot down fourteen of the Japanese aircraft and drove off the rest before the enemy planes did much damage.

General Imamura now consulted with Adm. Isoroku Yamamoto, the overall commander of the Japanese Combined Fleet in the Pacific. From his headquarters at Truk, 1100 miles north of Guadalcanal, Yamamoto agreed to send the Japanese Eighth Fleet out of Rabaul to strike back at the Americans.

General Gunichi Mikawa, the Eighth Fleet commander, sortied from Rabaul with seven cruisers and one destroyer at 1115 hours, on 7 August, carrying his flag on the cruiser *Chokai*. Mikawa also took along the transport *Meiyo Maru* that carried the 229th Jungle Battalion, who would strike back at the Guadalcanal invaders.

Despite several sightings by American search planes, Mikawa came down The Slot unmolested. In fact, Admiral Fletcher had already retired his carriers to the south to refuel. At about 2200 hours, on 8 August, a scout plane reported the Japanese fleet clearing the Russell Islands. Admiral Turner hastily withdrew his supply freighters even though they were only half unloaded. At 0043 on 9 August, Mikawa's lookouts sighted an American destroyer and gave an alarm. At 0133 hours, Japanese star shells blossomed over the six Allied destroyers and six cruisers protecting the Lunga Point landing site. Moments later, the Japanese opened fire, using adept night tactics and long lance torpedoes.

By 0215 hours, Mikawa's gunners had sunk or severely damaged the cruisers RAN *Canberra*, RAN *Astoria*, USS *Quincy*, USS *Vincennes*, and destroyer USS *Bagley*. Still, because an American submarine sank transport *Meiyo Maru*, Admiral Mikawa failed to follow up this smashing victory in the Battle of Savo Island with a bombardment of the American

Guadalcanal beachhead.

Yet, the Savo Island disaster left Gen. Alex Vandegrift and his marines on Tulagi and Guadalcanal with no air cover, no sea cover, no five-inch coastal guns, or airfield construction equipment (still aboard the withdrawn freighters).

"They left us bare-assed," Vandegrift said later.

The marine commander expected a Japanese counter invasion at any hour and he quickly set up a five-mile defense perimeter from the Tenaru River to Kokum on Lunga Point. The perimeter encompassed the two-mile-by-one-mile spread of kunai plain that included the un-finished runway, buildings, and Japanese roads. Vandegrift used 37mm halftrack and 37mm field pieces along with captured Japanese three-inch guns to bolster the perimeter.

Meanwhile, on the wide kunai plain, the First Marine Engineer Battalion worked feverishly on the airbase. Lacking their own equipment, they used captured enemy 'dozers to scrape away razor sharp kunai grass. They used abandoned Japanese trucks to haul fill to the airstrip, and they used Japanese rollers to tamp down the fill to smooth the runway. By 12 August, the first plane, a navy Catalina, landed on the hastily built 2600-by-160-foot runway. Vandegrift himself greeted the pilot and told him they had called this new base Henderson Field, in honor of a marine hero at the Battle of Midway. The next day, 13 August, nineteen Wildcat fighters and twelve Dauntless dive bombers of the Marine 223rd and 232d Squadrons arrived at Henderson from the jeep carrier USS *Long Island*.

At Rabaul, Gen. Hitoshi Imamura now ordered the crack Twenty-eighth Infantry Battalion along with supporting engineer companies to depart for Guadalcanal. Col. Kiyone Ichiki commanded this force, which Imamura believed could oust the two thousand-odd marines he believed were on the island (instead of the actual ten thousand).

After consultation with Imamura, Adm. Isoroku Yamamoto established the Guadalcanal Reinforcement Group, an amphibious fleet to bring men and supplies to the Solomons. Yamamoto named Adm. Raizo Tanaka, a man quiet in speech and calm in disposition, to command this amphibious unit. Tanaka had learned well the art of avoiding the enemy and thwarting air attacks to deliver men to destinations in either transports or destroyers. He had a high respect from both his sailors and the soldier charges, for he would disrupt any schedule or accept any danger to rescue survivors from sinking ships. Raizo Tanaka welcomed this assignment, but he did not like the idea of making piecemeal commitments of troops and supplies, a strategy that eventually proved fatal in the Pacific war.

"We were flushed with victories and we never imagined we could lose," Admiral

Tanaka told Interrogator Roger Pineau after the war. "We had victory disease; a blind arrogance, supreme confidence, and utter contempt for the enemy. My superiors were certain that single battalions and a few guns would easily dislodge the enemy from Guadalcanal. In the end, this tactic of piecemeal reinforcements led to tragic consequences."

The thin, narrow faced Tanaka left Rabaul on 15 August with Colonel Ichiki and 900 soldiers aboard nine destroyers. Two maru transports carried the 250 artillerymen and engineers. Tanaka planned to come down The Slot from Rabaul to arrive at Guadalcanal after dark. He successfully discharged the men and supplies and retired his ships back up The Slot before American surface ships or air units could respond during daylight. The 15 August mission became the first of many such nighttime missions, and the Americans referred to this Japanese strategy as the Tokyo Express. Time after time, Tanaka would thwart U.S. air and sea units with his cunning Tokyo Express runs, and the Americans soon referred to this sly Guadalcanal reinforcement group commander as "Tanaka the Tenacious."

At about 0100 hours, on 20 August, Col. Kiyone Ichiki sent probes to the Tenaru River. Then, at 0310, Ichiki's troops came out of the jungle forests in a screaming banzai charge, splashing over the Tenaru River, sparkling from a full moon. They came like black phantoms, but the First Marines greeted the attackers with machine gun fire, rifle fire, and pointblank 37mm artillery. The withering barrage pulverized the onrushing Japanese in this Battle of the Tenaru River. Over a hundred of the attackers soon lay dead or wounded on the river's banks. The fallen soldiers looked like scattered gray rocks on the mud. Twice more the Ichiki Regiment tried to break through the marine perimeter across the Tenaru and twice more the U.S. Marines threw them back.

The next morning, Wildcats and Dauntlesses raked the patch of jungle west of the Tenaru with bombs and strafing fire. By dusk of 21 August, 800 of Ichiki's troops were dead. The colonel and a handful of survivors reached Taivu where Kiyone burned the regimental colors and then committed suicide.

Despite the destruction of the Ichiki Force, the Japanese JCS decided to send another piecemeal force to Guadalcanal. This time fifteen hundred troops of the Fifth Yokosuka Landing Force and the Second Echelon of the Ichiki Department boarded four patrol boats and the auxiliary cruiser *Kinryu Maru*. A war fleet under Adm. Nobutake Kondo escorted Tanaka's reinforcement group. The enemy flotilla was sighted in The Slot about 250 miles from Guadalcanal at 0905 hours on 24 August. Adm. Frank Fletcher immediately launched planes from his Task Force Eleven that lay about 150 miles southeast of Guadalcanal. The American planes sank two of Kondo's cruisers and the carrier *Ryuju* while severely damaging several other warships. Japanese planes, in turn, failed to sink a single American vessel in this Battle of the Eastern Solomons. a miniature replay of the Battle of Midway.

Despite the disaster of Kondo's warships, Tanaka the Tenacious continued towards Guadalcanal until he was ordered back to Bougainville. Three days later, in the dead of night, Tanaka barreled down The Slot in another Tokyo Express and landed his fifteen hundred men from nine destroyers. With his nighttime landing success, Tanaka intensified his Tokyo Express. Between 30 August and 6 September he landed some thirty-two hundred men of the Twenty-fourth Infantry Division under Gen. Kiyotake Kawaguchi.

Meanwhile, during daylight hours and protected by carrier planes, Adm. Richard Turner successfully brought to Guadalcanal his own piecemeal reinforcements of U.S. forces: the First Paratroop Battalion and the Seventh Raider Battalion. These new units, under Col. Merrit Edson immediately dug in along the inland ridges bordering Henderson Field. There, they waited for a Japanese attack out of the jungle.

At about 2100 hours, on 13 September, Japanese float planes dropped flares over the ridge, and moments later a destroyer shelled Henderson Field. Then, at 2130 hours, two battalions of General Kawaguchi's infantry charged into the ridge. The Japanese pushed back the marines, but they rallied and pushed the enemy back into the jungle. By dawn, hordes of dead from both sides lay along the bloody ridge. On the night of the fourteenth the Japanese attacked again, but once more marines beat them back with pointblank artillery and tank fire.

On 15 September, Vandegrift sent the newly arrived Fifth U.S. Defense Battalion southwest of Henderson to search and destroy any remnants of Kawaguchi's Twenty-fourth Division. The marines found them along the Matanikau River and fought the Japanese in several sharp skirmishes. As the Japanese retreated, marine artillery fire raked the patch of jungle, killing dozens of Twenty-fourth Infantry troops. The Japanese scurried out of the jungle to escape the artillery barrage and tried to cross the river, but the American marines cut them to pieces on the Matanikau River bank.

The Japanese lost 700 men according to a captured diary, while the U.S. marines lost 125.

General Kawaguchi returned to Rabaul to explain his defeat, while General Vandegrift returned to New Caledonia to explain why he could not follow up his victory at the Matanikau River. Both men offered similar reasons.

Admiral Tanaka had done a good job, General Kawaguchi admitted, but his Tokyo Express runs had only enabled The Tenacious to bring in limited men and supplies. Tanaka only came down the Solomon Strait at night in order to avoid American aircraft from Henderson Field, U.S. carriers, or Espiritu Sancto during daylight hours. The Battle of the Eastern Solomons had shown that Japanese surface ships could not operate around Sealark Channel during the day.

General Vandegrift gave Admiral Ghormley a similar tale. Admiral Turner had done a good job in bringing in men and supplies, Vandegrift acknowledged, but he brought them in dribbles and only during daylight when air cover over Ghormley's transports could protect them against Japanese surface ships. The dark hours belong to the Japanese as evidenced by the Battle of Savo Island. Since that naval defeat in Ironbottom, the Japanese had confidently sent their warships into Sealark Channel at night to bombard Henderson Field and marine defense perimeters. Tanaka the Tenacious, meanwhile, had brazenly come down The Slot about twice a week at night to discharge men and supplies on Guadalcanal.

General Kawaguchi and General Vandegrift essentially agreed—only a massive reinforcement of troops and supplies, of at least division strength, could break the Guadalcanal stalemate. Yet, both Tanaka and Turner said they could not unload a full division of men and supplies during the twelve hours of darkness or the twelve hours of daylight. They would need at least twenty-four to thirty-six hours. But, how could Tanaka avoid the deadly American dive and torpedo bombers during the day, and how could Turner avoid the accurate

Japanese warship guns and long lance torpedoes during the night?

Since August, in addition to the major Savo Island and Eastern Solomons battles, both sides had engaged in minor battles: Japanese destroyers and cruisers bombarding Henderson, American planes attacking warships or transports, or a few destroyer and submarine attacks. None of these battles had been decisive.

By mid-October, Admiral Nimitz, CINCPAC chief, had received heavy criticism from Washington for the Guadalcanal stalemate. Nimitz reacted by relieving Admiral Ghormley as COMSOPAC, citing Ghormley's alleged failure to inspire his men in the Solomons campaign. Thus, Nimitz had acted as many baseball owners: fire the manager when the team cannot perform against tough opposition.

Nimitz appointed Adm. Bill Halsey to head up COMSOPAC. Halsey, after listening to Admiral Turner, agreed that the major problem in the Solomons was the lack of heavy reinforcements in one major landing.

Thus, both Halsey in New Caledonia and Admiral Yamamoto in Truk explored ways to discharge a fully equipped division of men and supplies on Guadalcanal. Halsey deplored the need to confine American amphibious reinforcements to daylight hours and Yamamoto disliked the few witching hours for Tokyo Express runs. But how could they change this routine? The hope came for both commanders in two naval battles that convinced both men they could send massive reinforcements into Guadalcanal during the day as well as at night.

In mid-October, Admiral Turner made another of his many runs to disembark troops and supplies at Guadalcanal, with four cruisers and six destroyers screening the transports. Because of storm conditions, the transports did not arrive at Guadalcanal until midnight. Turner unloaded his men and supplies uneasily, hoping to get through the night without interruption from Japanese naval vessels. At about 0100 hours, however, a Japanese flotilla of two cruisers and eight destroyers steamed into Ironbottom Sound.

In the ensuing engagement, the battle off Cape Esperance, the U.S. fleet sank the Japanese cruiser *Furutaka* and three destroyers. The Americans also damaged three destroyers and one cruiser. The Americans only lost the destroyer USS *Duncan*. The Japanese fleet was forced to retire and 2837 troops of the U.S. 164th Infantry, along with 10,000 tons of supplies, went ashore unmolested. Turner attributed this first nighttime naval victory in Ironbottom Sound to new radar equipment on the U.S. warships and the increased experience of U.S. sailors.

But, on 26 October, only a few days later, Admiral Yamamoto sent Tanaka the Tenacious down The Slot with a reinforcement group. Four carriers, *Junyo, Shokaku, Zuikaku*, and *Zuiho*, along with a dozen destroyers, escorted

Tanaka. The American carriers, *Enterprise* and *Hornet*, screened by six cruisers and twelve destroyers, came up The Slot to meet the Japanese, who hoped to land a new, one-thousand-man regiment of the Twenty-fourth Infantry Division. Heavy seas slowed Tanaka and he found himself off Guadalcanal at daylight.

Soon enough, American carrier planes as well as marine aircraft from Henderson Field attacked the convoy to begin the battle off Santa Cruz Island. The Japanese quickly launched carrier planes of their own and the engagement became another miniature Battle of Midway, where only aircraft participated against surface ships. This time, the Japanese won. They sank carrier *Hornet* and destroyer USS *Porter* with no losses to their own ships. The Japanese airmen chased the rest of the American armada south, allowing Tanaka to discharge his men and supplies at Cape Esperance.

Admiral Yamamoto was elated. "With this victory off Santa Cruz, we have shown that the Americans are not superior to us in daylight fighting. We have the strength to defeat our enemies and we must do so."

Admiral Halsey did not panic over the Santa Cruz Island setback. Despite the loss of *Hornet* and destroyer *Porter*, most of *Hornet*'s aircraft had landed safely on the carrier *Enterprise* or at Henderson Field. Halsey preferred to look at the nighttime victory in mid-October.

"Our victory at Cape Esperance dispelled the

myth that we couldn't defeat the enemy at night," Halsey told his staff at New Caledonia.

Each side thus saw its October victory as an omen to break the stalemate. Yamamoto convinced himself that he could disembark men and supplies during daylight if their aircraft were used wisely as they had been used in the Santa Cruz victory. Conversely, Halsey believed they could operate at night as well as during the day, if his surface ships performed as deftly as they had performed during the battle off Cape Esperance.

At his headquarters in Truk, Adm. Isoroku Yamamoto eyed the combat-honed Thirty-eighth Hiroshima Division scattered in tent encampments throughout the Truk atolls. They were eager for a fight. At his headquarters in Noumea, Adm. Bill Halsey looked at the endless rows of tent quarters where fresh, heavily equipped marine and army units had come in from the United States in recent weeks. The Americans waited not so eagerly to enter the battle.

Four men, heretofore obscure in the Guadalcanal operations, would gain notoriety in an upcoming sea battle that would become the most vicious naval clash of the Pacific war, a sea fight that ironically took place on Friday the thirteenth.

Adm. Hiroaki Abe was a respected naval strategist among the personnel of the Japanese Combined Fleet. The sober-faced, stockily built officer rarely raised his voice. Yet, when he spoke, men listened, for he was one of the most successful warship flotilla commanders in the Japanese Navy. He did have one fault—he was often overly cautious. His decision in this sea battle on Friday the thirteenth would make or break the Japanese efforts on the island of Guadalcanal.

Capt. Tameichi Hara had devoted most of his time in the Ironbottom Sound naval engagements as a destroyer division commander. More than once his Desron 10 had chased U.S. aircraft and submarines from maru transports. And many times his scout destroyers had warned armada commanders of enemy surface fleets long before the Americans knew the Japanese were nearby. Such reports had often given the Japanese the advantage of surprise. Hara was a by-the-book officer, as well as an advocate of fight-to-the-death philosophy that prevailed among many Japanese commanders. He had convinced his sailors to follow him fanatically, even if it meant certain death. His claims during the Friday the thirteenth battle would shock the Japanese naval brass.

Adm. Daniel J. Callaghan, an austere man, had always insisted on perfection among his subordinates. He was a highly religious man who remained aloof from those under him. He had often shown a quiet moodiness which many fellow officers attributed to his distaste for a desk job. He had been on the navy general staff at COMSOPAC in New Caledonia and he had yearned to return to combat command. He would get his chance in the upcoming battle in Ironbottom Sound, but perhaps he should have remained in Noumea, New Caledonia.

Finally, Comdr. Bruce McCandles was a quiet individual. He had been out of Annapolis only six years and he had been in combat only since January of 1942, with all combat service aboard the cruiser USS *San Francisco* as a minor officer. He had accepted his subordinate duties without complaint, but he had often daydreamed of the time when he would command stalwart men of the sea in battle charges against the enemy. He would win such an awesome position much sooner than he thought, for on 13 November 1942 he would assume a responsibility that transcended his wildest dreams. He would make vital decisions and issue quick orders that would decide the fate of the historic Friday the thirteenth brawl.

One of these four men would be dead before the engagement ended. A second would become disillusioned, a third disgraced, and the fourth would win the Congressional Medal of Honor, one of *five* Americans to be so honored before the brawling sea fight ended.

The Japanese called this melee the Third Battle off Savo Island and the Americans called it the Naval Battle off Guadalcanal, but for the sailors of both sides who fought it, it was the most awesome half hour of naval destruction ever known by fighting sailors.

# Chapter Two

The Truk islands include twenty-one scattered atolls, none of which measure more than three or four miles in depth or width. In fact, the entire Truk coral island group extends no more than 30-by-20 miles in length and width. But, an almost perfect ring of shoals surrounds the group, making Truk one of the best anchorages in the Pacific. Thus, the small island group lying almost 110 miles north of Guadalcanal became the most formidable Japanese naval base in the Pacific.

On any given day, at least twenty or thirty Japanese warships, maru transports, or maru freighters lay at anchor in the Udot or Tol lagoons of Truk. Sometimes, an observer might see as many as a hundred vessels anchored in Truk's several anchorages. Also, two large airfields lay at Truk, one on the Udot Atoll and the other on Tol Atoll. Swarms of Mitsubishi fighter planes (Zeros), Aichi dive bombers

(Vals), or Nakajima torpedo bombers (Kates) usually sat along the airstrips or behind coral built revetments. Finally, scattered about the other atolls of Truk were repair shops, supply buildings, harbor facilities, and troop encampments.

Aside from numerous small Polynesian villages, Truk offered only one town of any size, Falabequets, which nestled along the lagoon of Udot Isle, the largest of the Truk group. In Falabequets, out of a large metal building, Adm. Isoroku Yamamoto, supreme commander of the Japanese Combined Fleet in the South Pacific, maintained his headquarters.

The twenty thousand Polynesians, who lived on the Truk islands, housing themselves in grass shacks or in coral igloos, barely raised an eyebrow with the onset of World War II. They had been Japanese subjects since World War I, when the League of Nations wrested the islands from Germany and designated them as Japanese mandates as they had designated other Pacific islands of the Carolines to Japan. For years, Truk natives had seen military construction, warships, aircraft, and combat troops in and around the islands. So, the villagers had paid little attention to events at the start of the Pacific war.

By 1941, in fact, Truk had become the Japanese counterpart of America's naval base at Pearl Harbor. Inevitably then, Truk served as the distribution point for countless tons of military equipment, troops, and hardware that flowed south from Japan in support of the Japanese conquests of the Western Pacific. From Truk, naval commanders planned many of their operations, or staff officers planned ground force, Eleventh Air Fleet, or Eighth Fleet operations that staged out of Rabaul, 700 miles from Guadalcanal.

A plan for a massive reinforcement operation to Guadalcanal seemed too important to leave to subordinates in Rabaul. So, Admiral Yamamoto called a conference at Falabequets to organize this operation. The Japanese commander of the Combined Fleet, with the help of his staff, drew up Operation Seventy-three, a plan to reinforce Guadalcanal with a full division of combat troops, in addition to a massive supply of guns and ammunition.

On the morning of 6 November 1942, admirals and generals funneled over the coral roads that led to Admiral Yamamoto's headquarters. Among the first to arrive at the Combined Fleet headquarters was Adm. Gunichi Mikawa, commander of the Eighth Fleet and the hero of the Battle of Savo Island, and Adm. Junichi Kusaka, commander of the Eleventh Air Fleet in Rabaul.

In the harbors of Udot and Tol sat two aircraft carriers, four battleships, eleven cruisers, thirty destroyers, and eleven maru transports. Yamamoto, besides calling the meeting at Truk, had already worked with Admiral Mikawa to amass at Truk the dozens of ships for Operation Seventy-three. The commander of the Japanese Combined Fleet was leaning over a huge map on a table when, at 0830 hours, Admirals Mikawa and Kusaka stepped into the conference room and bowed before the supreme commander.

"I greet you humbly, Honorable Yamamoto," Vice Admiral Kusaka said.

"I appreciate your presence," Yamamoto answered. "Your aircraft will be important to this operation."

Next, Mikawa stepped forward and bowed. "Good morning, Honorable Admiral."

"Are the vessels prepared?" Yamamoto asked.

"Fully prepared," Mikawa answered.

Yamamoto did not answer. He looked again at the huge map on the table, but then looked up when more officers entered the staff room: Adm. Hiroaki Abe of Raiding Group Two, along with Capt. Tameichi Hara of Desron Ten; Adm. Raizo Tanaka of Reinforcement Group Two, along with his communications officer, Cmdr. Tadashi Yamamoto. Next came Cmdr. Minoru Tokoto of Group D submarine patrol. Finally, Gen. Kiyotake Kawaguchi, commander of the Twenty-fourth Division now on Guadalcanal, and Gen. Tadayoshi Sano, commander of the Thirty-eighth Hiroshima Division, entered the room. Last into the room came Adm. Nobutake Kondo and Capt. Shoji Nishimura of the Main Attack Group.

When the officers were seated about an oblong table, Yamamoto spoke to them.

"Gentlemen, I called this conference for 0900 and all of you have arrived before the appointed time. I thank you. I can assume that each of you has thoroughly read the proposal for Operation Seventy-three and you have prepared yourselves for your part in this vital mission." The admiral leaned back in his chair. "We will first take refreshments and then consider the business of this conference."

Aides served refreshments and the officers sipped tea and munched rice cakes for nearly a half hour. Some of them ad-libbed with each other or extended greetings to fellow officers they had not seen in some time. At 0930 hours, Admiral Yamamoto rose from his chair at the head of the table.

"We will now begin the conference." When those about the table looked up, Yamamoto continued. "Since you have had copies of this operation for some time, you should be familiar with your role in this endeavor. Let us hope that all of us do our part with efficiency and determination. Should any of us fail," the admiral gestured, "we will jeopardize the entire operation."

Admiral Tanaka nodded vigorously, for he above all others understood the disasters that often followed if supporting combat warships or combat aircraft failed to protect his maru transports. Tanaka the Tenacious still remembered the disaster of 24 August when the Eleventh Air Fleet failed to send planes from Buin to intercept American air strikes that had sunk carrier *Ryujo* in the battle off Cape Esperance. Tanaka had been forced to disembark the Fifty-fifth Yososuka Landing Force on Guadalcanal at night via destroyers.

Tanaka also recalled the failure to disembark elements of the Second Division in early October because the Eleventh Air Fleet had not supplied enough aircraft to neutralize American carrier planes that attacked the convoy. In both cases a misinterpretation of orders and poor communications had led to the failures. So, Tanaka liked this face-to-face conference where each commander became fully informed of his part in Operation Seventy-three. Each man would know exactly what he must do, when he must do it, and where he must strike.

"I must insist," Yamamoto continued, "that we have no failures in communications among the various elements of this operation such as we suffered in previous efforts. Operation Seventy-three is clear enough: we must destroy the enemy airfield at Lunga Point and destroy any American surface fleet that might interfere with Admiral Tanaka's mission to disembark the Hiroshima Division." He looked at Mikawa. "Have you planned coordination for this mission?"

"Yes, Honorable Yamamoto," the Eighth Fleet commander answered. "I have held a preliminary conference with Eighth Fleet officers." He rose from his chair and gestured. "My own Support Group Two will bolster Admiral Kondo's Main Attack Group and Admiral Abe's Raiding Group Two. Admiral Abe will bombard the enemy airfield at Guadalcanal at approximately 0100 hours on 13 November. Admiral Kondo will conduct a second bombardment with his cruiser group against this enemy installation just before dawn on 13 November. The two bombardments will render useless the enemy airfield. When Admiral Tanaka begins to disembark the Thirty-eighth Division, he need fear no air attacks from American aircraft."

"Do you agree with this plan?" Yamamoto looked at Admiral Abe.

"Yes, Honorable Yamamoto," Admiral Abe said, rising from his chair. "We know that in the engagement off Santa Cruz Island the American carrier *Enterprise* was badly damaged and the carrier *Hornet* was sunk. The Americans therefore have no carrier planes to harass Admiral Tanaka's Reinforcement Group Two. Thus, if we destroy the enemy airfield at Guadalcanal, there can be no air assaults on the marus. The Honorable Tanaka should have a minimum of thirty-six hours to put ashore the Thirty-eighth Division and its equipment."

Admiral Yamamoto scanned some papers on the table and then looked at Mikawa again. "As we discussed earlier, we cannot discount the possibility that the Americans may send a surface fleet into the Sealark Channel to obstruct Reinforcement Group Two or Main Attack Group. Admiral Mikawa, are you clear on your own responsibility in the event of such a possibility?"

"Should the enemy challenge us with warships," Mikawa said, "I will sortie my own Support Group Two from the Shortlands and attack such an enemy surface fleet with battleship guns and carrier aircraft. Meanwhile, the two bombardment groups will complement each other. While one group bombards the enemy airfield, the other group will remain alert to intercept any American surface fleet that might try to interfere.

"The battleships of Raiding Force Two will carry 500 rounds of fourteen-inch shells, including both armor piercing and the new type Zero incendiary for airfield bombardment. This will provide ample fire power to deal with both enemy surface ships and the target airfield. Admiral Kondo's cruisers will carry about a thousand rounds of eight-inch shells, including both armor piercing and incendiary explosives."

The type Zero shells for 36cm battleship guns and 24cm cruiser guns were designed to destroy enemy runways and parked aircraft. These quick-fused projectiles with thin-skinned casings exploded in a wide, hot shrapnel burst that ignited and destroyed anything within 30 feet. Thus, if only a few hundred of these explosives rained down on the American airfield nothing could escape destruction. After the two anticipated bombardments, coupled with a planned air attack on November 12, Henderson Field would be totally useless.

"I should remind you, Admiral Mikawa," Yamamoto said, "the Americans have shown unusual aggressiveness and accuracy in the engagement off Cape Esperance. They have learned to fight at night; they must not repeat this performance."

"I do not believe they can," Admiral Mikawa said. "The Eighth Fleet is too powerful. Admiral Abe's Raiding Group Two includes battleships *Hiei* and *Kirishima*, heavy cruiser *Nagara*, and eleven destroyers. Admiral Kondo's Main Attack Group includes six excellent cruisers with tested crews and six combat-ready destroyers. My own Support Group Two, the most powerful of these three combat elements, includes carriers *Junyo* and *Hiyo* with nearly a hundred total aircraft, battleships *Kongo* and *Huruna*, and eight veteran destroyers. Finally, Admiral Tanaka will have a screen of eleven destroyers for his eleven maru transports of Reinforcement Group Two. Our ships are ready and our crews are eager."

"Hopefully," Yamamoto said, "if we destroy the enemy airfield we may find no need to commit the carriers." Then he looked at the Eleventh Air Fleet commander. "Admiral Kusaka will furnish us with forty of the new Fujiyama Two night fighter planes (Hamps) that can accurately attack an enemy surface fleet during the darkest nighttime hours. We will also have a heavy complement of aircraft at both Rabaul and Buin for this operation."

Many of those at the table now threw icy stares at Admiral Kusaka, the commander of the Eleventh Air Fleet. Too often during the

Solomons campaign, as in the disaster off Cape Esperance, Kusaka had failed to provide land based air cover to support the Japanese attack groups and the naval reinforcement groups. Admiral Kusaka could not help but notice this coolness and he reacted bitterly.

"I know that many of you in the past have expressed disappointment because the Eleventh Air Fleet did not provide air cover for some vital missions in the Solomon campaign. But," he gestured, "the failure lies in the words of the Honorable Yamamoto himself—a lack of proper communications. Too often, many of you failed to notify us at Rabaul of the need for air support. We were not informed of upcoming operations and we therefore did not prepare ourselves to offer air support. How can you call us in a desperate moment to ask for instant support? Rabaul lies nearly 700 miles from the Sealark Channel (Ironbottom Sound), and we cannot have aircraft over Guadalcanal at once.

"And remember," Kusaka continued, "the facilities at Buin are limited and we keep few aircraft here on a permanent basis. Only if we know well in advance that you require air support will we temporarily overcrowd this airfield. But even Buin lies 350 miles from the Sealark Channel," he gestured curtly, "so we would need at least an hour's notice to come even from Bougainville."

"Admiral Kusaka has a point," Yamamoto said.

"I am grateful for the opportunity to participate in this conference today," Kusaka continued. "I will leave here knowing full well what you expect. I will know that Admiral Abe's raiding force will begin his bombardment at about 0100 hours on 13 November, and I will know that Admiral Kondo will follow up with his own bombardment of the enemy airfield a few hours later. Our night fighters at Buin will be on full alert. I will know that on the evening of 13 November Admiral Tanaka will begin disembarking the Thirty-eighth Hiroshima Division at Cape Esperance so our night fighters will be on the alert again. Yes," Kusaka nodded vigorously, "I will know all these things and our bombers and fighters at Buin will be prepared to cover these operations. By 11 November," Kusaka gestured, "we will have several squadrons of aircraft from the Twenty-sixth Air Flotilla jammed on the Buin airfield. The very capable Capt. Hideo Shoji will command this air flotilla at Bougainville."

"What is the current complement of the Eleventh Air Fleet?" Yamamoto asked.

"Between the Twenty-fifth and Twenty-sixth Flotillas we will have nearly 300 operational aircraft, of which forty are the new Fujiyuma Two night fighters. Fifty Mitsubishi fighter planes and fifty Aichi dive bombers will be deployed at Buin where they can reach the areas of Lunga Point or Cape Esperance in little over an hour."

"It will be the responsibility of all ship commanders to keep the Twenty-sixth Air Flotilla at Buin fully informed of your needs," Admiral Yamamoto said. He then looked at Cmdr. Minoru Yokoto. "Do you understand the mission of the submarines?"

"Fully," Yokoto replied. "The I-boats of Patrol D will be on alert. I-7 will patrol at Santa Cruz, I-20 will be off Savo Island, and my own I-26 will lay off San Cristobal. We will keep the commanders fully informed should any American surface fleet sail up the Solomon Strait or through the Sealark Channel."

"Fine," Yamamoto said. He now looked at General Kawaguchi. "Are you satisfied with these plans?"

"With such reinforcements we can surely win a decisive victory," Kawaguchi said.

"Good," Yamamoto nodded. "I suggest, general, that you leave for Guadalcanal at once by seaplane to prepare encampments for these new troops."

"I will leave as soon as this conference ends," the Twenty-fourth Division leader said.

Yamamoto now looked at the others. "Let us review our plans. The Eighth Fleet will consist of four groups: Raiding Group Two with two battleships, a cruiser, and fourteen destroyers; Main Attack Group with six cruisers and six destroyers: Admiral Mikawa's own Support Group Two of two aircraft carriers, two battleships, and a screen of eight destroyers; Admiral Tanaka's Reinforcement Group Two of eleven destroyers and eleven maru transports. Finally, the Eleventh Air Fleet will furnish 300 aircraft, 140 of them at Buin and the rest at Rabaul. And of course, the submarines will report any American fleet movements.''

Operation Seventy-three would begin on the afternoon of 12 November 1942 when fifty Val dive bombers from Buin and fifty Betty bombers from Rabaul would bomb Henderson Field. The aircraft would then return to Buin or Rabaul and remain on alert to aid surface ships if necessary.

The surface ships themselves would leave Truk as soon as this conference ended, with the I-boats moving at all speed to take up patrol stations in the lower Solomons. Admiral Abe's Raiding Force Two would leave Truk on 8 November and sail directly south through the open sea to enter Sealark Channel between Santa Isabel and the Florida Islands. Admiral Abe should arrive at Lunga Point shortly after midnight during the first hour of 13 November to bombard the enemy airfield. Admiral Abe would then circle Savo Island and return to Truk.

''Meanwhile,'' Yamamoto gestured, ''Admiral Mikawa will sortie the remaining elements of the Eighth Fleet in the Shortlands on 12 November. The Main Attack Group will sail down the Solomon Strait (The Slot) to bombard the enemy airfield shortly before dawn on 13 November, with Admiral Tanaka's Reinforcement Group Two following Main Attack Group to arrive at Cape Esperance on the evening of 13 November to discharge our troops and supplies. Since the two bombardment groups will have destroyed the American airfield by this time," Yamamoto pointed, "Admiral Tanaka should suffer no harassment from American aircraft while he carries out his mission. As soon as the troops are landed, the Thirty-eighth Division will move quickly east from Cape Esperance to attack the American perimeter at the Tenaru River."

"The soldiers of the Thirty-eighth, along with my own Twenty-fourth," General Kawaguchi suddenly spoke, "will be enough. These troops, along with massive artillery support, will easily overwhelm the American positions and overrun the enemy airfield."

When Admiral Yamamoto concluded the review of Operation Seventy-three, he looked about the oblong table. "Is there anyone not clear of his responsibility?"

None.

Yamamoto nodded. He then looked at Admiral Mikawa, the man ultimately responsible for the success of the operation. "Honorable Mikawa, may the Gods aid you in this endeavor."

Mikawa straightened proudly. "We will not fail, Honorable Yamamoto."

"I assure you, admiral," General Tadayoshi Sano suddenly spoke, "the Imperial troops of the Hiroshima Division are eager and faithful, ready to fight with determination and honor against our enemies. They were carefully trained in jungle fighting and they are fully capable of recapturing Guadalcanal.''

Yamamoto nodded and then gestured to an aide. "Bring wine, so that we may drink a toast to our Samurai ancestors and ask that they favor us with success.''

Ironically, neither Adm. Isoroku Yamamoto nor his admirals in the Combined Fleet conference room suspected that the Americans were planning a similar Operation Seventy-three of their own.

On the evening of 8 November 1942, Admiral Abe left Truk with Raiding Force Two. The next afternoon, 9 November, heavy swirls of smoke again spiraled skyward into the bright day, and heavy clanks of rising anchors again echoed across the Udot and Tol lagoons. On the shoreline, service troops watched as sailors scurried about their vessels, preparing to get their ships under way. In less than an hour, the loaded maru troop and supply transports of Reinforcement Group Two glided out of Udot lagoon, their destroyer escorts clinging to their sides as they would cling for nearly 1100 miles to Cape Esperance on the northwest tip of Guadalcanal.

When Reinforcement Group Two had cleared Udot lagoon, the cruisers and destroyers of Admiral Kondo's Main Attack Group slowly plowed out of Tol lagoon. Within an hour the cruisers and destroyers had cleared Truk and turned south.

Next, the destroyer screen of Admiral Mikawa's Support Group Two steamed out of Udot lagoon, followed by *Kongo* and *Huruna*. The big battleships rumbled as they glided forward at five knots and sent heavy swells across the water and into the shoreline. Finally, Mikawa's carriers, *Junyo* and *Hiyo*, wallowing like giant whales in Udot lagoon, followed the battleships. By dusk, when the setting sun covered Truk with an orange hue, *Junyo* and *Hiyo* were underway. Explosive orange sparkles blinked from the folded wings of Vals, Zeros, and Kates that jammed the decks of the two Japanese carriers.

Admiral Yamamoto stood on the shoreline with an aide, Captain T. Ohmae, and watched the last of his warships clear the Truk complex. Then, as the last rays of sun darkened in the west, Yamamoto watched a small launch carry Adm. Junichi Kusaka to a bobbing seaplane that would take the air chief back to Rabaul, as a seaplane had taken Gen. Kiyotake Kawaguchi back to Guadalcanal on 6 November. Yamamoto could not help but think that the success of Operation Seventy-three would depend on Kusaka. If the Eleventh Air Fleet commander did not supply air support with timely accuracy, the operation could be another failure.

When the seaplane and the last of the sixty-seven vessels was gone, Yamamoto squinted into the growing darkness, the sky now in limbo with no blue or daylight and no sparkles of stars. He knew the Eighth Fleet, by this time, had made its 90 degree turn around Udot Island. The chief of the Japanese Combined Fleet, South Pacific, sighed and then turned to Captain Ohmae.

"Perhaps it is time for the evening meal."

"You have done all you could, Honorable Yamamoto," Ohmae answered. "The rest is up to them," he gestured towards the empty sea.

Admiral Yamamoto nodded and walked away from the shoreline with his aide.

# Chapter Three

The island of New Caledonia lies 800 miles south of Guadalcanal. Noumea, Caledonia's principal city, was a crowded, unpainted ramshackle town of seventeen thousand people, part French, part Polynesian, and a few hundred mixed Orientals. But there were consolations amidst the squalor that prevailed throughout most of the town. A sweet springtime fragrance from the niaculi trees that lined the mostly unpaved streets radiated through Noumea. The comfortable temperatures, never rising above 85 degrees, enhanced the invigorating sea breezes that whiffed from the South Pacific across New Caledonia to render cool nights and the absence of the malaria mosquito. And beyond the ramshackle Noumea were cultivated yam and taro fields, indented with coves with dazzling white coral sand beaches, and patches of quaint vales and wood forests.

The French colonials who dominated New Caledonia for nearly a century had expressed mixed views when the Allies seized the island at the onset of World War II under the guise that the island belonged to the Free French, de Gaullist government. Some French residents supported the Allies, but others supported the Vichy government, now supposedly neutral in this global conflict. The Vichyites expressed a distaste for the Allied occupation.

The French governor on the island, a Vichy booster, sulked in his hilltop palace home when the American and Australian military descended on New Caledonia. Grudgingly, but with little choice, the governor conceded a villa to Adm. Richard Ghormley, the COMSOPAC commander. The villa had been the former residence of the Japanese consul.

Other pro-Vichy French administrators and residents had also snubbed the "invaders," cooperating with them only under pressure or threats. But the small businessmen, the barkeeps, the merchants, and the prostitutes had welcomed the influx of sailors and soldiers with plenty of money to spend. The arrival of the Allied military had turned the quaint island into a teeming, restless area where the Yankee dollar increased the supply of wine and women, as well as the price of taxi fares, restaurant food, movie houses, hotel rooms, and prostitutes.

The Anamite laborers of New Caledonia, native Polynesians, could not have cared less whether the Vichy French or the Allied military wielded control over them. The Americans paid them as well or better than the French colonialists. The lives of the natives had not been changed materially. They simply did their work and vanished into their hovels at night, taking their young women with them.

As soon as the Americans arrived, seabees transformed the wooded grounds of the commander in chief's villa into a bureaucratic complex. Quonset huts sprouted like huge silver mushrooms on the grounds to house the senior officers. The seabees also built a long barracks, Havoc Hall, to house the junior officers. Near the waterfront, an old warehouse and an adjoining stable were transformed into the COMSOPAC headquarters. Here, Admiral Ghormley, fifteen staff officers, and fifty bluejacket enlisted men ran the entire South Pacific show. They directed navy, marine, and army personnel; they directed the movement of ships, aircraft, supply, and service. They ran the base hospital, military camps, officers and enlisted men's clubs, and even the units of the army air force.

In the beginning, the U.S. and Australian soliders loved the relative idleness at New Caledonia. When they were not taking drill exercises or working at routine chores, they could usually wheedle passes to spend their time amidst the strings of bars, restaurants, and brothels in Noumea.

With the onset of the Guadalcanal campaign,

however, a tension spread over the military in New Caledonia. Ships and men left Noumea harbor regularly, many never to return. Almost daily, during September and October of 1942, damaged vessels brought wounded and neurotic personnel back from the Solomons war zone to join other haggard marines and sailors in the fleet landing barracks. The bloody fights on Guadalcanal or in Ironbottom Sound (Sealark Channel), had physically injured and mentally tortured hundreds of men.

Each night, the same conversations seemed to prevail in the military camps, the French bars, or, for the more affluent, the Grand Hotel de Pacifique.

"Bill was buried at sea after a Nip shell wiped out the number four turret."

"The sufferin' bastards held off a whole banzai charge, but only a third of 'em were still standing when it was over."

"That poor son of a bitch! When that fourteen-inch shell hit, there wasn't enough of him left to bury in a shoebox."

"Yeh, all 700 guys went down on the Vincennes."

But there were also the occasional happy reunions, "Christ, Harry, you still alive?"

Now, in early November of 1942, amidst the bustling harbor and shoreline activities at Noumea, amidst the apprehensions in the bars and barracks, and amidst the hectic uncertainties in the COMSOPAC headquarters, Adm. Bill Halsey had gone on the sick list with dermatitis, and the navy had wavered between giving him a command or sending him back to a Washington desk job. But in the fall his dermatitis had cleared up and Admiral Nimitz sent Halsey to Noumea to supposedly command a carrier force. However, when he arrived at fleet headquarters on 15 October 1942 and reported to Admiral Ghormley, Halsey found an order from Washington waiting for him.

"You will take command of South Pacific Force (COMSOPAC) immediately."

Halsey had read the order in astonishment. He had heard rumors that Admiral Ghormley had fallen into disfavor with CINCPAC JCS in Hawaii. However, Bill Halsey had no idea he would head up COMSOPAC. He suspected that Admiral Nimitz had used Ghormley as a scapegoat for the problems in the Solomons campaign. Halsey guessed that he too would be expendable if he did not make progress in the campaign. Still, Halsey assumed command, promising himself to do his best.

Halsey had spent most of his time analyzing the action reports in the Solomons and consulting with marine and naval commanders. He agreed with his subordinates: they needed a huge reinforcement of men and supplies on Guadalcanal to break the standoff. But how? The Japanese Combined Fleet, operating out of Truk and Rabaul, had simply outgunned the fleets of the Allied South Pacific Force, especially in night actions. The Japanese had also possessed twice as many aircraft, although

American airmen generally had thrashed their Japanese counterparts in air actions. When Halsey reported this problem to Nimitz, CINC-PAC commander, Nimitz still believed they could succeed in Guadalcanal.

"Not unless we get a massive dose of men and supplies into Guadalcanal," Halsey said, "and we haven't had any success at night."

"We wouldn't want to evacuate the Solomons unless it became absolutely necessary," Nimitz said. "What does Vandegrift say?"

"He says he needs more than piecemeal rein-forcements."

"We'd hate to give up this foothold in the Solomons," Nimitz had repeated. He told Halsey that he had been in conference with the Joint Chiefs of Staff in Washington as well as with the president himself. The president and the military recognized the seriousness of the Guadalcanal fight. They had promised stronger reinforcements for the South Pacific. In fact, in a memo from President Roosevelt to the JCS, Roosevelt had ordered them to send all available men and weapons to the South Pacific, even if it meant reducing commitments elsewhere, save for the upcoming invasion of North Africa. Already on the way, Nimitz had told Halsey, were a battleship, two destroyers, six cruisers, twenty-four submarines, seventy-five navy fighter planes, and fifty-six navy dive bombers. The navy would also send thirty transport ships to the South Pacific by the end of November, with twenty additional 7,000-ton transports by the first of the year.

The army air force had promised the president to send twenty-three heavy bombers and fifty-three fighter planes from Hawaii to meet the emergency in the Solomons, along with the temporary diversion of three heavy bombardment squadrons from Australia to New Caledonia. The aircraft would be here in a few weeks.

Finally, Nimitz had told Halsey, the army had promised to send the Twenty-fifth Army Combat Division to the South Pacific, while the navy would send a marine regimental combat team to join the Solomons ground fighting. These forces should arrive by early December.

Then had come the Cape Esperance victory in which the Americans had won their first night action against the Japanese. "This action proves we can operate around Ironbottom Sound at night," Halsey had elatedly told his aide. "If we can get a massive reinforcement of troops into Guadalcanal we can do more than maintain the status quo. We could win a major land battle. We should have enough reinforcements by the end of December for a decisive victory in the Solomons. We'll need to devise a plan to get massive troop reinforcements into Guadalcanal in one amphibious operation.

"I want to meet with the entire COMSOPAC staff to draw up a plan for this massive reinforcement operation," Halsey said. "If we got a horde of troops ashore on Lunga Point and more aircraft at Henderson and Espiritu Sancto, we'll be in a good position to beat the Japanese at Guadalcanal.''

"That would help, Sir," the aide said.

Thus did Adm. Bill Halsey and his staff at Noumea draw up Operation Orange. On 2 November 1942 Halsey sent copies of this plan to all fleet commanders and ground troop commanders of COMSOPAC. He would muster all available naval vessels into Task Force 67, which in turn would deliver huge ground troops and arms to Guadalcanal. Halsey had an array of surface ships under his command: the carrier *Enterprise*, two battleships, several cruisers, twenty-two destroyers, and several transport ships. This fleet, although much smaller than the fifty-eight Japanese vessels that had left Truk, could be effective with the aid of air support from Henderson Field and Espiritu Sancto.

On 4 November, Halsey held a conference at his villa quarters in Noumea. Few people in Noumea paid any attention to the brass that converged on the villa grounds. Most of the sailors and marines in Noumea, if they were not absorbed in assigned tasks, were absorbed in seeking diversions in the ramshackle town. Nor did the fleet lying at anchor in the harbor arouse much curiosity. The South Pacific Force, far inferior in numbers to the Japanese, used hit-and-run tactics in the Solomons, so the Allied naval vessels usually spent more time in the harbor than they did in the Solomons combat zone. Conversely, the Japanese Combined Fleet, more confident than the Americans, often scattered itself throughout the Solomons, spoiling for a fight. Its warships were more likely to be at sea than in the anchorages at Truk, Rabaul, or the Shortlands.

Admiral Halsey's Operation Orange was a relatively simple plan. Task Force 67 would be split into four groups. The force would include an amphibious force of transport vessels, two cruiser-destroyer warship units, and an attack unit that included the lone carrier *Enterprise*, two battleships, and several cruisers and destroyers as screens. Halsey's plan would depend heavily on aircraft based at Henderson Field and on Espiritu Sancto. Also, a squadron of twelve submarines would support the surface ships.

Operation Orange took into account the possibility that a Japanese armada might destroy Henderson Field in a night bombardment. If such a calamity occured, the operation would be called off.

By 0900 hours on the morning of 4 November 1942, an array of officers had seated themselves about an oval table in Admiral Halsey's staff room: Rear Admiral Turner, who would not only lead the 67.1 transport group, but who would also be the overall operations tactical commander (OTC) of the Orange Operations: Rear Adm. Daniel Callaghan of Task Force 67.4; Rear Adm. Norman Scott of Task Force 62.4; Adm. Thomas Kinkaid of Task Force 16, the carrier group; Adm. Aubrey Fitch who commanded the Cactus Air Force, the land based aircraft at Henderson Field and Espiritu Sancto; Adm. Allan McCann, commander of the Squadron Two submarine group on loan from Australia; and the two marine ground force generals, Alex Vandegrift and Alex Patch.

"Gentlemen," Halsey began, "I realize that some of you are not quite accustomed to me as your commander in chief. Perhaps you're not sure what I expect from you in this painful Solomons campaign. I can assure you, I want the same thing you want—victory. I gave each of you an opportunity to read thoroughly the proposed Operation Orange. In essence, the plan calls for massive ground troop reinforcements to Lunga Point to break the back of the Japanese at Guadalcanal. All of you know Generals Vandegrift and Patch," the admiral gestured to the two marine generals on either side of him. "They can tell you how important this mission will be."

When General Alex Vandegrift rose from his chair, the admirals studied him carefully. He had been known as Mr. Marine, having served in the U.S. Marine Corps since World War I. He had fought in Nicaragua, Vera Cruz, and Haiti when the United States had elected to intervene in the internal squabbles of these Central American countries. By 1933, Vandegrift had risen to assistant chief of staff of the marine coprs, and at the outbreak of World War II, he received command of the First Marine Division that made the initial landings on Guadalcanal and Tulagi. Vandegrift had called his troops a force of rude humanity, trained only for fighting and destruction; a force of tough guys who asked for nothing less than a fight. In the Solomons they had found that fight.

Vandegrift himself, a quiet, unassuming man, had learned his trade in the marine school of hard knocks during the Central American incursions around World War I. Because he would march anywhere with his men, his troops had shown a total loyalty to him. He had often been compared to Stonewall Jackson of Civil War fame, and like that Confederate general who rode at the head of his troops, Vandegrift had personally led his marines in the Solomons Campaign.

To the right of Halsey sat Gen. Alex Patch, the commander of the American Force that was currently fighting the Japanese and hostile terrain of Guadalcanal. For weeks, Patch had complained that reinforcements had come to him in dribbling doses, never enough to overwhelm the enemy.

"We've been in a struggle for almost three months with an enemy that fights tenaciously," General Vandegrift told the assembled admirals. "More than once we considered an evacuation of Guadalcanal. True, we whipped them good at the Tenaru, Bloody Ridge, and at the Matanikau. However, their Tokyo Express keeps bringing more troops. The fight on the island has been touch and go and we need a major operation if we're to conquer Guadalcanal."

"We know you've tried hard," General Patch now spoke. "Without your air and naval support, they might have forced us out of Guadalcanal. Certainly, the arrival of the 155 artillery evened the odds against their long range Pistol Petes. But, we've been unable to chase the Japanese off the island. We need a big infusion of men and arms for a quick, massive assault on the enemy."

"I believe," Vandegrift spoke again, "that Operation Orange will give us the superior forces we need to conduct such an offensive. I therefore ask all of you to support this plan. None of us can feel satisfied with the campaign thus far: the loss of men, planes, supplies, and naval vessels with no apparent progress. The reinforcements included in this plan can score for us a decisive victory."

When Vandegrift reseated himself, Halsey regarded the admirals at the table. "General Vandegrift and General Patch must conduct the day-to-day, face-to-face fight on the island. We certainly have a responsibility to help them. We've been playing checkers so far. We win a few and lose a few. We get a few troops ashore and they get a few troops ashore. Common sense would tell us—if we can land one huge army, with massive fire power, we can turn the tide." Halsey looked at Admiral Turner who would be OTC for Operation Orange. "Do you see any faults with this operation?"

"No," Turner said, "unless the Japanese can wipe out Henderson Field before we carry out the plan. They've done some awful damage to planes, installations, and runways with their nighttime bombardments. Fortunately, they've been too squeamish so far to use their battleships with their fourteen-inch guns because of our aircraft. Japanese surface commanders fear air attacks more than anything else and if we can have an edge in aircraft, we should succeed with this operation."

"How many operational planes do we have?" Halsey asked Admiral Fitch, the commander of the land based planes, dubbed the Cactus Air Force.

Fitch looked at some papers in front of him. "We've got ninety-one navy and marine aircraft and six army planes assigned to Henderson, but only twenty-one are there. We usually keep them at Espiritu Sancto because the Japanese hit Henderson so often. But, the planes at Espiritu Sancto can be at Henderson within an hour."

"How about army air units?"

"We have twenty-seven B-17s of the Eleventh Bomb Group and twenty-three fighter planes of the Sixty-seventh Fighter Squadron at Espiritu Sancto. They can be over The Slot in an hour."

Halsey now looked at Admiral Kinkaïd.

"How about your carrier?"

"The *Enterprise* isn't quite fit for duty yet. Repairmen have been working on her elevator around the clock and she should be ready in a few days. We've got forty dive bombers and forty fighters in her storage deck."

"That means we have over 200 aircraft to support Orange," Halsey mused. "That should be sufficient." He shuffled through some papers. "Do any of you have any comments?"

"The plan is reasonable and logical," Admiral Turner said again.

The others nodded in agreement.

"Good," Halsey said. "Let's review to make certain we all understand our respective responsibilities."

Operation Orange, the plan to disembark massive American ground troops and supplies on Guadalcanal would include two warship groups, a transport group, and a battleship-carrier support group. The warship TG 64.4 under Admiral Scott would include the cruiser USS *Atlanta* and four destroyers, TG 67.4 under Admiral Callaghan included four cruisers and ten destroyers, and the transport group under Admiral Turner included three AKA troop-freighters and four large troop transports. All three task groups would be under the overall command of Admiral Turner in Task Force 67. A support warship-carrier group, Task Force 16, under Admiral Kinkaid, included carrier *Enterprise*, battleships USS *South Dakota* and USS *Washington*, two cruisers, and ten destroyers.

Turner's transport group, TG 67.1, would be split into two groups. The three AKAs would be screened by Admiral Scott's TG 64.4, and the four troop transports would be screened by Admiral Callaghan's TG 67.4. The AKA cargo ships would carry the First Marine Aviation Battalion, the First Marine Air Wing, and several thousand tons of material, ammunition, provisions, and guns, including a battery of 155 artillery. The four 10,000-ton troop transports would carry the 182nd Army Combat Regiment, the Second Marine Raider Regiment, and the Fourth Marine Replacement Regiment, nearly fifteen thousand fighting men.

The first group, the three AKAs, would begin unloading at Lunga Point on the morning of 12 November. The four troop transports, screened by Callaghan's TG 67.4, would begin unloading at Lunga Point on the afternoon of 12 November. The transport vessels would then scoot back to Espiritu Sancto.

Admiral Fitch's TG 63, the 200 land-based planes at Henderson Field and Espiritu Sancto, would be on alert throughout 11 and 12 November to intercept any Japanese naval vessels or aircraft that attempted to interfere with the unloading process. The short range Dauntlesses, Avengers, and Wildcats would sortie from Henderson Field against such enemy interception. The long range B-17 bombers and P-38 fighters would fly up The

Slot out of Espiritu Sancto to attack any Japanese fleet coming down from the north.

The twelve submarines under Admiral McCann would station themselves down The Slot from Bougainville southward to report and attack any Japanese surface vessels that might be seen heading for Guadalcanal.

Finally, Adm. Thomas Kinkaid's Task Force 16, the carrier-battleship force, would lay to in the lower Solomons, some 300 miles southeast of Lunga Point. If necessary, Kinkaid would use his carrier planes and battleships to challenge any Japanese naval or air units that attempted to harass the disembarkment of troops and supplies at Lunga Point—the object of Operation Orange.

After reviewing the plan of operation, Admiral Bill Halsey looked up at his generals and admirals. "We can't have any slipups. Our submarine and patrol planes covering The Slot should give us plenty of warning against any Japanese fleet coming down from the north."

"We'll utilize eight PBYs and four B-17s as scouts," Admiral Fitch said. "Two of them will shuttle up and down The Slot around the clock. We'll also have constant F-4 air patrols in the strait during daylight hours. If anything is coming down from the Shortlands, we'll know well in advance."

"Very good," Halsey nodded. Then, he motioned to a steward who brought two bottles of wine and a tray of glasses to the table. Halsey picked up one of the bottles and grinned.

"Burgundy, Cote', 1898, a good year. We managed to wheedle a few bottles from a local wine shop. A toast, gentlemen; and remember, '98 was also a good year for us—Dewey at Manila Bay.''

A burst of ad-libs erupted about the table.

Everybody knew that the Japanese often had war flotillas prowling around the Sealark Channel. However, neither Halsey nor anyone else in this conference room knew that almost the entire Japanese Eighth Fleet, fifty-eight vessels, would be sailing down The Slot; nor did these Americans know that the Japanese would also have heavy air power; nor that the Japanese had planned a similar Operation Orange of their own—reinforce Guadalcanal with massive ground troops to bring a decisive victory in the Solomons.

On this 4 November day, 1942, neither Adm. Bill Halsey nor Adm. Isoroku Yamamoto knew of the other's plans. Neither the Americans nor the Japanese wanted a sea fight, for they both had a more important mission. Still, despite reluctance on both sides, they would clash in a nightmarish nighttime sea battle on Ironbottom Sound (Sealark Channel). The battle that nobody wanted would deteriorate into a disorganized brawl that was unique in naval warfare. And, for one of the adversaries, Friday the thirteenth would be an unlucky day indeed.

# Chapter Four

At 1500 hours, 8 November 1942, the seven transports of Admiral Turner's TG 67.1 weighed anchor and sailed slowly out of Noumea Harbor. Only the cruiser *Atlanta* and the four destroyers of TG 62.4 escorted the transports into the open sea north of New Caledonia for the Japanese surface ships or submarines were not likely to be lurking this close to Noumea.

The remainder of Task Force 67 had already left Noumea on the sixth and seventh. Halsey had slyly sent the rest of the armada out of New Caledonia ahead of the transports in fragmented fashion to minimize suspicion of the Orange operation. Now, Callaghan's TG 67.4 and Kinkaid's TF 16 carrier-battleship force lay in the twin harbors of Espiritu Sancto to await Turner's TF 67.1 transports and Scott's TG 62.4. The American fleet would then sail northward in three columns, with

Scott's TG 62.4 and the AKA transport-freighters in the lead. Callaghan would sail some two hours behind Scott with the four transports, and Kinkaid's TF 16 would sail several hours behind the other two.

By 10 November 1942, Turner's TG 67.1 transport group reached Espiritu Sancto to rendezvous in the twin harbors with the rest of TF 67. By first light, with the sun rising over a calm sea, the thirty-nine vessels of TF 67 and TF 16 lay quietly at anchor. At 0700 hours, Admiral Turner, from his flag transport USS *McCawley*, called USS *San Francisco*, the flagship of 67.4.

"It's Admiral Turner," a communications mate told communications officer Bruce Mc-Candles.

McCandles picked up the TBS radio phone, the system of communications between land and ships. "Yes sir," McCandles answered Turner, "I'll get Admiral Callaghan immediately." McCandles switched the call to the JV phone on the bridge and then, out of curiosity, the communications officer listened in.

"We'd like to aweigh by 0800," Turner said. "Is that okay?"

"No problem," Adm. Daniel Callaghan answered.

"We're sending the AKAs in first with Admiral Scott, as you know," Turner said. "They should reach Lunga Point by noon of the twelfth to start unloading. You can bring in the transports by late afternoon of the twelfth to start your own unloading."

"Yes sir," Callaghan answered. "What about Kinkaid?"

"His carrier and battleships will lay in the lower Solomons, some 250 miles from Lunga Point. Halsey and Kinkaid are worried about our single carrier and they don't want to commit *Enterprise* unless they absolutely have to. But, we should get plenty of air support from Henderson Field and Espiritu Sancto."

After the conversation with Turner, Admiral Callaghan ordered Bruce McCandles to maintain station on the bridge to expedite any further TBS communications. An hour later, at 0800, McCandles watched the three AKA transports form into single file and leave the harbor with cruiser *Atlanta* and four destroyers. Then, the JV phone buzzed.

"This is the captain," the deep voice of Capt. Cassin Young croaked into the intercom. "Notify all ships to get underway."

Cassin Young had been one of America's first naval heroes of World War II when he directed the crew of USS *Raleigh* during the Japanese attack on Pearl Harbor. He had worked alongside the bluejackets in the midst of flames and destruction to save the cruiser. His efforts had won him the respect of his men and one of the first Congressional Medals of Honor of World War II. Young had taken over command of *San Francisco* in May of 1942 when Callaghan had joined Ghormley's staff at

Noumea in the new COMSOPAC command.

Cmdr. McCandles quickly transmitted Young's order over the TBS to the other thirteen ships of 67.4: three cruisers and ten destroyers. By 1000 hours, the fourteen vessels under Admiral Callaghan had established themselves in a screen alongside the four heavily laden transports. Callaghan sent destroyer USS *Cushing* ahead to act as scout and he ordered destroyer USS *O'Bannon* to take up the rear as a trailing picket. Two groups of four destroyers each and one cruiser sailed in single lines off the starboard and port sides of the transports while cruiser *San Francisco* sailed behind picket *Cushing*.

The heavy warship screen, rather than comforting the troops aboard the transports, actually brought an uneasiness to the men. Why so many screening warships? Was COMSOPAC expecting heavy opposition from Japanese surface ships somewhere in Ironbottom Sound?

At about 1200 hours, Callaghan's armada was well at sea, some 30 or 40 miles behind Scott's armada. When another officer relieved the communications officer and McCandles retired to an officer's ward room, he sat next to Lt. Cmdr. Herb Shonland, the cruiser's damage control officer.

"What's the word upstairs?" Shonland asked.

"We're taking the long way round, east and north of San Cristobal," McCandles said.

"That's why we'll need almost two days to reach Lunga Point. But, Turner figures we can avoid Jap detection with an end run."

"Hell," Shonland sneered, "the Nips have submarines all through the goddamn Slot. Some of the I-boats even carry those seaplane scouts. They'll know our position, strength, and destination before we even reach Guadalcanal."

"Maybe," McCandles answered.

Lt. Cmdr. Herb Shonland was correct. Northeast of San Cristobal Island lay the Japanese submarine I-26. Cmdr. Minoru Yokoto surfaced his boat at about 1300 hours on the afternoon of 10 November and he immediately catapulted a scout seaplane to make a routine search of the lower Solomons. The seaplane flew at 10,000 feet, scouring the sea, vast and open on this cloudless day. By 1330 hours, the seaplane had flown 100 miles southeast of San Cristobal and then arched in a 180-degree turn to begin its flight back to I-26, northeasterly of San Cristobal.

Soon, the spotters aboard the seaplane observed specks off their starboard at about two o'clock, just beyond San Cristobal Island, the land mass furthest south in the Solomon Islands chain. The Japanese plane veered further east and within three minutes the pilot and two observers gaped in astonishment. Below them was Scott's warship group escorting the three AKAs.

"Enemy scout!" the lookout aboard *Atlanta* cried.

Within a minute, whoop alarms echoed through the American cruiser and 700 men scrambled about her decks to battle stations. "Goddamn it!" Admiral Scott cursed from the flag bridge, "we've barely cleared San Cristobal and the bastards have already spotted us. Bring that plane down!"

Abruptly, a barrage of 40mm pom-pom and five-inch ack-ack fire spewed upwards from *Atlanta*, the destroyers, and even the attack cargo ships. Countless exploding black puffs turned the sky into a blue canvas riddled with black holes. The very sea under the American vessels shuddered from heavy concussions and the men aboard the ships winced from the deafening gunfire.

But, the solitary Japanese seaplane remained high in the sky, circling and swooping above the American task group like a defiant hawk. The Japanese pilot even maneuvered his aircraft 30 or 40 miles south of Scott's flotilla where the Japanese observers got another visual shock—Callaghan's TG 67.4: four cruisers, ten destroyers, and four huge troop transports.

"We have seen enough," one of the observers told the pilot.

"Then we depart," the Japanese pilot answered.

The seaplane arched upward to 12,000 feet and then zoomed west through a second gauntlet of antiaircraft fire. One of the observers quickly radioed the sightings to Cmdr. Yokoto. "We observed two enemy flotillas, sailing in tandem with the rear column some 30 to 40 miles behind the first. Each flotilla includes transport vessels and warship screens."

"Where?" the Group D submarine patrol commander asked anxiously.

"The first flotilla is on a bearing of 164 degrees east and 10.2 degrees south; sailing northwest on a 168 track, perhaps 12 to 15 knots. The second flotilla is at a 164.2 east by 10.4 south bearing, also on a 168 track and also at a 12 to 15 knot speed."

"A reinforcement fleet, and a large one!" Cmdr. Yokoto gasped. He immediately radioed Admiral Mikawa over the UBR (ultra beam radio), the Japanese counterpart of the American TBS communications system. The Eighth Fleet had left Truk on the eighth and all but Abe's Raiding Force Two were now assembling around the Shortlands below Bougainville, about 300 miles north of Lunga Point.

"Honorable Admiral," the I-26 commander said, "our scout plane has sighted two enemy armadas about 40 miles apart and perhaps 100 miles southeast of San Cristobal Island. They are sailing northwest up the Solomon Strait. The combined enemy flotillas include seven large transports with escorts of several cruisers and at least a dozen destroyers. They are on a 168 track, at about 164 east by 10 degrees south, making 12 to 15 knots."

"Are you certain, commander?"

"Both the pilot and the observers aboard the scout plane agree."

"There were no battleships or carriers?"

"No, Honorable Mikawa."

"As soon as your scout plane returns, proceed at once to a position of 163.6 west by 9.4 south to maintain a track on their movements," the Eighth Fleet commander said. "It is vital that we do not lose sight of these enemy flotillas. You must be our eyes from this moment on."

"We will not fail you," Yokoto promised.

"We were foolish indeed not to expect the Americans to share our own beliefs," Mikawa told an aide. "They too recognize the need for massive reinforcements on Guadalcanal to win a decisive victory. The irony lies in their timing—they began their effort at the same time as ourselves." He paused. "You will report these American flotillas to the Twenty-sixth Air Flotilla at Buin and to our surface ship commanders."

"Yes, Honorable Mikawa," the aide said.

The aide immediately called Captain Hideo Shoji of the Twenty-sixth Air Flotilla at Buin. "Our scout plane observers report that seven transports of the ten-thousand-ton class, with warship escorts, are sailing in tandem columns up the Solomon Strait. We can assume the Americans plan to disembark troops and supplies on Guadalcanal with a reinforcement group as large as our own. Your aircraft must be on full alert." Then, the aide called Admiral

Abe of Raiding Force Two and Admiral Kondo of Main Attack Group, relaying the same information. "This sighting, however, is not to deter our current plans," the aide told the surface ship commanders.

Aboard battleship *Hiei* of Raiding Force Two, now on the wide open sea between Truk and the Solomons, Admiral Abe stroked his double chin and turned to the ship's commander, Capt. Masao Nashida. "It appears, captain, that our mission is beset with complications."

"True," Captain Nashida answered.

Abe had barely spoken when he received a personal call from Admiral Mikawa. "You must not allow this new development to detain you. At their speed and course, the Americans may reach Lunga Point shortly before you do. Therefore, you now have a two-fold mission. You must not only destroy the American airfield, but you must also destroy the enemy transport vessels before they disembark troops and supplies. I will ask Admiral Kondo to increase his speed so that Main Attack Group can strike the enemy airfield earlier than planned."

"Yes, Honorable Mikawa," Admiral Abe said.

"I will also request the Twenty-sixth Air Flotilla to attack the enemy fleets as well as the enemy airfield on Guadalcanal."

"A wise decision," Abe said.

Mikawa now called Captain Shoji. "You have heard the reports of the enemy flotillas. I will expect your aircraft to conduct strong sorties against these enemy units as well as against the American airfield.''

"We are prepared for both," Captain Shoji answered.

To the south, Admiral Turner appeared quite shaken by the sightings from the Japanese search plane. But, the sighting did not lessen his determination. He ordered both TG 62.4 and TG 67.4 to increase speed to 16 knots so they could reach Guadalcanal earlier than planned. "If you arrive at Lunga Point by dawn of the twelfth, we'll have a couple of days before the Japanese can send a surface fleet down The Slot from Rabaul and even more time if they send a fleet from Truk.''

"Those transports are pretty jammed," Admiral Scott answered Turner.

"We don't have any choice," Turner said.

Admiral Callaghan did not like the idea of upping the speed of his four transports to 16 knots, but he agreed with Turner. They needed to reach Lunga Point and unload before the enemy could intercept with warships. In fact, Callaghan increased speed to 18 knots and he was soon on the tail of Scott's TG 64.2 warships and AKAs.

Callaghan stood on the bridge of *San Francisco* throughout the night of 10 and 11 November. Almost every hour he turned to Cmdr. Bruce McCandles for a report on their position.

"We're now 150 miles from Lunga Point, sir."

"The time, commander?"

"0830 hours, sir," McCandles said.

Adm. Daniel Callaghan was obviously apprehensive. Callaghan, the former CO of *San Francisco*, had led this cruiser in several earlier engagements, including some sharp night actions where the Japanese had done serious damage with starshells, turret guns, and long lance torpedoes. Thus, the quiet rear admiral felt no inclination to meet a Japanese surface fleet, especially at night.

But, as the morning of 11 November wore on, Callaghan grew more relaxed. He saw no more Japanese planes, he received no more reports of I-boats, and no word of Japanese surface ships in the area. By mid-morning of the eleventh, he felt relatively safe. No doubt, the Japanese were probably mustering a war fleet at Truk or Rabaul, but such a fleet could not reach Lunga Point before the transports had unloaded and departed.

However, only a few hundred miles up The Slot, two PBY scout planes, on this mid-morning of 11 November, at 1035 hours, suddenly spotted Admiral Kondo's Main Attack Group cruiser force. Only five minutes later, at 1040 hours, the same PBY spotted Reinforcement Group Two to the rear of the cruiser force. In single file were eleven maru transports with a screen of some dozen destroyers.

"Holy Christ!" one of the PBY American

observers hissed.

"Baby One to Cactus; Baby One to Cactus," the pilot called Henderson Field. "We've got a big Japanese cruiser fleet below the Shortlands."

"It can't be," the voice from Henderson said. "They only spotted our fleets yesterday. They couldn't come down so soon from Truk or Rabaul."

"All we know—they're down there," the pilot insisted, "and maybe 300 miles from Lunga Point."

"Maybe it's only a Tokyo Express."

"Like hell," the pilot scoffed. "The sea is covered with cruisers and destroyers; and there's a huge maru convoy right behind them, a dozen transports with a dozen destroyer escorts."

"Are you sure?"

"We're sure." Then, before the PBY pilot spoke again, the sky erupted in numbing explosions of antiaircraft fire from Japanese surface fleet guns. The sky became pocked with black puffs and the PBY shuddered from the deafening ack-ack concussions. The American patrol plane dipped, turned, and arched to avoid the antiaircraft fire.

"Baby Two, Baby Two," a voice now came from the second PBY, "we count eleven transports to the rear of the cruisers; eleven transports."

"Any carriers?" the voice from Henderson Field asked.

"We don't see any."

"What's their position?"

"Bearing at 159.1 west by 6.8 south; they're on an 073 track, southeast at 15 knots."

"Okay," the Guadalcanal radio man said. "Get your ass out of there before they shoot it off."

The pilots of the two PBY planes did not hesitate. They arched high into the sky, above 12,000 feet and out of ack-ack range. Then, the planes zoomed southwards towards Guadalcanal. The PBYs had not seen Admiral Mikawa's huge carrier-battleship Support Group Two because this armada was still far up The Slot; nor had the PBY observers seen Admiral Abe's Raiding Force Two because this force was far to the north of the Solomons instead of northwest up The Slot.

When the communications officer at Henderson Field relayed the PBY sightings to Admiral Turner aboard the flagship *McCawley* of TG 67.1, the admiral gasped, "It can't be! It can't be!" He immediately called *San Francisco* where Cmdr. Bruce McCandles listened in awe: a horde of Japanese cruisers, destroyers, and maru transports. The Japanese obviously were sending a huge reinforcement convoy to Guadalcanal themselves. McCandles knew that their carrier-battleship force was far to the south. Neither the battlewagons nor *Enterprise* could arrive in time to attack the Japanese armada coming down The Slot. He was not sure their own TG 67.4 could handle six cruisers.

When McCandles brought his report to the flag bridge, both Admiral Callaghan and Captain Young read the reports in astonishment. They guessed at once that the Japanese had planned the same kind of operation as Operation Orange. Callaghan and Young, like Mikawa, also saw the irony: their reinforcement missions had come off at the same time.

Before Callaghan digested the implications of this Japanese armada, he got another TBS call from Admiral Turner. "We maintain full ahead. Those Jap cruisers are 300 miles north of Lunga Point. We can make Guadalcanal by 0900 tomorrow and discharge most of our men and supplies before they reach us. If the weather stays calm, we can unload and be gone by midnight. Meanwhile, I've ordered aircraft from Henderson Field and Espiritu Sancto to sortie against this enemy fleet. We can at least disrupt them and slow them down."

"Aye, aye, admiral," Callaghan said. But he, Captain Young, and Bruce McCandles doubted the feasibility of Turner's plan. The Americans possessed a mere forty-five aircraft at Henderson Field of which only twenty-four were torpedo or dive bombers. The B-17s at Espiritu Sancto could bomb the enemy fleet, but the Flying Fortresses had never succeeded too well against enemy surface ships.

Nonetheless, on the afternoon of 11 November, Adm. Aubrey Fitch, the American OTC of the Cactus land based aircraft, ordered air strikes on the enemy fleets. Aircraft from

Guadalcanal located Kondo's Main Attack Group in The Slot at about 1400 hours. However, heavy antiaircraft fire and skillful Japanese helmsmen aboard Kondo's cruisers and destroyers thwarted the American pilots who made only a few minor hits. And soon, Zero fighters from Buin pounced on the twenty-four American light bombers. Escorting American Wildcat fighters fought off most of them, but some of the Japanese fighter pilots got through the U.S. fighter screen to effectively scatter the American bombers. An hour later, sixteen B-17s out of Espiritu Sancto, from high altitude, dropped 20 tons of bombs over the Main Attack Group. But, the Fortress pilots scored hits on only two destroyers, neither of the hits fatal.

Meanwhile, Capt. Hideo Shoji sent twenty-four Val dive bombers with twenty-four Zero escorts out of Buin at 1500 hours to bomb Henderson Field. But, Wildcat fighter planes rose from the field to meet them. The marines on Guadalcanal, instead of ducking into fox-holes, watched the aerial dogfight between the Americans and Japanese planes over Ironbottom Sound. The air battle lasted a half hour, with the Wildcats knocking half the Vals out of the air and damaging seven of the Zero escorting fighters. Some of the Japanese dive bombers tumbled into Sealark Channel to join the bones of ships and men already on the bottom of Ironbottom. Other Vals fell in flames and exploded in the Guadalcanal jungles. The

Zeros knocked three Wildcats out of the air, but the surviving Vals did little damage to Henderson Field before they and their Zero escorts scooted back to Buin.

Thus, neither the American nor Japanese air attacks on the afternoon of 11 November changed anything. Both American Task Force 67 and the tandem Japanese fleets continued towards Sealark Channel. The carrier groups of both sides, Kinkaid's TF 16 and Mikawa's Support Group Two, wallowed and waited far to the rear, hoping to avoid the need to commit carrier planes.

The Americans, of course, were still unaware that Admiral Abe was steaming south from Truk over the open sea with two battleships.

Then, at about 0200 hours, 12 November, Col. LeVerne Saunders led twenty-four B-17s from Espiritu Sancto to the Japanese airfield at Buin. The Flying Forts dropped nearly 30 tons of bombs, using H2X radar as their bombardment guide. A deluge of 250-pound incendiary bombs tore up every square yard of the airstrip and taxi ways on Buin. The bombardment had also destroyed half of the Japanese aircraft on the ground.

"A damn good job, boys," Colonel Saunders told his airmen. "Let's go home."

When the dust cleared, and the drone of B-17 engines faded to the south, Capt. Hideo Shoji surveyed the utter destruction to his air field.

"Unfortunate," he told one of the pilots.

"True," the pilot answered Captain Shoji. "We will need at least two days to repair the runway and taxi ways so that aircraft may again fly from Buin. The battle, if there is one, will surely be over by then." Shoji squeezed his face. "I fear the Honorable Mikawa will need to use his carrier planes to aid our surface ships against an enemy fleet."

Thus, with the elimination of the Buin airfield, the B-17s had scored the first serious blow in the upcoming Friday the thirteenth battle.

When Admiral Mikawa learned of the destruction at Buin, he scowled in disappointment, but he did not lose his resolve. He told both Abe and Kondo to continue southward with all haste. He would follow with his carrier force to support both bombardment groups, if necessary. Should he lose aircraft, Mikawa would request Rabaul to send replacement aircraft to carriers *Hiyo* and *Junyo*.

Aboard the Raiding Force Two flagship, battleship *Hiei*, Abe hoped the loss of the Buin airfield would not affect a possible engagement with an American fleet. He consoled himself from two advantages: the American armadas had no battleships or carriers and his own battleship fourteen-inch shells carried for a distance of twenty-one miles. Secondly, the probability of a sea battle would take place at night when the Japanese were generally superior.

On destroyer *Amatsukaze*, Capt. Tameichi

Hara, commander of Desron 10, felt an excited exhilaration. The loss of the Buin airfield did not faze him for he was certain that Raiding Force Two, with its superiority in battleship fire power, could win a decisive naval battle against an American cruiser force. Hara stood on the bridge of his destroyer throughout the night, taking mere catnaps on a bunk and gulping bowls of rice or cups of tea. He scanned the southern horizon eagerly, although he knew he was a full day away from the American fleet.

Far to the south, less than a hundred miles from Lunga Point, Admiral Callaghan stood on the bridge of *San Francisco*, scanning the dark sea round him. He did not relish star shells blossoming over his ship or searchlight beams settling on his cruiser's superstructure. He also knew he was still a day away from the enemy, but each passing hour made him more tense. He looked at his watch: 0230 hours. In a dozen hours he would be at Lunga Point to discharge his men and supplies. He only hoped that he could do this before the Japanese intervened.

Below the bridge, in the radio room, Cmdr. Bruce McCandles sat quietly, drinking coffee. He looked at the radio man. "Anything new?"

"Nothing since the report of the B-17 air attack on Buin a half hour ago," the communications mate said.

The round-faced, stockily built Bruce McCandles took another sip of coffee and he then looked at the radio clock: 0240. He knew that each passing moment brought them closer to the Japanese cruiser force coming down The Slot. TG 67.4 and the Japanese fleet might well confront each other before the transports could get in and out of Lunga Point. For a moment, McCandles envisioned a smashing victory over the Japanese armada. In the next moment, however, he envisioned total defeat, a rout in which *San Francisco* was sunk and he was killed.

McCandles wrestled with these images for several minutes, until an ensign came into the radio room. "I'm here to relieve you, sir. You better sack out; tomorrow evening may be the start of a long night."

"Yeh, a long night," McCandles nodded. He left the radio room and returned to his quarters and hoped to fall asleep.

## Chapter Five

After the B-17 attack on Buin, the remainder of the night and early hours of 12 November passed uneventfully. Scout planes and submarines from both sides kept a watch on Kondo's Main Attack Group and Turner's TF 67, but no aircraft or submarines attacked the surface ships. Then, at about 1030 hours on 12 November, a B-17 reconn plane reported what appeared to be an enemy surface fleet far out at sea, some 350 miles due north of the Solomons. PBYs spent the next several hours trying to verify this report, but they found nothing. Admiral Turner thus shrugged off the B-17 report as incorrect, especially since the Japanese always seemed to sortie their fleets around the Shortlands and then send them down The Slot.

Nonetheless, Turner decided to hasten Admiral Callaghan forward. So, by 1300 hours on the afternoon of 12 November, the four transports reached Lunga Point almost simultaneously with the American AKAs. Admiral Callaghan's warships along with Admiral Scott's now loitered off the coast in the waters of Ironbottom Sound to protect the unloading. Callaghan's fleet had been reduced to four cruisers and seven destroyers when the rest of his tin cans had been detached to join the destroyer screen of Kinkaid's TF 16.

On the bridge of *San Francisco*, Callaghan, Young, and communications officer McCandles watched the transports anchor off the shoreline. Then, small launch boats puttered out from the beach to pick up men and supplies to shuttle them back to the island.

"What do you think, Dan?" Captain Young asked.

The admiral peered through binoculars at the transports off Lunga Point and then scanned the sea, churning up three to four foot breakers from sudden winds that had been sweeping across Sealark Channel. Above, dark, low hanging clouds raced across the sky.

"We might get a storm," Callaghan told Young. "That means they'll have trouble unloading."

Capt. Cassin Young also stared at the low hanging clouds and the worsening swells on the surface of the sea. "I don't know how long we can hang around here," the *San Francisco* skipper said. He turned to McCandles. "Bruce, how far away is that Japanese cruiser force?"

"They were 300 miles up The Slot at 1000

hours this morning," McCandles answered.

Callaghan looked again at the dense clouds, picked up a TBS and called Henderson Field. He spoke to the communications officer of the 142nd Marine Group. "This is Admiral Callaghan. Do we have scout planes tracking that Japanese armada?"

"Yes sir, admiral," the voice answered. "We've had reconnaissance planes out all day. Right now we have two PBYs and a half dozen Wildcats up The Slot. They've been out for most of the afternoon. Our last report, about an hour ago, showed the Japanese fleet off Santa Isabel. We don't think they can reach Lunga Point before tomorrow, especially in this weather."

"If you get anything new, let me know immediately," Callaghan said.

"Aye aye, sir," the MAG 142 communications officer said.

Now, Callaghan looked at Cassin Young. "Are we on full alert?"

"We've been at battle stations all afternoon," Young said. "Every gun in both our own and Admiral Scott's group is on the ready. If we see anything, we'll be set." The *San Francisco* skipper then looked again at the dense, low hanging clouds. "Those bad skies may discourage any air attack and those heavy seas may slow down the Japanese cruiser fleet."

But Cassin Young was wrong. At 1317 hours, coast watchers reported enemy bombers with fighter escort coming down The Slot. Admiral Turner immediately stopped unloading and ordered all transports out of Sealark Channel. The transports, however, had only reached the middle of the channel when, at 1400 hours, twenty Val torpedo bombers circled the Florida Islands and zoomed in two groups over Ironbottom Sound. Fortunately, Turner's transport helmsmen successfully veered their ships to avoid the torpedo wakes.

Meanwhile, every ack-ack gun aboard the American warships and transports opened up on the attacking Vals. The gunners knocked down six planes in just over one minute. More important, Wildcat fighter planes rose from Henderson Field and roared into the Vals as the bombers circled again for a new attack.

Capt. Joe Foss, a burly, corn fed, curly haired farmer from Sioux Falls, South Dakota, led the American fighter planes of MAG 142. Foss had been a boxer and wrestler in high school and college. Since early childhood, his father had taught him to take care of himself. The strapping Midwesterner had done so ever since he joined the Marine Air Corps in August of 1940. He had arrived in the Solomons with the first marine air units in late August of 1942, exactly two years after he began pilot training. In the Solomons campaign, he had already shot down thirteen Japanese planes and won a Distinguished Flying Cross. The pilots in the MAGs VFS 121 fighter unit held Foss in high esteem, despite his ragged, and often unorthodox attire. Foss had taught his pilots to meet the enemy head on, a strategy that had enabled his pilots to defeat and scatter superior numbers of aircraft in aerial combat.

Now, in just moments, Joe Foss and his fighter pilots had knocked all but two of the remaining Vals out of the air and downed several of the escorting Zeros.

But the Vals did make scores on three warships. The destroyer USS *Buchanan* took so many 250-pound bomb hits that Turner ordered her out of Ironbottom and back to Noumea. Another bomb hit USS *Monssen* and damaged her SG radar gear, but the destroyer did not need to retire. Finally, a wounded enemy plane crashed into *San Francisco*'s after control station with the ensuing explosion killing several men and destroying the station.

"Damage! Damage!" Young yelled into his JV.

"They got our fire control radar and flak direction," Lt. Cmdr. Herb Shonland answered, "but our damage control crews have fires under control."

Fortunately, the hit on *San Francisco* did not materially damage the cruiser and she was able to remain in the battle zone. Casualties were transferred to transport USS *President Jackson* that had extensive hospital facilities.

A half hour after the attack, Admiral Turner angrily called Henderson Field. "What the hell were our scout planes doing? Why weren't fighter interceptors up sooner? And where the hell is your Combat Air Patrol?"

"We'll keep a CAP out from now on, sir," somebody answered the admiral.

By 1700 hours, with no more reports of Japanese planes coming down The Slot, Turner sent his transports back to Lunga Point to complete the unloading. But now, darkness was approaching and darkness was often the witching hour for American ships, despite the recent victory at Cape Esperance.

Aboard *San Francisco,* Admiral Callaghan watched the launch boats now struggling through the heavy swells to reach the anchored transports for more men and supplies. Callaghan frowned, wrinkling his face. In these heavy breakers, unloading activities would be slowed to a snail's pace. The launches would not even dent the jammed holds of the American transports by midnight. But, perhaps these same heavy swells would keep the Japanese cruisers away until morning until planes from Henderson Field could attack the enemy surface fleet.

Less than a 150 miles north of the Solomons, Adm. Hiroaki Abe stood on the flag bridge of battleship *Hiei* with his chief of staff, Capt. Susumu Kimura, and the ship's commander, Capt. Masao Nashida. Abe peered through binoculars at the eleven destroyers strung in a long single line. Then, he looked at *Kirishima,* some 5,000 meters to his rear, with the fellow battleship becoming a growing silhouette in the waning afternoon. Finally, Abe looked at the cruiser *Nagara*, riding some 3,000 meters in front of *Hiei*. He turned to Captain Nashida.

"Is everyone at battle stations?"

"Yes, Honorable Abe," Nashida answered.

Abe now studied the growing swells that rocked even the 32,000 ton *Hiei*, He stared at the sky and the low hanging clouds, but they gave him no comfort. He knew that American aircraft could attack at surface height, and Abe still felt uneasy about the loss of the Buin airfield. Further, Abe remembered the B-17 this morning and he feared the Americans now knew he was coming down directly from Truk to bombard Henderson Field. He rightly suspected that the Americans would spare nothing to stop such action.

"What is our bearing?" Abe asked the navigation officer.

"160.1 east by 8.6 south. We are 123 miles from our destination."

Abe nodded. Then, he peered through his binoculars at the empty sea. "It is time to muster into the Ita pattern, for we are entering dangerous waters. Such a pattern will assure us protection against submarine attacks."

Thus, less than 120 miles from Lunga Point, the orders went out from the bridge of *Hiei*. Raiding Force Two would assume Ita pattern, a tight horseshoe formation, eleven destroyers spread out in a half-circle, three to port, three to starboard, three as trailing protectors and destroyers *Yudachi* and *Marasame* in the van point position. Cruiser *Nagara* took the forward position inside the horseshoe ring, while the battleships remained in tandem behind *Nagara*. Destroyer *Samidare* scurried far ahead, perhaps 25 to 30 miles beyond the horseshoe, to report any activity by the enemy. The vessels in this Ita pattern remained about 2,000 meters apart and moved at 26 knots. When the pattern had been completed at about 1710 hours, a premature darkness, the result of dark clouds, descended over Abe's Raiding Force Two.

The Japanese armada sailed only a short distance when a heavy rain squall struck the war fleet. Nonetheless, Abe launched a scout plane from *Hiei*. Two observers shared the cabin with the pilot.

"You will report the enemy's position," Admiral Abe said.

"It will be done," the pilot promised.

The scout plane had barely disappeared to the south when the storm worsened. Drenching sheets of rain soaked Abe's ships; sailors slipped and slid about the wet deck as they carried out their duties. In the heavy rain, bridge commanders could barely see the vessels next to them and nerves stiffened among the sailors. But the officers and men in the raiding force also welcomed the poor weather for no American planes or submarines would likely attack the armada.

"Perhaps we should slow down," Captain Nashida told Admiral Abe.

"We must maintain speed to reach the target area on schedule," Admiral Abe answered. He squinted at the driving rain beyond the bridge. "In any event, this squall is local in nature and we should come out of it soon."

But, as the armada continued its southern sail at 26 knots, the squalls continued unabated. About a half hour later, Captain Kimura, Abe's aide, received a UHR call from the scout plane. "A dozen enemy warships loiter about Lunga Point in the Sealark Channel and at least a half dozen transports lay anchored off Lunga Point. At least a half dozen small launches are disembarking men and supplies, but they operate with difficulty in the heavy seas and driving rain."

"What is the complement of warships?" Captain Kimura asked.

"They appear to be cruisers and destroyers. We have seen no battleships or carriers numbered among the enemy warships."

When Kimura brought the report to Abe, the admiral's dark eyes brightened. "There are no carriers or battleships?"

"None, admiral."

Admiral Abe nodded and then grinned at Captain Nashida, *Hiei*'s commander. "No battleships or carriers; Heaven favors us. We can easily deal with this American warship force and their transports, and then bombard the airfield."

"Yes, admiral;" Nashida said.

"Maintain present speed and pattern," Abe said.

The Japanese armada continued over the

open sea. However, by about 1800 hours, the rains still pelted ships and men and Admiral Abe expressed surprise. Abe had confidence in his commanders. He knew they could hold this speed in heavy seas and still control their ships. He hoped they could maintain their Ita pattern until the last moment, just before any engagement with the enemy.

At 1810 hours Capt. Susumu Kimura received a radio message from Guadalcanal. "On this island, the rain squalls remain fierce and the storm shows no evidence of abating. Our scouts say the Americans are experiencing extreme difficulty in unloading their transports because of the heavy swells that now prevail in Sealark Channel."

With this report from Guadalcanal, a sudden change came over Admiral Abe. He had always shown a trait of uncertainty in poor weather, unexpected opposition, or some other unforeseen development that interfered with his schedule. Now, his sense of caution overcame his thirst for battle. He stared at the destroyers around him, watching them heave and list in the heavy seas. Then, he rationalized. Perhaps they could not complete their mission in this weather.

Then, Captain Kimura handed Abe another message. "The scout plane cannot find *Hiei* in this storm. The pilot will fly to Bougainville and try to land there."

The message convinced Abe. "The weather will make a bombardment of the enemy airfield impossible," he told Captain Kimura. "We will reverse course."

"Reverse course!" Captain Kimura gasped.

"Yes," Abe answered.

When the order went out to all ships for a 180-degree turn, astonishment struck every sailor in Raiding Force Two. Yes, the weather was bad, but they needed only to slow their speed and change into a single attack column. They could still reach Lunga Point during the depths of darkness and macerate the enemy transports. But, despite the advice of his flag officers, Abe held to his order to reverse course.

Soon, the Japanese fleet swung into a 180-degree turn, a difficult maneuver in the complex Ita pattern. But the fourteen vessels deftly made their full half-turn. Then, the armada reduced speed to 16 knots.

Aboard *Amatsukaze,* Capt. Tameichi Hara, commander of Desron 10, had been pacing the bridge irritably for several minutes. Then, his patience exhausted, he called Abe over the UHR, the Japanese counterpart of the American TBS.

"Admiral, I implore you," Hara said, "our purpose is to destroy the enemy and we must carry out this mission."

"The weather is too unfavorable."

"Honorable Abe," Hara continued, "please reconsider. Only shame will come to you and every sailor in this flotilla if we return to Truk with no attempt to strike our enemies. We have two battleships to make short work of both the American warships and their transports. We must grasp this opportunity."

"I appreciate your enthusiasm, captain, but under the circumstances . . . "

"No, admiral," Hara persisted. "Remember that Admiral Tanaka carries thousands of Japan's sons to Guadalcanal. If we fail, he too will fail."

"I will reconsider," Abe said, obviously embarrassed by the reprimand by his destroyer screen commander.

Meanwhile, *Hiei*'s commander, Capt. Masao Nashida, looked disapprovingly at Abe, but the Raiding Force Two commander only turned his embarrassed face. However, the captain continued to stare at Abe until the admiral finally spoke.

"You think I am wrong, captain?"

"You must excuse my impudence, admiral," Nashida said, "but your decision to reverse course is astonishing. If it is your aim to disgrace yourself and the men of our command, you will succeed. We cannot ignore this American armada at Lunga Point. We must destroy it."

"Every man aboard *Hiei* and in this armada will fight to the death," Capt. Susumu Kimura now spoke. "We must fight, even if you do so in a typhoon. Please, admiral, I urge you to reverse course and fulfill this mission."

"I will think about it," Abe said, turning away from his subordinates.

Truk 525 miles

Japanese Bombardment
Group
Adm. Abe

1030/12
Sighted by B17

FIRST BATTLE OF GUADALCANAL
Nov. 12-13, 1942

0 20 40 60 80 100
NAUTICAL MILES

BOUGAINVILLE

CHOISEUL

1800/12
SHORT-
LAND IS.

Adm. Tanaka

SANTA
ISABEL

NEW
GEORGIA

THE SLOT

1815/12

MALAITA

FLORIDA
IS.

0130/13        1815/12

GUADALCANAL

Adm.
Turner

Then, when the commander of Raiding Force Two looked at the others on the the bridge of *Hiei*, he could see the disappointment and even scorn in their eyes, although they said nothing. Abe turned away again, obviously embarrassed by the rebukes from Nashida and Kimura. He leaned over the chart table and studied the maps again. Finally, he straightened and walked to the starboard porthole of the bridge. He stared at the raging storm and the boiling sea. Then, he sighed, turned, and looked at Captain Kimura.

"Is every man at battle station?"

"Yes admiral," the chief aide answered eagerly.

Abe nodded and looked at the bridge clock: 1815 hours. He walked back to the chart table, stared at the map and then looked again at Captain Kimura. "You will send out instructions to all vessels. We will again reverse course to 180 degrees and continue south. We will remain in the Ita pattern."

"Yes, admiral," Kimura answered, grinning.

Abe lowered his head. "May the Gods favor us," he mumbled to himself, "and allow us to reach our ememies without detection."

But the Gods did not favor Abe. At 1800 hours, after Abe's flotilla had just reversed course to the south again, a PBY droned over the Japanese fleet. The pilot and observer stared in horror: two battleships! And they were only 125 miles from Guadalcanal. Admiral Abe scowled and ordered antiaircraft fire. However, the PBY dipped into the clouds before the pilot called Henderson Field.

"Cactus, this is Baby Six, Baby Six; hang on for this one! We just spotted a Japanese fleet with two battleships barreling south. Two battleships! They're about 125 miles out and about 160 east by 8.9 south."

"You're crazy," a voice from Henderson Field said. "You must be seeing the same mirage that Fortress saw this morning."

"No mirage; and they're blackening the sky with ack-ack."

Two more PBYs immediately flew to the area where, at about 1930 hours, they too saw Raiding Force Two: two battleships, perhaps two cruisers, and maybe a dozen destroyers. When Henderson Field got the verification, they relayed this ominous information to Admiral Turner aboard *McCawley*. Turner remained in shock for a full minute before he called Admiral Callaghan.

"We've heard the worst, Dan," Turner said, "a Japanese fleet of battleships and cruisers are about a hundred miles from Guadalcanal. They came straight south instead of coming down The Slot. They figure to come between Santa Isabel and the Floridas. This latest sighting must be the real bombardment fleet with the cruiser fleet up The Slot a mere decoy. Dan, we've got to stop loading and abort."

"Abort?"

"We've got to get out," Turner continued.

"We'll weigh anchors on our transports and sail south. I hate to do this, but you're on your own with TG 67.4. I'll leave behind *Atlanta* and two destroyers from 62.4 to help out. The other 62.4 destroyers will escort us south." Admiral Turner paused. "That Japanese armada will reach Ironbottom Sound a little after midnight at their present speed, and you'll have to stop them. If you can, we'll come back in the morning to continue unloading."

"What's their position now?" Callaghan asked.

"One hundred sixty east by 8.9 south," Turner answered. "They're northeast of Santa Isabel. I've called Admiral Kinkaid, and he's bringing up *Enterprise* and the battleships at full ahead. But he can't reach you until midday tomorrow. Meanwhile, you'll have to do the best you can tonight and in the morning."

"Any suggestions?"

"A few prayers, Dan," Turner said. "I'll leave the battle plans to you. And Dan, good luck," Turner said before he switched off.

No one on the bridge of *San Francisco* said anything: not Captain Young, not the tracker, not the assistant, not the bluejackets, not Bruce McCandles. In the silence, the splash of pelting rain sounded much louder. But then, the pelting suddenly stopped for the squalls had abruptly ceased. Callaghan opened the flag bridge bulkhead and walked onto the open deck. He peered into the sea where the waters of Ironbottom had begun to calm after the storm.

Callaghan soon walked back inside and leaned over some charts while every eye on the flag bridge followed him. Finally, Callaghan and two assistants retired to the plotting room where they spent two hours drawing up a battle plan. They decided to use a B-1 battle formation, a snakelike, single column, with destroyers in the van, cruisers in the middle, and other destroyers completing the tail. The admiral would send USS *Cushing*, USS *Laffey,* USS *Sterett*, and USS *O'Bannon* forward. Behind these destroyers would come his cruisers: antiaircraft cruiser *Atlanta*, followed by *San Francisco*, USS *Portland*, USS *Helena*, and USS *Juneau*. In the rear of the snake would follow destroyers USS *Aaron Ward*, USS *Barton*, USS *Monssen*, and USS *Fletcher*.

Callaghan believed that the snake pattern, reminiscent of old line-of-battle sailing ships, would make navigation easier in the restricted waters between Savo Island and Guadalcanal. Further, in this disposition, Callaghan could communicate easier with other ships.

However, Callaghan failed to take advantage of his superior radar equipment on some of his ships. Callaghan did not place in the van the cruiser and two destroyers that carried search radar. *Atlanta*, with inferior radar, steamed ahead of flagship *San Francisco*, while *Helena*, with the latest radar equipment, sailed fourth in the cruiser column. Further, destroyers *O'Bannon* and *Fletcher*, with good search radar, sailed to the rear of the column.

As the transports weighed anchor and moved away from Lunga Point, the sailors of TG 67.4 watched fearfully. They were left alone to deal with two Japanese battleships and none of the bluejackets looked forward to this kind of chore. Throughout the early evening, the men said little to each other as they prepared for battle and wondered how Callaghan would handle this crisis.

Finally, the darkness deepened over Ironbottom Sound. By the time Callaghan had set his plans the clock read 2343 hours. Friday the thirteenth would arrive in little over an hour. Callaghan was not a superstitious man, but he did fear a Japanese fleet that included two battleships. On the bridge of *San Francisco*, the TG 67.4 commander drew a cup of coffee and looked at Bruce McCandles.

"Anything new on that Japanese fleet?"

"No sir," McCandles answered. "But we do have a report from Maj. Bob Richards of MAG 142. He says he has forty dive and torpedo bombers ready to intercept the Japanese fleet as soon as he gets the word."

Callaghan glanced through the rain soaked portholes. "A hellava lot of good he can do in this weather, especially at night."

"He'll try, sir."

Bruce McCandles now glanced seaward beyond the bridge. He stroked his round face, shuddering slightly. TG 67.4 would be no match against battleships. But, perhaps the heavy weather had slowed them down and even though the sea had now calmed, the enemy battleships might not be here until morning. Planes from Henderson Field might then help out significantly during the daylight hours.

McCandles looked at the bridge clock: 2247 hours. They had eight hours before welcome daylight.

Then, a call came over the TBS and McCandles handed the phone to Callaghan. "Admiral, it's Admiral Turner."

Callaghan nodded and picked up the TBS. "Yes, Rich?"

"Wildcats have sighted the Japanese fleet less than a hundred miles north of the Floridas. The complement was verified as two battleships, possibly two cruisers, and a dozen destroyers. No carriers. They're coming south at about 20 knots, ignoring the weather."

By 2350 hours, moments before midnight, Turner's transports had cleared Ironbottom and now sailed south to avoid the Japanese battle fleet. Turner would return in the morning if Callaghan could dispose of this fleet.

For the next hour and a half the sailors of TG 67.4 waited tensely aboard their vessels. Clad in helmets and lifejackets, they stood rigidly at battle stations, while the snaking column sailed northward in Sealark Channel. By midnight, the clouds had broken up, the sea had calmed, and a placid 9-knot southerly breeze rippled across Ironbottom. Jagged flashes of lightning exploded over the silhouetted Savo Island and Guadalcanal, the final flickers of the evening's tropical storm. Sailors peered into the darkness, but saw no sign of the enemy.

When Admiral Callaghan returned topside, Bruce McCandles looked at the admiral's sober face and McCandles then stared at the clock: 0117 hours. They were now over an hour into Friday, 13 November 1942.

McCandles watched Callaghan peer through a porthole while he held his hands behind his back and tapped his fingers nervously on his palms. And why not? He must stop battleships with cruisers.

For seven minutes a tense quiet prevailed on the flag bridge of *San Francisco*, even though the ship now moved easily over calm Ironbottom. Then, a TBS call came from *Helena*, the radar cruiser. McCandles ogled at the message: "Contact of enemy fleet at 0124 hours; bearing 310 and 312 in some kind of circular formation; distance 27,000 to 32,000 yards." After Callaghan read the radar report, he ran his tongue around his lips.

In a few minutes heavy night action would begin, something Callaghan had dreaded. And in truth, this Friday the thirteenth would be the last day of life for eight warships and hundreds of sailors, including two admirals.

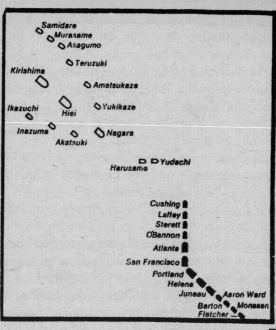

Samidare
Murasame
Asagumo
Teruzuki
Kirishima
Amatsukaze
Ikazuchi
Hiei
Yukikaze
Inazuma
Akatsuki
Nagara
Harusame
Yudachi

Cushing
Laffey
Sterett
O'Bannon
Atlanta
San Francisco
Portland
Helena
Juneau
Aaron Ward
Barton
Monssen
Fletcher

**BATTLE OF GUADALCANAL**

Nov. 13, 1942
0124 – 0140

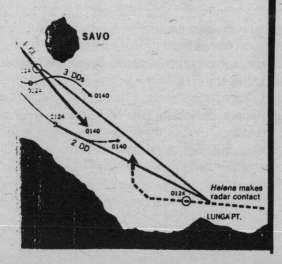

SAVO

3 DDs

0124
0140

0124
0140

2 DD
0140

Helena makes
radar contact

0124

LUNGA PT.

## Chapter Six

Adm. Daniel Callaghan walked to the open deck and peered at the calm sea as well as the broken clouds overhead. In the cleared night, he could easily make out the silhouetted peaks of Savo Island and the dark, rugged shoreline of Guadalcanal off to his left. When the admiral returned to the bridge, those inside saw the cold, sober look on his handsome face. A determination now beamed from his eyes. He stroked his chin and then turned to Cmdr. Bruce McCandles.

"Give me an open channel on the TBS to all ships."

"Aye aye, sir."

Bruce McCandles opened the communication control and then spoke into the open line. "This is the flag; stand by for instructions."

Callaghan now spoke slowly and softly. "Every man should be at battle station. Enemy is now about 25,000 yards to the west of the

Floridas and swinging around the lee of Savo Island into Sealark Channel. We'll alter course to 300 degrees and hit them head on. Up speed to 20 knots and maintain single column, but do not fire until ordered to do so.''

The men on the bridge paled. The admiral would sail straight into the teeth of the enemy fleet, instead of circling the enemy for a port side end around run and torpedo attacks. However, Bruce McCandles was not surprised. He understood Callaghan's thinking. The best chance against the superior firepower of big guns was at close range where the eight-inch guns of the American cruisers would be more effective against the battleships, whose fourteen-inchers were accurate and deadly up to a range of 21 miles. Further, the American cruiser and destroyer crews, only recently trained in the use of torpedoes, would be at a disadvantage against the Japanese crews who had mastered the use of the long lance torpedo with unusual accuracy up to a range of 20,000 yards.

Yes, Callaghan had made the right decision. Get in close and slug it out, like a light heavyweight using swift in-fighting against a powerful heavyweight.

By 0130 hours, Callaghan's fleet assumed its single thirteen vessel column on a 310 course at 20 knots, with destroyer *Cushing* in the lead and destroyer *Fletcher* taking up the rear. At this same 0130 hours, the radar man aboard *Helena* began an ominous countdown: ''Range,

14,500 yards, bearing 105 degrees, speed 23 knots." Less than two minutes later: "Range, 12,000 yards, bearing still at 105, speed 23 knots." In two more minutes: "Range, 9500 yards, bearing 105, speed 23." Every sailor aboard TG 67.4's cruisers and destroyers stiffened with each new report of the approaching enemy armada.

At their complementary speeds of some 20 knots, the two adversaries were closing on each other at the rate of 40 knots per hour. As the range diminished, the American sailors wondered why Callaghan had not used their radar advantage to open shell fire or to launch torpedo attacks.

Conjectures among the task force sailors and officers prompted a heavy exchange of chatter over the TBS radio. Men from the various American vessels called one another, discussing Callaghan's tactics, seeking word on a visual contact of the Japanese fleet, or wondering when they'd open fire. The interfering chatter cut off or disrupted the steady reports from *Helena*'s radar men who constantly gave course, speed, and distance of the enemy fleet. Finally, an exasperated Callaghan barked authoritatively into the TBS.

"All hands, get the hell off TBS! Stay off TBS! We'll report a visual sighting as soon as we have one. We'll tell you when to commence firing."

Those aboard the other American vessels quickly ceased their intership chatter and the

TBS channels remained clear for radar reports.

Yet, some of the TG 67.4 officers believed that Callaghan's delay to commence fire had given an advantage to the Japanese who lacked the efficient radar system of the Americans. At 0124 hours, Admiral Abe still had no idea of Callaghan's location. Now, as Abe sailed at 23 knots into Sealark Channel without reports of enemy warships, he tended to relax. Abe had received a report from shoreline scouts on Guadalcanal that the American transports had weighed anchor and sailed south. Was it possible the American warships had also sailed south with the departing transports? To bolster this hope, he turned to his aide, Capt. Susumu Kimura.

"You have no contact yet?"

"None, Honorable Abe."

"Nothing? Nothing at all?"

"None, sir."

Admiral Abe nodded, satisfied. Perhaps he would find no opposition to a bombardment of Henderson Field. As Raiding Group Two cleared Sealark Channel, Admiral Abe maintained his Ita horseshoe pattern. Three thousand meters to the van were destroyers *Yudachi* and *Marasame*, ahead of cruiser *Nagara* and battleships *Hiei* and *Kirishima* in tandem. Capt. Tameichi Hara's flag destroyer *Amatsukaze* along with destroyers *Yukikaze* and *Terusuki* sailed on the port side of the pattern, while destroyers *Akatsuki, Inazuma,* and *Ikazuchi* sailed on the starboard side of the big ships. The trailing pickets, destroyers *Asugumo* and *Harusame*, sailed about 800 yards behind *Kirishima*. Destroyer *Samidare* had left its tail position to scoot far ahead as a scout.

Unfortunately, Cmdr. Yusuhide Setoyama, *Samidare*'s commander, had already swept through Sealark Channel, heading hell-bent for Lunga Point. He had found nothing because the transports had already sailed south and Callaghan's warships had already sailed northeast in the B-1 pattern. So, Cmdr. Setoyama had inaccurately reported to Admiral Abe that there were no enemy ships in the Sealark Channel. The American ships were gone, Setoyama had reported. So, Abe assumed that the U.S. warships as well as their transports had deserted Lunga Point.

Thus, at 0139 hours, fifteen minutes after *Helena*'s radar had picked up the location of the oncoming Japanese fleet, Admiral Abe still had not learned of Callaghan's presence. Raiding Force Two continued on, and after the flotilla had cleared Savo Island, Admiral Abe ordered his armada into a 20-degree turn to port so that his warships could make a wide arc and come into Lunga Point for a port side bombardment of Henderson Field. The lead destroyers, *Marasame* and *Yudachi*, made the turn first and sailed eastward.

The time was 0140 hours and the nighttime brawl of Friday the thirteenth was about to begin: the most vicious half hour of death and destruction ever recorded in the annals of naval sea fights.

At 0140, a radar man on USS *O'Bannon*, the fourth ship in the van destroyer column, picked up three Japanese warship columns on his screen, one group heavy at 287 degrees, 11,000 yards; another group on a 318 bearing at 8500 yards; and the third group at 042 degrees at a mere 5,000 yards. Even as the radar man rushed the information to the bridge of *O'Bannon*, the lookout aboard the lead destroyer USS *Cushing*, at 0141 hours, gaped in astonishment.

"Holy Christ! They're here! They're here!" He quickly picked up a JV and called *Cushing*'s bridge. "Captain, two enemy destroyers off the bow, no more than 3,000 yards."

The destroyer's skipper, Lt. Comdr. Ed. Parker, rushed out of the wheelhouse and quickly climbed a ladder to the upper bridge. He peered through his binoculars at the two enemy destroyers, jagged silhouettes in the distance at a mere 3,000 yards. He picked up a JV and called the wheelhouse. "Hard to starboard! Hard to starboard!" Then he called the mid-deck torpedo officer. "Ready torpedo launch!"

The helmsman turned the wheel sharply and *Cushing* plowed across the sea, leaving a huge wash in its wake. The quick, unexpected turn by *Cushing* to avoid a collision with the apparent enemy ships threw the 67.4 column into disarray. No one on the other American vessels had yet seen the Japanese and no one expected

*Cushing* to make a sudden starboard swing. Destroyer *Laffey*, steaming behind *Cushing* at more than 20 knots, bounced over the heavy swells of *Cushing*'s wash and the *Laffey* skipper ordered a quick reduced speed to ten knots to avoid the serious wash and perhaps capsize. Destroyer *Srerett*, right on *Laffey*'s heels, swung hard to port to avoid a rear end collision, and *O'Bannon* turned hard to starboard to prevent a collision with the slowed *Jaffey*.

Behind the destroyers, cruiser *Atlanta*, heavier than the tin cans, could not slow or turn as fast as the sleek destroyers. She found herself trapped behind the slowed up *Laffey*, and *Sterett* and *O'Bannon* on her left and right. Capt. Sam Perkins, *Atlanta*'s skipper, scowled at the confusion in front of him. "Goddamn it! What the hell are those destroyers doing?"

"I don't know, sir," the helmsman answered.

"Hard left rudder—hard left!"

"Aye, sir."

Now, the cruiser made a sharp turn, spewing up a wash that raised six to ten foot waves in her wake. *Atlanta* barely missed destroyer *Sterett*, but her wash sprayed tons of water over the destroyer's decks. *Atlanta*'s quick maneuver had rattled the sailors aboard *San Francisco*, next in column.

Admiral Callaghan picked up a TBS and quickly called Captain Perkins. "Captain, what the hell's going on up there? Why are you sweeping left?"

111

"To avoid collision with our destroyers," Captain Perkins answered. "They're turning all over the sea."

"What for?"

"I don't know, but I think we've run smack into the enemy fleet."

Before the admiral could speak again, a TBS call came from Lt. Cmdr. Parker of *Cushing*. "Admiral, sir, we've made visual contact. Two enemy destroyers are practically on top of us. Can I let them have a few fish?"

"Permission granted." Then, Callaghan called other ships. "Resume B-1 column and fire at will. All ships. Resume column and open fire!"

But, surprise was lost. Capt. Hara raced his *Amatsukaze* to the forward where Cmdr. Kiyoshi Kikkawa, skipper of *Yudachi*, reported the presence of American warships at a mere 3,000 yards. "Enemy destroyers off starboard and coming directly at us," Kikkawa had told Hara over the UHR.

When Captain Hara received the report and reached the van position, he was flabbergasted to see USS *Cushing* in the darkness. Like other officers of this raiding force, Hara had understood that the American war fleet had sailed south with its transports. And now, suddenly, the enemy was in their midst. Still, Hara was quite puzzled. He knew the Americans possessed superior long distance radar and they must have known the Japanese fleet had come within range. Why hadn't the American fleet opened fire? And why was this American destroyer rushing head on? Further, Hara could not understand why the Americans had not made a smooth 90-degree turn to starboard to get their turrets and torpedo launchers into position. Finally, Hara was sure the American commander knew that heavy battleship guns and better torpedo tactics by the Japanese would prove superior to the Americans. Why had the American ships sailed directly into the Ita horsehoe where the U.S. vessels could be hit in an unmerciful crossfire?

Hara was about to order a quick 90-degree turn when he saw destroyer *Cushing* make a quick turn itself. Then, Hara was more astounded. He saw the American column turning left and right in erratic movements. The Americans appeared to be in utter confusion, in no position to launch torpedoes or to fire gun salvos. Hara called Admiral Abe.

"Enemy fleet off starboard quarter, perhaps a mere 5,000 meters. But, they appear utterly confused. May we commence fire?"

"At your pleasure, captain," Abe answered.

Then, Adm. Hiroaki Abe squeezed his face; he suddenly remembered they had stacked incendiary shells and not armor piercing shells on the gun decks of the battleships, for *Hiei* and *Kirishima* had expected to bombard an American airfield and not enemy surface ships. Abe quickly called *Hiei*'s gunnery officer, Cmdr. Hideo Sekino. "Replace incendiaries with armor piercing shells at once."

Then, Abe turned to his aide, Captain Kimura. "Call *Kirishima* and order her to immediately replace incendiary shells with armor piercing shells."

"Yes, admiral."

Sailors aboard both battleships sprang into action. Every available man scurried about the ships, carrying armor piercing shells to the gun decks and removing the incendiaries. For a moment, Abe watched sailors scurry about *Hiei*'s decks. Then, he peered into the sea through his binoculars. He saw no sign of the enemy ships on the southern horizon and he was sure his sailors would have armor piercing shells on the gun decks before the enemy commenced firing. But then, another thought struck Abe. He had no time to change his Ita pattern into an attack pattern. He called all ships and warned them to begin fire as soon as American vessels penetrated their horseshoe.

Meanwhile, aboard *Amatsukaze*, Captain Hara squinted at the disorganized American ships and then looked at the outline of Guadalcanal to his right. He now recognized still another American error. Why didn't the American ships steer close to Guadalcanal where their silhouettes might have been obscured by the island's dark background, and where the Americans could have opened fire on the Japanese silhouettes in the middle of Sealark Channel? Surely, with superior radar, the Americans could have acted in time. But, Hara shrugged. He would waste no more time on conjecturing about the Americans' foolish strategy.

"Prepare aft torpedo launch and aft turret fire!"

When Hara's orders echoed through *Amatsukaze* over the loud speaker, the Japanese sailors stood momentarily rigid, looked at the bridge, raised their arms skyward, and then cried in unison: "Banzai! Banzai!"

"Commence fire," Captain Hara cried over the loudspeaker.

"Banzai!" One last cry came from the crew before the sailors swung the aft turret to starboard and sent a salvo of five-inch shells across the sea. Seconds later, a half dozen torpedoes whooshed off the rear deck of *Amatsukaze* and sped towards the approaching American vessels.

Thus, at 0148 hours, these first shots opened the Friday the thirteenth brawl.

But, neither the torpedoes nor the salvo of shells from *Amatsukaze* hit anything. However, the opening round prompted Adm. Norman Scott to order *Atlanta* at near full ahead to 30 knots. The American destroyers in front of him had also straightened and increased speed. Soon, *Atlanta* and the four destroyers had cut into the middle of the Japanese horseshoe to loosen salvos of five- and six-inch shells at the obscure Japanese destroyers on either side of them. But, all shells fell short.

Adm. Abe, on hearing these salvos, called Captain Hara. "Where is the enemy?"

"They have apparently regrouped and now come recklessly into our midst," Hara answered. "They have opened fire, but without success."

"Maneuver your destroyers for torpedo launches," Abe said.

"Yes, Honorable Abe," Hara answered.

As destroyers *Amatsukaze* and *Yudachi* maneuvered to starboard and port turns to launch torpedoes, the American ships plowed onward. In the darkness, Scott's lookout on *Atlanta* spotted the huge pagoda superstructure of *Hiei* looming in front of him, with the battleship no more than 5,000 yards away. The *Hiei* lookout almost simultaneously saw the American destroyers and the bigger *Atlanta*. However, before the Japanese lookout reported the sightings to *Hiei*'s bridge, *Atlanta*, along with destroyers *Laffey* and *O'Bannon*, loosened more salvos of shells at the silhouetted *Hiei*. The series of b-blooms sent up huge geysers of water around the battleship, washing the main decks. One five-inch shell struck *Hiei* amidship, but merely knocked out a supply compartment.

"Illuminate! Illuminate!" Admiral Abe shouted.

A moment later, powerful searchlight beams from *Hiei* blinked open and swept Ironbottom Sound from left to right until the beams fell on *Atlanta*'s superstructure like rays of sunshine. The sailors aboard *Atlanta* froze. The illumination was a Japanese night tactic familiar to

Americans, a prelude to generally accurate turret salvos and torpedo launches. Lt. Cmdr. Hank Bell, the gunnery officer aboard *Atlanta*, did not wait for orders from the bridge.

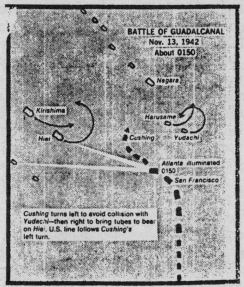

**BATTLE OF GUADALCANAL**
Nov. 13, 1942
About 0150

*Nagara*

*Kirishima*

*Harusame*

*Hiei*

*Cushing*    *Yudachi*

*Atlanta* illuminated 0150

*San Francisco*

*Cushing* turns left to avoid collision with *Yudachi*—then right to bring tubes to bear on *Hiei*. U.S. line follows *Cushing's* left turn.

"Counter illuminate and fire!" he shouted.

When Bell checked range, he gaped. The cruiser had come within 1600 yards of *Hiei*. *Atlanta*'s gunners sent a double salvo of six-inch shells at both *Hiei* and her escorting destroyers on the starboard side, for the American column of ships was now sailing between the big ships and their port escorts. Some of the shells hit destroyers *Akatsuki* and *Inazume*, but did minor damage. A port salvo sailed over *Hiei* and exploded in the sea beyond. The cruiser's gunners had fired too far from this close quarter.

Then, *Atlanta* paid dearly for these first salvos.

"Fire! Fire!" Capt. Masao Nashida cried from the bridge of *Hiei*. Then, he picked up his UHR phone and called destroyers *Akatsuki* and *Inazume*. "Torpedoes! Launch torpedoes at once!"

Sailors aboard *Hiei* and the two Japanese destroyers quickly responded. Unfortunately for *Atlanta*, the Japanese set their gun turrets and torpedo launches for close range since the American cruiser was a mere 1500 yards away. A salvo of fourteen-inch shells from *Hiei*'s port, twelve one-ton projectiles, spewed out of the mammoth tubes. The shells came from a mere 1600 yards, almost pointblank range for such big guns. Eight of the big shells struck *Atlanta*, disintegrating her superstructure in one minute. One shell hit the bridge and blew it away, including Adm. Norman Scott and all of the admiral's staff. Another shell struck the con room, killing three men outright and seriously wounded *Atlanta*'s skipper, Capt. Sam Perkins.

In seconds, *Atlanta* was dead in the water, her superstructure a mass of smoke and flames. The heavy explosions had lifted the 6,000-ton antiaircraft cruiser literally out of the water and then set her down again, shuddering and crippled. In the plotting room, fire control crews saw the speed indicator plummet to zero. Two of the shells had ripped open the engine room, destroyed the engines, and killed every man there. In the damage control room, the ship's terrier mascot, Lucky, whimpered fearfully from the deafening concussions and heavy smoke.

The damage control officer, coughing from dense smoke and wiping asphyxiating tears from his eyes, yelled into a JV, calling several areas. "Damage! Report damage!"

Nobody answered him.

Then came two torpedo spreads from *Yudachi* and *Amatsukaze.* Most of the long lances missed, but one from *Amatsukaze* struck stricken *Atlanta* in the aft starboard and shook the cruiser again. Damage control men, pressed beyond capacity, fought raging fires throughout the American cruiser, sealing off starboard compartments to stem a gush of sea water into the holds.

Meanwhile, *Atlanta*'s gunnery officer, Lt. Cmdr. Hank Bell, scrambled through the smoke and debris that had once been the cruiser's superstructure. He tiptoed over hot, twisted metal and the bodies of American dead and wounded. "Pharmacist! Pharmacist!" the gunnery officer cried during his dash forward. He hurried on until he reached the area that had once been the cruiser's bridge. He squeezed his face in anguish as he surveyed the damage and slaughter. Bell could see bloodied arms, legs, torsos, macerated heads, and wads of flesh scattered about the warped deck and

119

smashed wheelhouse. Amid the rubble, he could not recognize anyone because their faces had become bloody, burned flesh.

The gunnery officer stood aghast when a communications mate stumbled next to him. "They're gone, sir," the enlisted bluejacket said. "All of 'em gone."

"Can the ship move?"

"No sir," the sailor shook his head vigorously. "We ain't got a single engine and half the turrets are gone."

"Goddamn it!" Lt. Cmdr. Bell cursed.

"What're we gonna do, sir?" the bluejacket asked anxiously. "We're sittin' ducks. They killed over a hundred men with their first salvos and they'll get all of us if they send another salvo after us."

The gunnery officer poked his head through the debris on the bridge and pulled loose a pair of binoculars, perhaps a pair that Admiral Scott himself had used. The officer peered to the south where he saw the outlines of the other American cruisers steaming towards him. "They're coming," Bell told the communications mate. "Help is coming."

"They won't do no good against them battleships, sir."

Lt. Cmdr. Hank Bell looked hard at the bluejacket and gripped the man's shirt. "We aren't dead yet, and we're still afloat. So long as we've got one gun, we'll fight." He paused. "Now move!"

"Aye sir," the man answered before he scooted away.

But a moment later another salvo of fourteen-inch shells struck *Atlanta*, once more lifting her out of the water and igniting a new batch of fires from bow to stern. And five inchers from the Japanese destroyers pummeled the cruiser once more. One shell knocked Hank Bell off the mangled bridge, dumping him to the poop deck and breaking his leg so that he could not move.

Within two minutes, by 0150 hours, *Atlanta* had taken countless hits from the Japanese, including nearly a dozen fourteen-inch shells. Destruction lay behind every bulkhead in almost every compartment. Below deck, horrified sailors groped in the darkness, coughing from acrid smoke and sloshing through oily, gushing water that rose on every deck below. More than 200 of the 700 crew men were dead and another 200 injured. In a mere 120 seconds, Japanese gunners had transformed *Atlanta* from a sleek light cruiser into a burning wreck.

Pharmacists and volunteers worked desperately to treat the bleeding wounded while the rest of those still able toiled frantically to seal ruptures or to contain fires.

The communications mate, meanwhile, found most of the JV phones useless. He therefore sped about the smashed decks, stepping over burned and eviscerated corpses. Or, he stepped lightly over severed limbs and chunks of flesh mixed with steel debris. Finally, he reached an undamaged gun pit where the sailors were loading six-inch shells into the barrel.

"Commander Bell is the only officer left," the communications mate said. "He says to keep firing."

"We'll get the bastards," a gun chief answered.

Meanwhile, a damage control mate had reached the wounded Hank Bell and hoisted the gunnery officer to his feet. Bell then squinted again to the south where he saw the American cruisers still coming on. Then, he peered north at the silhouetted masts of *Hiei*. If the American cruisers did not engage *Hiei* soon, Bell and everybody else aboard stricken *Atlanta* would be dead.

"Find a searchlight," Bell told the damage control bluejacket. "Get a light on that battleship, even if you have to use a flashlight. Our cruisers have to see that target or all of us on this ship are going to the bottom."

"Aye sir," the sailor said before he bounded away.

# Chapter Seven

*Special Note*: The next several chapters cover the main action of the naval battle on Friday the thirteenth. The engagement began and took place for the most part in a half hour. However, the particulars of spewing shells, whooshing torpedoes, sudden death, widespread destruction, and sinking ships often occurred almost simultaneously. Thus, in narrating the ordeal of ships and men of both sides, the story will often regress in time.

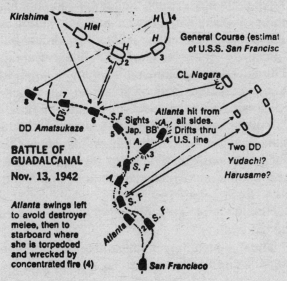

Kirishima

Hiei

General Course (estimat of U.S.S. *San Francisc*

CL *Nagara*

*Atlanta* hit from all sides. Drifts thru U.S. line

S.F Sights Jap. BB

DD *Amatsukaze*

**BATTLE OF GUADALCANAL**
Nov. 13, 1942

Two DD Yudachi? Harusame?

*Atlanta* swings left to avoid destroyer melee, then to starboard where she is torpedoed and wrecked by concentrated fire (4)

*Atlanta*

San Francisco

*Atlanta*, a hopeless wreck only two minutes after the battle began, hoped and waited for help from her fellow cruisers. Fortunately for Lt. Cmdr. Hank Bell, somebody aboard *Atlanta* managed to get a searchlight beam on *Hiei*'s huge pagoda masts. The cruiser lookouts on other U.S. ships thus saw the battleship. Capt. Cassin Young on the flag bridge as well as Cmdr. Bruce McCandles in the signal house of *San Francisco* ogled at the huge Japanese ship.

"Captain," McCandles called Young, "that battleship is no more than 3,000 yards off."

Young quickly called gunnery officer Don Ross. "Commence fire, 30 degrees to port! Commence fire!"

"Aye, aye," Lt. Cmdr. Don Ross answered. The gunnery officer had served under Cassin Young aboard cruiser *Raleigh* where he had earned a Navy Cross for his courage against air attacks on 7 December 1941. His efforts had helped to save the *Raleigh*. When Captain Young assumed command of *San Francisco*, he had asked Don Ross to join him, for Young considered Ross an excellent gunnery officer.

Ross's gunners now sent near point blank salvos of eight-inch shells towards *Hiei*. One shell knocked out a deck on the pagoda mast and another shell ruptured the deck of a secondary six-inch battery.

"Keep firing, keep firing!" Don Ross urged his gunners.

The forward turret unleashed another barrage of fire and two more eight-inchers struck

*Hiei*. One shell hit a magazine behind the forward fourteen-inch turret and erupted a fire that lit up the patch of sea. The other shell struck a portion of the conning tower and blew away the bulkhead.

Captain Nashida yelled into a JV. "Idiots! Why do you not respond?"

Captain Nashida called the damage control officer, Lt. Cmdr. Horishi Yokumo. "Are you all drinking sake?" he scolded. "Extinguish the fires behind the gun turret. At once! At once!"

"Yes, captain, yes," Yokumo answered.

Captain Nashida had barely spoken when Sekino's gunners sent a salvo of fourteen-inch shells at *San Francisco*. One shot hit the ready service locker five-inch AA ammunition and sent a whoosh of exploding flames skyward like a fireworks display at a Fourth of July picnic. A second shell hit the cruiser's rudder control system and sent the *San Francisco* veering erratically to the right.

"Damage control! Damage control!" Captain Young cried.

"We're getting on it, sir," Lt. Cmdr. Herb Shonland answered.

However, by the time Shonland and his crews began repairs, switching the cruiser to manual steering, *San Francisco* had lost sight of *Hiei*. But the two flagships would meet again in just fifteen minutes and on this next occasion, neither ship would escape as easily as they did this time.

Meanwhile, destroyers *Cushing* and *Laffey*

had come about to ply forward towards the Japanese ships. The bulk of *Cushing*'s crew had been squinting at the dark sea when the navigation officer took a reading and gaped. "My God," he told the skipper, Lt. Cmdr. Ed Parker. "We're within 2,000 yards of enemy destroyers."

Parker squinted through his binoculars and spotted two shapes skimming off the starboard bow. He had sighted *Yudachi* and *Amatsukaze* that had also come about.

"All gunners, set to starboard," Parker cried.

At 0149 hours, turret gunners swung their turrets right to unleash several salvos after the Japanese destroyers. However, one barrage landed short of *Amatsukaze*, but another shell hit the aft of *Yudachi* and started a small fire. Capt. Tameichi Hara, aboard *Amatsukaze*, ordered lights on the interloper. The booms from *Cushing* had also alerted the battleships. Soon, searchlights from both *Amatsukaze* and *Hiei* lit up Ironbottom Sound like floodlights over a football field. At 0153 hours, one Japanese beam fell squarely on *Cushing* to reveal her steaming swiftly parallel to *Amatsukaze*.

"She is after *Hiei*," Pilot Matsumoto told Captain Hara.

"Then she sails to her grave," Hara answered. "Commence firing."

The *Yudachi* lookout, meanwhile, had also seen *Cushing* and within a minute, the *Yudachi* gunners sent a barrage of five-inch shells at the American destroyer at about the same time that *Amatsukaze* unleashed a five-inch barrage at the speeding American destroyer. *Cushing* caught two hits amidship from the Japanese tin cans. The exploding shells rocked the destroyer and killed several American sailors before knocking out some of the destroyer's power. A moment later, another salvo from *Yudachi* smacked the U.S. destroyer's signal bridge and control room. The USS *Cushing* shuddered to a stop.

"Damage! Damge!" Lt. Cmdr. Ed Parker cried into his JV.

"We've lost power and signal apparatus," the damage control officer said.

"Can we maintain course by magnetic compass?"

"Yes sir."

"Then move it! Move it!"

"Aye sir."

A minute later, on manual control, *Cushing* again started northeast, but at a reduced 10 to 12 knots. Meanwhile, *Amatsukaze* and *Yudachi* sent new salvos of five-inch shells at the crawling *Cushing*. The salvos missed and Parker sighed in relief. However, Parker suddenly got a call from the deck officer.

"Holy Christ, captain, we're within a thousand yards of the battleship!"

Lt. Cmdr. Ed Parker and his executive officer, Lt. Tom Stokes, rushed to the port quarter of the bridge and stared in awe. The big hull of *Hiei* loomed out of the darkness like a black monster rising from the sea. In its evasive action against the Japanese destroyer, USS *Cushing* had closed on *Hiei*.

"Hard to starboard!" Lt. Cmdr. Ed Parker cried.

The helmsman, with the aid of hand control crews, swung hard right, sending up huge sprays of water. Within a minute, *Cushing* was off *Hiei*'s own starboard quarter. "Launch torpedoes!" Parker cried.

Again with local control, the crews sent a spread of six torpedoes off the midship torpedo deck. However, at that close a range, lookouts on *Hiei* saw the torpedoes plop into the water and the Japanese lookouts easily directed the helmsman to veer the big battleship out of harm's way. Parker scowled at his failure, but he felt relieved by the slow withdrawal of *Hiei*. Maybe Parker could get his stricken *Cushing* out of the area.

But *Cushing* had barely moved before star-shells exploded overhead and new searchlight beam exposed *Cushing*'s port quarter. Seconds later, several more shells from Japanese destroyers struck *Cushing*, setting off a series of explosions. The shells cut *Cushing*'s power lines and disintegrated a forward 20mm gunpit and its crew in exploding debris. Another shell tore up the P&S searchlight house along with the observation bridge. Fires erupted in the forward areas.

"Get us the hell out of here," Ed Parker cried.

Crewmen worked feverishly to keep manual control, while engine room crews shoved throttles to full ahead. But the damaged *Cushing* could only make a 15 knot speed. Still, she pulled away from the starshell glare overhead and the searchlight beam on her mid-quarter. She had almost lost the Japanese destroyers when a new searchlight beam from *Hiei* lit up *Cushing* like a sparkling white whale.

"Forward turrets!" Captain Nashida cried from *Hiei*'s bridge.

Two salvos of fourteen-inch shells boomed from *Hiei*, shuddering the inky surface of Iron-bottom Sound. A half dozen of the 1-ton shells struck the damaged American destroyer and her superstructure crumpled like a collapsing mountainside in an avalanche. *Cushing* almost bounced out of the water from the numbing concussions of heavy, close range explosions. In seconds, the lead destroyer of TG 67.4 had erupted into a burning graveyard that had claimed half of her crew.

All four five-inch turrets, two aft and two forward, caught direct hits or secondary explosions. One shell tore apart the wardroom with everyone inside. A third shell knocked out the forward observer station, the galley, the machine shop, and yeoman's quarters, leaving more than fifty dead and fifty wounded in these areas alone. Another fourteen-inch hit destroyed the fire room and crushed six men to death under the debris.

In the pilot house, still in one piece, Lt. Cmdr. Ed Parker and Lt. Tom Stokes called frantically for damage reports, but the fourteen-inch shells had knocked out all internal communications. Parker sent runners about the ship to gather information. However, the battleship salvos had set off so many fires, belching explosions, and heaps of debris, that no one could move very far.

"We may have to abandon ship, Ed," Lt. Stokes said.

"Maybe we can save her."

But, the holocaust aboard shattered USS *Cushing* soon intensified. The raging fires drew more enemy guns. Aboard *Amatsukaze*, Captain Hara grinned. "Aft guns will continue fire. We will finish her."

A moment later, another barrage of five-inch shells pummeled the badly damaged *Cushing*. Two shells hits the destroyer's living quarters, blowing away sleeping cots, stowed personnel gear, and writing desks. Another hit knocked out all steering and still another hit stopped all diesel power.

Ed Parker and Tom Stokes left the pilot house to personally direct repairs—if they could find enough men. The two officers had barely left the bridge when a five-inch shell from *Yudachi* smashed into this quarter and killed the helmsman and deck officer.

Parker found a squad of sailors and sent them aft to fight fires on the stern five-inch turrets. But, the dozen men had barely reached the area to spray water on the flames when another fourteen-inch shell from *Hiei* struck USS *Cushing* on the aft starboard and ripped open the hull before igniting her magazine. A deafening explosion rocked the destroyer and wiped out the entire stern section. All twelve men in the repair crew disappeared in a tremendous fireball. Parker and Stokes suffered lacerations from flying debris, but nothing serious. They wobbled along the ruptured deck, rounding up staggering, dazed men, but the cause was useless.

At 0156 hours, two minutes after Japanese searchlights had lit up *Cushing*, the American destroyer was finished. At 0157, Parker ordered the ship abandoned.

"Aye, sir," one of the sailors answered.

Every *Cushing* sailor who could crawl, walk, or hobble lowered himself into a whaleboat or a life raft, taking wounded with him. Dozens of other sailors had swarmed over the sides of the burning destroyer and plopped into the oily, debris-filled waters around the devastated U.S. destroyer.

"Get away as fast as possible," Lt. Cmdr. Ed Parker yelled from a lifeboat. "There might be more explosions."

About half of *Cushing*'s 250-man crew, including hordes of wounded, now huddled inside crowded whaleboats and lifeboats. But, as *Cushing* survivors moved away from the burning destroyer, tragedy followed them. Gunners on *Yudachi* and *Amatsukaze* continued to pound *Cushing* with five-inch shells. One of the shells overshot and scored a direct hit on a whaleboat, blowing the craft apart and killing all twenty sailors in the overcrowded boat. Three other boats caught shrapnel from near miss explosions, killing or wounding more *Cushing* sailors and sinking two of the boats. Survivors from these two boats bobbed in murky Ironbottom where they floundered throughout the night and into the next day before Higgins boats from Guadalcanal rescued most of them.

The sailors aboard USS *Laffey* had stared in awe as fourteen-inch shells blew apart *Cushing*. But, while the crew members of this second ship in the TG 67.4 column gaped at the obvious death blows to *Cushing, Laffey* moved unwittingly into a nest of Japanese warships. At about 0150 hours, the lookout on *Laffey* suddenly gaped when he detected no less than six silhouettes around the U.S. destroyer. The array of outlines included cruiser *Nagara*, four Japanese destroyers, and battleship *Hiei*. In fact, *Hiei* was so nearby the *Laffey* lookout feared a collision with her.

"We're right on top of that battleship," the lookout screamed into a JV.

Lt. Cmdr. William Hank, commander of *Laffey*, peered anxiously through binoculars in astonishment. *Hiei* was less than a thousand yards off. "Quick starboard! Quick starboard!" he cried.

The helmsman spun the wheel and the sleek

American destroyer quickly veered right, barely missing a collision with *Hiei* and just gliding past her starboard quarter. *Laffey* had come so close that sailors from both ships were near enough to leap aboard each other's vessels for a hand to hand brawl reminiscent of the pirate ships of yore.

"Torpedoes!" Lt. Cmdr. Hank cried.

*Laffey*'s crew quickly sent spreads of torpedoes into the water. However, the American destroyer had come so close to *Hiei* that the missiles did not even have time to arm before they struck the battleship's hull. The first spread bounced harmlessly off the side of *Hiei*. The second spread merely skidded up the hull of the battleship like salmon trying to leap over cascading rapids.

"Gunfire!" Lt. Cmdr. Hank now yelled.

In such close proximity, it was the topside gunners who responded first. The crews sent a chatter of 1.1 machine gun fire into the superstructure of *Hiei* forcing dozens of Japanese sailors to scurry for cover. Other topside *Laffey* gunners sent small 20mm shells into the superstructure of *Hiei*. The light fire merely clanged or pinged off the battleship's armor. However, one spray of machine gun fire penetrated *Hiei*'s bridge, chopped up the con room and wounded chief of staff Susumu Kimura, cut the face of Capt. Masao Nashida, and killed a deck officer with flying metal debris. Another machine gun bullet struck Admiral Abe himself, cutting a deep gash in his right leg, the second time this Japanese admiral had been wounded in battle. Abe fell to the deck and cringed in pain. He grimaced in anger when he saw the damage in the wheelhouse.

Abe reached for a dangling JV phone. "How can this be?" he cried angrily. "Where are the gunners? Where?"

"We are responding, admiral," gunnery officer Tokuno answered.

Seconds later, the battleship shuddered when a barrage of fourteen-inch shells left the number four turret of *Hiei*. Abe, with the help of two aides, struggled to his feet to squint out of the wheelhouse and witness an American destroyer's destruction.

The first fourteen-inch shell struck *Laffey*'s bridge, shattering the pilot house and con room. The helmsman, deck officer, and everyone else on the bridge died instantly from exploding shrapnel, flying debris, and collapsing metal. Fortunately, the *Laffey* commander was two decks below in the plotting room, helping gunnery officer Bill Doyle to direct fire. The explosions had merely knocked Hank and Doyle to the deck. Before they regained their feet, however, other fourteen-inch shells slammed into *Laffey*.

One shell hit amid-ship, piercing the aft fire room and electrical workshop. The explosions killed every man in both compartments and left a mass of smoking ruins. Another shell put out the number two and number three gun turrets, killing half the crews and injuring the others. A third shell blew away the number four turret, tossing gun, gun pit, and bodies skyward before plunking the dead sailors and debris into the sea. The next hit shattered the engine room where one survivor managed to crawl to a JV. "She's gone. All engines gone and steam is pouring out like crazy."

"We'll send a repair crew," Hank responded.

"No good, sir; it must be 200 degrees down here and there's no way we can stop the breach."

"Okay, get yourself out."

"Aye, sir."

Lt. Cmdr. Hank had barely digested this latest tragedy when another fourteen-inch shell tore *Laffey*'s stern apart, blowing away the aft deck and a dozen men, and then turning the propulsion system into a mangled mess. The American destroyer had now lost steering as well as power. And, before pharmacists could reach the aft section to aid survivors, rocking explosions turned the aft into an inferno. The injured there died in thick, oily fires.

"We can't save her, sir," the control officer called Lt. Cmdr. Bill Hank.

"Do your best."

The damage control officer rounded up whomever he could to fight the raging fires now engulfing the entire aft section of the ship. But moments later, two torpedoes from destroyer *Teruzuki* slammed into the port quarter of *Laffey*, knocking out all pressure and electrical power. The explosions also opened two gaping holes in the hull and sea water poured into the bowels of the

American destroyer bringing *Laffey* to a quick port list.

"We can't save her," the damage control officer again told Hank.

"Okay, pass the word," Hank said. "Abandon ship! Abandon ship!"

Thus, at 0153 hours, only three minutes after the first shells hit *Laffey* this second American destroyer had also become a victim of the big battleship.

Already, more than half the *Laffey* crew had died. Some of the dead lay in masses of bloody pulp under twisted debris in a dozen of the destroyer's compartments. Some were burned beyond recognition in flaming infernos, and some had drowned in flooded compartments below deck. Less than fifty men of the 250-man *Laffey* crew had escaped unscathed. While some of these able survivors lowered whatever whaleboats and life rafts they could, other sailors darted about the battered, burning decks to find wounded. They dragged injured men, many screaming from severe burns, from heaps of debris.

But the worst was yet to come.

Less than a hundred men, half of them wounded, managed to clamber into whaleboats and life rafts to escape listing, burning *Laffey*. The sailors in the several lifeboats rowed quickly away from listing *Laffey* before the destroyer keeled over and sucked some of the boats or rafts in a boiling eddy of water.

At 0230 hours, thirty-two minutes after the

vicious, disorganized battle began, the last life raft had pulled away from *Laffey*. But then, a thunderous explosion spewed from *Laffey*, lighting up Ironbottom Sound like an erupting volcano. The explosion tore the 350-foot, 1630-ton destroyer in one shattering blast. Flaming debris rained down on the men in the whaleboats and life rafts, killing more than half the survivors, including Lt. Cmdr. Bill Hank, *Laffey*'s skipper. Before the horrified survivors could react from this numbing ordeal, *Laffey* was gone, leaving behind a huge geyser of heavy steam on the surface of the sea.

"Oh my God!" one of the sailors whined.

"Good Lord!" another of the American sailors hissed.

Lt. Bill Doyle stared in awe at the dissipating steam, the last evidence of USS *Laffey* that now settled to the floor of Ironbottom. Then, he squinted to the south where he could see the outline of Guadalcanal. "Head for the island," Doyle told the oarsmen. "Let's hope the hell we can make it."

Doyle was not sure he would make Guadalcanal for the rattling concussion of shellfire still boomed all over Ironbottom while torpedoes still streaked all over the sea.

Meanwhile, at 0153 hours, while other ships had given *Atlanta* a respite, the American anti-aircraft cruiser continued through the gauntlet of enemy ships, *Hiei* and two destroyers on one side of her, with *Nagara* and two destroyers on the other side of the battered U.S. cruiser.

Wounded gunnery officer Hank Bell still had two turrets in operation and he ordered a renewed fire on *Hiei*, whose crews had been momentarily busy snuffing out fires caused by American gunfire.

Two salvos of six-inch shells from *Atlanta* boomed towards *Hiei*, less than 2,000 yards off and chopped out chunks of the battleship's superstructure. The *Hiei* again turned westward to avoid fire. Meanwhile, *Yudachi* quietly came about, stalking *Atlanta* like a wolf moving in on a wounded buffalo. *Yudachi*'s skipper, Cmdr. Kiyoshi Kikkawa stood on the bridge and stared fiercely through his binoculars at the burning American cruiser. "What is the range?"

"Five thousand meters and closing."

"We will launch torpedoes at 2,000 meters."

But, Kikkawa's delay was a mistake. As *Yudachi* came stealthily on, somebody aboard the flaming *Atlanta* got a searchlight on *Yudachi*. "Off starboard! Enemy ship!"

Gunnery officer Hank Bell, the surviving senior officer aboard *Atlanta*, peered through binoculars and turned to a runner. "Get a gun to starboard."

"Aye aye, sir."

Cmdr. Kikkawa, meanwhile, screwed his face when the searchlight illuminated his destroyer. He ordered an immediate torpedo launch. At 0154 hours, a whoosh of six missiles leaped off the deck of *Yudachi* and sped towards the cruiser. Spotters aboard *Atlanta* saw the wake and watched in horror. The cruiser's steering and power were gone, and *Atlanta*'s sailors could only gape.

"Brace for explosions!" Lt. Bell cried.

Fortunately, brisk winds sweeping across Ironbottom Sound threw the torpedoes slightly off course. And more important, Cmdr. Kikkawa did not know that *Atlanta* was dead in the water, so he had set torpedoes for a moving target. The missiles skimmed past the bow of the American cruiser.

Kikkawa frowned. He prepared a second torpedo attack, but two six-inch shells from *Atlanta* splashed and exploded in front of *Yudachi*. The near misses sent up sprays of sea water that washed over the decks of the destroyers. Before Cmdr. Kikkawa could react, *Atlanta*'s gunners had adjusted range and sent another pair of shells into *Yudachi*. One of the six inchers struck the pilot house, killing the helmsman and staff and starting fires. The second shell struck the forward fire room, knocking out an engine and starting a huge fire below deck.

"We must regain control and put out fires," Cmdr. Kikkawa shouted.

"Yes, commander," an aide answered.

Japanese sailors scurried frantically about the destroyer to put out flames. The damage had not been serious, for *Yudachi* could still maneuver. However, Commander Kikkawa did not like his destroyer lit up like a bonfire to draw enemy ships in this gloomy night. Kikkawa knew that a couple dozen ships, enemy as well as his own, were steaming about Ironbottom in disorganized confusion. Nervous gunners and uncertain ship commanders were firing at anything they could see, shooting first and asking later whether the target was friend or foe.

Within a minute, *Yudachi* damage control crews had snuffed out the fires in the pilot house and contained the flames in the hull's forward engine room. Cmdr. Kikkawa had also switched to manual control after the destruction of the pilot house so he appeared in good shape.

However, *Atlanta*'s gunners were not finished. They lobbed several more six-inch shells at *Yudachi*. Most of them fell short, but one of the six-inchers hit the fuel compartment and started a billowing fire, too big and too hot for the damage control crew, who had just finished putting out the fire room flames.

"We must escape, we must," the executive officer told Kikkawa.

The *Yudachi* commander scowled. He disliked the idea of leaving the fight, especially since he had an excellent opportunity to take another shot at burning *Atlanta*. "Is there no chance to put out this latest fire?"

"None, commander," the aide said. "And worse, our fuel supply may become exhausted by this fire. We must escape to the north before this happens."

Kikkawa nodded. "Set a 312-degree course

and steer north.''

The *Yudachi* turned to and steered northeast, for the flaming oil fire would indeed make the Japanese destroyer a tempting target. And in fact, the next two U.S. destroyers in the American TG 67.4 column, USS *Sterett* and USS *O'Bannon*, were following avidly in the wake of burning *Yudachi*.

# Chapter Eight

Moments before *Sterett* and *O'Bannon* began stalking flaming *Yudachi*, the USS *Barton*, in the rear position, had veered to starboard abruptly. USS *Aaron Ward*, in front of *Barton*, almost came to a full stop in order to avoid collision with cruiser *Juneau*, and *Barton* tried to avoid collision with her fellow destroyer. *Barton*'s commander, Lt. Cmdr. Douglas Fox, now found himself gliding eastward away from the other American ships of TG 67.4.

"How come *Aaron Ward* almost stopped dead?" Fox asked his executive officer. "What the hell's going on up ahead?"

"I don't know, sir," the executive officer answered.

*Barton* had veered off just a few minutes before when Lt. Cmdr. Fox had heard the scolding voice of Admiral Callaghan over the TBS at 0145 hours. "Get the hell off the TBS.

We'll tell you when to open fire." The order had puzzled Fox for he had seen nothing anywhere except *Aaron Ward* and *Juneau* beyond his port bow. Still, *Barton*'s skipper picked up a JV and called his gunnery officers, Lt. Wilbur Quinn and Lt. Harlow White. "Ready all turrets to engage."

A few minutes later, at 0148 hours, the crew aboard *Barton* saw the flashes of gunfire in the distance and then heard the rumbling booms echo across Ironbottom Sound. The sea fight had apparently begun, but where? Who was firing at whom? Lt. Cmdr. Douglas Fox stood rigidly on the bridge, searching the dark sea through binoculars. Each passing moment had increased the suspense. Fox then checked with his con officer.

"We're moving at about 18 knots on an 038 bearing," the con officer told Fox, "but I have no idea where the shooting is coming from."

Fox scowled and again stared at the dark sea. But still he saw nothing but the gunfire flashes in the distance off port.

*Barton* had only been commissioned on 29 May 1942, and after shakedown she had arrived in the South Pacific in September with a green crew and a commander with his first command. Thus, although Barton was a new ship with the latest radar equipment and gun control, her officers and crew had no combat experience. Lt. Cmdr. Fox therefore would play the game by the book when or if he engaged the enemy.

The anxious Fox looked at his executive officer who had also been scanning the sea through binoculars. "Do you see anything?"

"No," the executive officer answered.

Fox picked up a JV and called Lt. White. "Anything yet?"

"No sir," the forward gunnery officer answered.

"Stay alert." Then, Fox called Lt. Wilbur Quinn. "What do you see, Will?"

"Nothing, Doug," the aft gunnery officer said.

"Stay alert."

*Barton* sailed on cautiously for about a minute when, at 0149 hours, the destroyer had moved into range of a destroyer that had been exchanging fire with *Atlanta*. A moment later, the *Barton* lookout saw a fire erupt on the destroyer *Yudachi*. He called the *Barton* commander, who watched the Japanese vessel intermittently brighten from fire as she fired at USS *Cushing*.

"Off starboard, only a few thousand yards," the lookout called the bridge.

"Forward turrets, commence fire," Lt. Cmdr. Fox cried into a JV.

"Aye aye," Lt. Harlow White answered.

At exactly 0150 hours, *Barton* opened up on *Yudachi* with two salvos from her forward five-inch guns. Lt. White's gunners fired rapidly, expending a dozen rounds within seconds. Cmdr. Kiyoshi Kikkawa zigged and zagged his destroyer to avoid the spew of fire from *Bar-*

*ton*, and only one shell hit, striking the stern of *Yudachi* but causing little damage.

"Return fire," Cmdr. Kikkawa cried into his JV. He was now engaged with USS *Barton* as well as *Cushing*.

Seconds later, Japanese gunners fired furiously back at the American destroyer, but the engagement with two American ships disrupted their aim, and the shells missed *Barton*. A few seconds later, *Barton* returned fire, expending rapid rounds of five-inchers. However, none of the shells hit *Yudachi*. The *Barton* gunners had been thrown off target by the equally rapid gunfire response from the Japanese.

Both Lt. Cmdr. Fox and Cmdr. Kikkawa ordered torpedo launches, but the five torpedoes launched from *Barton* never came close to *Yudachi*, and those launched from the Japanese destroyer were equally inaccurate. The two destroyer skippers now resumed five-inch shell fire, while both ships steamed swiftly eastward over Ironbottom on a parallel course, and *Yudachi* still firing at USS *Cushing*.

For six minutes the exchange of gunfire between the two destroyers continued unabated, with *Barton* loosening a total of sixty rounds. In the meantime, both *Cushing* and *Laffey* had been badly battered by *Hiei*, and *Yudachi* had suffered the oil fire from *Atlanta*'s six-inch guns. Lt. Cmdr. Fox was elated by the bright oil fire; he could see his target clearly. He ordered engine rooms to increase speed for a better shot at the retreating *Yudachi*.

But at 0156 hours, *Barton*'s helmsman screamed, "Ship ahead!"

"Cut engines." Lt. Cmdr. Fox yelled. "Heave to!"

The *Barton* came to an almost complete stop as fellow destroyer *Aaron Ward* suddenly loomed out of the darkness and cut across *Barton*'s bow. *Aaron Ward* had been wandering aimlessly about Ironbottom after the B-1 column fell apart. Now, she had returned to investigate the gunfire exchanges and had nearly run into her fellow destroyer. When *Barton*'s helmsman successfully avoided collision, the crew sighed in relief, while *Aaron Ward* steamed out of sight.

Unfortunately, *Barton* had come within 2,000 yards of *Amatsukaze*, whose eager crew had already pulverized *Atlanta* and *Cushing* in the first moments of battle. In the next moment, *Barton* would suffer a fate never before witnessed in naval combat.

Capt. Tameichi Hara stood stiffly on the open deck in front of *Amatsukaze*'s wheelhouse, his shirt slapping against his chest from the gusts of wind. The wash of water kicking up from the bow sprayed damp mists on his face.

"Captain," Hara's executive officer suddenly pointed. "Flares!"

Captain Hara looked upward and saw star shells bloom in the sky to the forward and then explode in a spread of light. The brightness lit up four scattered vessels from 3,000 to 5,000 yards of *Amatsukaze*'s starboard aft. The ships were burning *Laffey*, burning *Cushing*, confusing *Aaron Ward*, and probing *Barton*. The Desron 10 commander picked up a JV and called his torpedo officer, Lt. Masatoshi Miyoshi. "Prepare torpedo launch."

"Yes, Honorable Hara."

The sleek Japanese destroyer veered right to maneuver into launch position, but during the turn the star shell light diminished and Hara could no longer see the American destroyers. But suddenly heavy gunfire flashes only a couple thousand yards away exposed *Barton* firing at the retreating *Yudachi*. Hara had also seen, through the gunfire flashes, the near abrupt stop of *Barton* as she avoided *Aaron Ward*. The combat-experienced Hara slyly closed on USS *Barton* while her crews centered their attention on *Yudachi* and *Aaron Ward*. When Hara came within a thousand yards of the American destroyer, he yelled into a JV. "Launch torpedoes!"

A spread of ten torpedoes, five from the aft pad and five from the mid-ship pad, sprang off *Amatsukaze*'s deck and swished towards *Barton*. Two of the torpedoes scored devastating hits. One torpedo struck *Barton*'s forward engine room and another struck the forward fire room.

In an uncanny single second, two heavy explosions erupted huge pillars of fire on *Barton*. The American destroyer broke completely in two and sank immediately to the bottom of Ironbottom Sound. *Barton*'s entire combat life had lasted exactly seven minutes, from 0150 hours to 0157 hours, Friday, 13 November 1942. The 347-foot length of steel went under in a hiss of steam and explosions only *ten seconds* after the torpedo hits. Lt. Wilbur Quinn and Lt. Harlow White, the two gunnery officers, were the only officers to survive. Only forty enlisted men survived, blown clear from topside decks and into the water. The forty-two U.S. sailors suffered varying degrees of burns and deep wounds from flying metal debris. The other 205 crew members had been killed instantly by the blasts or drowned in the abrupt sinking.

And, to worsen the horror, USS *Monssen*, sailing behind *Barton* in the B-1 column, shot past the quickly sunk ship in front of her and plowed through bobbing survivors, killing 25 of them. *Monssen*'s crew, so utterly astonished by the swift demise of *Barton*, were not aware of these men in the water. Later in the night, when the battle was over, USS *Portland* would pick up a couple of the survivors, and at daybreak, a Higgins boat would pick up more. Two would somehow swim to shore.

Both the crews aboard *Amatsukaze* and *Yudachi* stared in disbelief at the sudden death of *Barton*. These Japanese sailors were combat veterans, but none of them had ever seen a warship burst into flames and sink in a matter of seconds. The Japanese sailors had caught a mere glimpse of the flashing explosions and then nothing on the surface of Ironbottom. They could not believe that any warship, no matter how badly hit, could sink so fast.

But, neither Captain Hara nor Cmdr. Kikkawa had time to wait and gape. Hara continued eastward looking for more American targets and Kikkawa hurried northward to avoid American gunfire until he could snuff out the fuel compartment fire.

USS *Monssen* had been following *Barton*, when her fellow destroyer and *Yudachi* began their exchange of fire and torpedo launches. Lt. Cmdr. Charles McCombs, *Monssen*'s skipper, had assumed that *Barton* set the Japanese destroyer afire while the two ships shot at each other. Thus, at about 0154 hours, McCombs closed in on *Yudachi* to engage. He called his gunnery officer.

"Forward turrets, 30 degrees left; burning target off the port bow."

"Aye aye," the gunnery officer answered.

McCombs then ordered the helmsman to alter course 3 degrees. He also called the engine room. "Reduce to flank speed."

"Aye, sir."

Even though Lt. Cmdr. McCombs wanted to join *Barton* against the burning enemy destroyer in the distance, the *Monssen* commander did not want a collision with *Barton*. McCombs could not get a radar fix on either nearby *Barton* nor distant *Yudachi* because *Monssen* had suffered an SG radar malfunction from the Japanese bomb hit on the afternoon air attack. The gunnery officer would need to make visual guesses against *Yudachi*.

At 0156, the first salvo of five-inch shells thundered from *Monssen* towards *Yudachi*, who did not even know that a third American ship was now attacking her. The shells all missed. Then, at 0157, before the *Monssen* gunnery officer adjusted range for a new salvo, the crew aboard *Monssen* felt a shudder, like a tremendous underwater earthquake, as *Barton* exploded from the torpedo hits. On the bridge of *Monssen*, Charlie McCombs, his executive officer, and his helmsman gaped in numbed horror as the 1670 tons and 347 feet of complicated combat warship, with a crew of 247, vanished in a quick, double burst of light and a hiss of steam.

"Oh my God!" McCombs gasped.

Then, a lookout yelled into a JV. "Torpedoes off port quarter!"

The warning prompted McCombs to forget *Barton* and rush to the port side of the bridge, where he saw wakes in the distance. "Full ahead!"

The engine room crew responded and *Monssen* lurched forward, almost toppling Mc-Combs and his executive officer. But they and the crew sighed in relief. The torpedo wakes skimmed just beyond the stern of the American destroyer. The launch had apparently come from *Amatsukaze*'s busy crew.

But as the U.S. destroyer raced away from

the torpedo wakes, *Monssen* plowed through *Barton*'s survivors. The slicing bow of *Monssen* had killed some of the American sailors outright, while the heavy wash from the increased speed had drowned others. But nobody aboard *Monssen* had even seen the *Barton* survivors on the dark surface of Ironbottom Sound.

Now McCombs scanned the sea, looking for other American warships or other enemy ships. He spotted neither. However, lookouts aboard two Japanese destroyers, *Harusame* and *Ikazuchi*, spotted the faint outline of *Monssen*. The skipper of *Ikazuchi*, Cmdr. Naka Ikeda, studied the American destroyer through his binoculars and he then closed *Ikazuchi* for an attack.

"Prepare torpedo launch," Ikeda cried into a JV.

A moment later, a spread of six torpedoes leaped off the mid-deck of the Japanese destroyer. However, the torpedoes skimmed beyond the stern of *Monssen*. A second spread of torpedoes, apparently from *Harusame*, had been set too deep, and a pair of the four torpedoes that were on target shot under *Monssen*'s keel, since this *Barton* class destroyer had a shallow draft. The two torpedo spreads alerted the American sailors, and Lt. Cmdr. McCombs searched the starboard until he saw the silhouettes of the two destroyers against the dark horizon. He called his gunnery officer.

"Turrets 30 degrees to starboard; range 3,000 yards. Open fire!"

"Aye aye."

Seconds later, a twin salvo of five-inch shells sailed towards the Japanese warships, but all eight fell short. However, the forward gunners continued to pour shells eastward, and two of them finally struck *Ikazuchi*. One shell knocked out her forward gun mount on the main deck, killing the entire crew there. The second shell struck the mid-ship torpedo tubes, erupting heavy fire and sending torpedoes skyward like huge rockets. A half dozen men died in the explosions. Cmdr. Ikeda squeezed his face in annoyance. He had lost a dozen torpedoes with their mount, seriously reducing the ship's effectiveness. But even as Ikeda grumbled over the damage to his ship, USS *Monssen* had come within a half mile of *Ikazuchi*, and topside American gunners sent a withering stream of 20mm fire into the Japanese destroyer. The heavy barrage shattered *Ikazuchi*'s signal bridge, tore holes in the pilot house, and destroyed one of the ship's life boats. Fires suddenly blazed from mid-ship storage compartments, prompting Cmdr. Naka Ikeda to scowl. He called the engine room.

"Full speed!" Then he yelled to the helmsman. "Hard to port! Hard left!"

The sleek Japanese destroyer, now minus its forward gun mount and signal bridge, and with fires blazing on her topside, plowed a wide arc and away from *Monssen*. The gun crews of

*Ikazuchi*'s aft turret sent a barrage of five-inch shells after pursuing *Monssen*, but all missed, merely erupting geysers of water that washed over the decks of the U.S. destroyer. The near misses, however, prompted Lt. Cmdr. McCombs to break off pursuit and alter course.

As McCombs watched burning *Ikazuchi* zigzag away, he spotted *Harusame* some two miles off his starboard bow. "Come about 20 degrees to launch torpedoes," the skipper yelled.

When *Monssen* had reached launch position, aft torpedo crews sent a spread of five torpedoes that whooshed towards the Japanese destroyer in the distance. However, the Japanese lookout had seen the wakes in plenty of time and the helmsman easily maneuvered *Harusame* away from the torpedoes.

*Harusame*, in turn, launched a pair of torpedo spreads of its own at the hazy outline of *Monssen*, but the launch had been too hasty and too erratic. None of the torpedoes hit the U.S. destroyer. *Monssen* moved westward and lost sight of the second destroyer as she had earlier lost sight of the damaged *Ikazuchi*. As *Monssen* maneuvered about the patch of Ironbottom, Lt. Cmdr. Charlie McCombs retired to the navigation room to consult with his navigation officer.

"Where are we?" McCombs asked.

Before the navigation officer could take a reading, star shells suddenly exploded a few hundred yards off the American destroyer's aft. Lt. Cmdr. McCombs rushed to the open deck, the navigation officer behind him.

"Where did those goddamn star shells come from?" McCombs cursed.

"I don't know," the navigation officer said.

"We haven't seen any more Japanese ships around," McCombs said. "They must be from our own cruisers or from *Aaron Ward*." He picked up a JV and called the signal officer. "Flash a recognition signal before those idiots start throwing shells and torpedoes at us."

"Aye aye, sir."

A few seconds later, the signal officer switched on a light that became *Monssen*'s death warrant. The recognition light fell on the huge battleship *Kirishima* that had been steaming cautiously some 2,000 yards behind *Hiei* and now found herself a few thousand yards off *Monssen*'s port quarter. *Kirishima* immediately responded with two huge tentacles of light that bared *Monssen*, and drew destroyers, *Harusame*, and the ever alert *Amatsukaze* towards the American destroyer.

"My God! My God!" Lt. Cmdr. McCombs cried.

He had barely spoken when a barrage of five-inch shells from the two Japanese destroyers and a salvo of fourteen-inch shells from *Kirishima* boomed towards the exposed USS *Monssen*.

In less than a minute, a staccato of explosions shattered the American destroyer with 37 shell hits, including a half dozen fourteen-inchers. Shells smashed into both engine rooms, killing the crews instantly, setting fires, and unleashing a hiss of scalding steam. A fourteen-inch shell destroyed the fire room and killed every man there. Other shells knocked out gun turrets, torpedo launch areas, ward rooms, the galley, and ammo loading quarters. More shells knocked out all power pumps and gun controls. Another fourteen-inch shell struck the bridge, killing the executive officer, the deck officer, and the helmsman. All steering was gone, manual or otherwise. All power was gone, all turrets were masses of smoldering wreckage with distorted corpses in every warped gunpit. One shell had even shattered the dispensary, killing the pharmacist and bed-ridden wounded.

In sixty seconds, the U.S. destroyer became a burning hulk, dead in the water, listing to port, with 130 of her crew dead.

Survivors, many of them burned or bleeding profusely from shrapnel wounds or flying debris, scurried about the flaming ship to seek safety. Sailors weaved past grotesquely burned bodies, scorched torsos, or heads with surprised looks on their faces. Too often, the able who tried to help the wounded became themselves corpses from new shell hits.

Ironically, Lt. Cmdr. McCombs and his navigation officer had been on the open deck and had only suffered lacerations from flying debris when the shells wiped out the bridge and its occupants. McCombs picked up a JV to call the pilot house, but no one answered, for a half dozen five-inch shells had turned the pilot house into a death tomb for every one of the six men inside.

"Damage control!" McCombs yelled into a JV, even while he bled from his left arm and left leg. "Report damage! Report damage!"

But nobody answered. McCombs and his navigation officer now stepped over the twisted, warped deck. They moved slowly and warily, coughing from heavy smoke, hanging onto twisted metal because of *Monssen*'s list.

"We can't do anything, commander," the navigation officer said.

"We'll try," McCombs answered.

The skipper gathered whatever men he could to attend wounded, snuff out flames, and seal flooding compartments. Fortunately, the Japanese gunners from *Amatsukaze*, *Harusame*, and *Kirishima* had ceased fire once they saw the listing, burning *Monssen* aflame from bow to stern. They had accurately concluded that the American destroyer was finished and they saw no need to expend further ammunition on her.

*Monssen* had entered the fray at 0156 hours, one minute before the sudden, spectacular demise of *Barton*. Three minutes later, at 0159 hours, USS *Monssen* herself was a burning, useless wreck. One hundred and thirty-eight men lay dead in crumpled compartments throughout the below and topside quarters. Injured lay in small heaps in the few undamaged sections of the destroyer.

For a half hour, Lt. Cmdr. Charlie Mc-Combs and his surviving sailors tried to fight fires, repair damage, contain flooding, and care for wounded. But the Japanese shells had battered *Monssen* beyond salvation.

"We can't save her, sir," one of the surviving gunnery officers told the skipper.

McCombs, his body reeking with perspiration from the hot fires around him, squeezed his face. "We've got an awful lot of wounded aboard."

"We'll just have to get them off."

McCombs sighed and then nodded. Then, at 0220 hours, when the night action was about over, McCombs yelled into a PA. "Abandon ship! Abandon ship!"

Within ten minutes, survivors had lowered whaleboats and rafts to drift in the murky waters of Ironbottom Sound. Many aboard the rafts and whaleboats, badly burned or wounded, would die before rescue. In fact, more than 60 percent of *Monssen's* crew would perish. The USS *Monssen* herself would burn throughout the night until she exploded and sank at about noon on 13 November 1942.

## Chapter Nine

Meanwhile, USS *Sterett* and USS *O'Bannon* continued to trail flaming *Yudachi*.

Aboard *Sterett*, the ship's commander, Lt. Cmdr. Jesse Coward, peered from the bridge at the burning Japanese destroyer. "It looks like we've got a pigeon."

"Yes sir," the deck officer said.

Then Coward picked up a JV. "Increase speed to 30 knots."

"Aye sir," came the response from the engine room.

As *Sterett* lurched forward, Lt. Cmdr. Ed Wilkinson of USS *O'Bannon* also ordered increased speed to close on the apparently disabled Japanese destroyer. At 0158 hours, when *Sterett* and *O'Bannon* closed to 3,000 yards on the limping *Yudachi*, both American destroyers opened with forward five-inch turret guns. The first salvos missed, except for two shells that knocked out a rear gun turret and a torpedo rack on the Japanese destroyer. The crews aboard the two American ships cheered.

But in the darkness of early 13 November 1942, on the murky, sinister surface of Ironbottom, nothing was certain. The Sealark Channel cradled a multitude of warships that loomed out of the night from nowhere, seeking friend or foe. All these ships, American or Japanese, plied about Ironbottom with uncertainty, their nervous, trigger happy gun crews waiting to pounce on anything. *Sterett* and *O'Bannon*, hunters at the moment, would themselves soon become targets.

After *Sterett*'s first salvo at *Yudachi*, the SG radar man aboard the American destroyer got sudden blips on his screen, the readings ranging from 1,000 to 5,000 yards. "Captain, enemy ships all over the place," the radar man called to Lt. Cmdr. Jesse Coward.

Coward rushed to the bridge and peered through his binoculars to both starboard and port. He saw nothing on the dark surface of Ironbottom and he squeezed his face, confused. Then he got another call from the radar man.

"A big one, closing on port quarter," the radar man cried.

Now, Lt. Cmdr. Coward peered harder and saw a searchlight off starboard sweeping the sea. The beam came from the Japanese cruiser *Nagara* that was trying to find *Sterett* and *O'Bannon*, the two ships shooting at burning *Yudachi*. The *Nagara* was steaming at 30 knots, apparently bent on protecting the Japanese destroyer. Suddenly the searchlight beam fell on *Sterett*'s starboard.

"Full ahead left! Full ahead left!" Coward cried.

The helmsman spun the wheel while engine room crews pushed up speed to nearly 30 knots. *Sterett* plowed in a wide arc just as two salvos of six-inch shells from *Nagara* screamed towards the American destroyer. Most of the six-inchers missed, but one of the shells smashed into the port aft, disabling *Sterett*'s steering gear. Then, another salvo from *Nagara* screamed towards *Sterett*. Again, most of the shells plopped into the sea off the destroyer's starboard bow and erupted geysers of water like huge white ghosts popping out of the sea. But one shell snapped off the destroyer's mast, including the radar antenna. Debris tumbled into the sea. The furious fire at *Sterett* chased off *O'Bannon* and she soon lost sight of *Sterett*.

"Hit 'em back!" somebody yelled from *Sterett*'s pilot house.

The aft turret swung right and the gunners unleashed two salvos of five-inch shells at *Nagara*. Most of the shells plopped harmlessly into the sea, but two of the five-inchers struck *Nagara*'s bridge and forward turret respectively. The bridge hit killed two staff members and wounded *Nagara*'s commander, Capt. Masakane Suzuki. Flying debris struck Suzuki's left arm and opened a deep gash. But miraculously, the falling chunks of metal collapsed in front of him.

Suzuki struggled to his feet through the debris to a JV. "Damage! Report damage!

"The turret on the main deck forward is disabled, Honorable Suzuki," the damage control officer said. "The guns are frozen and the turret will not turn."

"Casualties?" Suzuki asked.

"Two slightly wounded."

The commander scowled. He picked up his binoculars and stared at the sea. However *Sterett* had escaped the searchlights. Suzuki thought the American ship had run off, but suddenly another salvo boomed from USS *Sterett*. Two more shells hit the plotting room below the bridge and erupted a huge fire that sent flames pouring skyward and exposing *Nagara* like a moose caught in a poacher's headlights. Captain Suzuki scowled again. Like every other commander in this confused melee, he knew that a burning ship became a quick target for enemy gunners, especially amidst the chaos that now reigned in Ironbottom Sound during these first hours of Friday the thirteenth. He yelled into a JV.

"You must put out the fire!"

"We are trying, Honorable Suzuki," somebody responded from the deck beyond the burning plot room. "There has been an oil leak that nourishes the flames."

"Retire to the north," Suzuki told his helmsman. "We must retire until we can put out these fires."

"Yes, Honorable Suzuki."

Meanwhile, a repair crew on USS *Sterett* worked frantically to restore the steering apparatus. They cheered from the stern of the destroyer, for they had left *Nagara* burning and pulling away. But the rasping voice of a chief jerked the crew from their momentary lapse of watching the Japanese cruiser.

"Move it! Move it!" the grizzly chief barked at the repair crew. "Do you think this is a god-damn floor show?"

The crew quickly resumed work and soon repaired one of the rudders.

"Okay," the chief yelled to the pilot house through a JV. "We've made emergency repairs, and you can turn her at least 20 degrees."

"Good job, chief," the *Sterett*'s deck officer answered.

Now, as *Sterett* moved westward, the crew squinted at burning *Nagara* to the north and flaming *Yudachi* to the east. They had not seen the huge, black silhouette until the hulking shadow was almost on top of them.

"Oh my God! My God!" the lookout hissed. He picked up a JV and yelled to the bridge. "Battleship! Battleship dead ahead!"

"Hard right, hard right!" Coward cried.

But, with damaged steering, *Sterett* came within 2,000 yards of the battleship before the helmsman brought the ship around.

"Torpedo launch! Torpedoes!" *Sterett*'s skipper cried.

Six torpedoes quickly skimmed across the

inky surface of Ironbottom Sound towards the battleship. Four missed, but two slammed into the hull and exploded, shuddering the Japanese warship. However, the huge *Hiei* had only been slightly hurt and her repair crews quickly sealed off two compartments to avoid serious flooding.

Admiral Abe, bandaged from thigh to calf from the early injury to his right leg, hobbled to a JV. "Where are the gunners? Are they asleep? How can these pesky Yankee destroyers attack us with no response?"

Yet, before the Japanese gunners aimed their big turrets at *Sterett*, the American gunners sent two more salvos of five-inch shells into *Hiei* from within 2,000 yards. The effort was like throwing rocks at a giant, creating more nuisance than serious damage. A half dozen five-inchers smashed into the forward area of *Hiei*, but only killed a few Japanese sailors and caused light damage on the bridge because of the battleship's heavy armor. Lt. Cmdr. Jesse Coward frantically called for distance between themselves and the battleship, while inciting his gunners to pump round after round into *Hiei*. The furious barrage of five-inch shells finally chopped away a breast plate, knocked out a small gun, tore away pieces of the superstructure, and killed or maimed more than two dozen sailors of the 3,000-man battleship crew.

Then Coward and his spunky gunners paid for their efforts. *Sterett* had opened to 4,000 yards from *Hiei* when a searchlight beam from

163

the battleship struck *Sterett* like a death ray. A salvo of fourteen-inch shells from *Hiei*'s forward turret hit the American destroyer like blasts from a heavy gauge shotgun at point-blank range. Three of the monstrous shells exploded on *Sterett*'s rear quarter and knocked out everything from the mid-quarter to the stern. The fourteen-inchers destroyed the aft gun turret, the 20mm gunpit, the stern depth charge rack, the handling room below the aft deck, the mid-quarter 40mm guns, and the aft fire direction compartment. Blazing oil fires and dense smoke smothered the entire rear half of the American destroyer. More than 20 percent of *Sterett*'s crew, over fifty men, died at their posts. Pharmacists dragged away another dozen bloody or burned wounded.

"Damage! Report damage!" Lt. Cmdr. Jesse Coward yelled from the con room.

"The whole aft is gone, smoking and burning," Ensign Pete Hall, the fire control officer, answered Coward.

"What can we do?" Coward asked.

"Get the hell out of here, sir," Pete Hall answered.

Lt. Cmdr. Jesse Coward sighed and then looked at his helmsman. "Turn another four degrees and make for Tulagi." Then to the engine room, "Give us all you've got—on the double!"

"Aye aye, sir," came the reply from below.

At 0200 hours, less than a minute after the battering from *Hiei*'s fourteen-inch guns, the

American tin can steamed into the darkness of Ironbottom Sound. But the brilliant aft fires clearly lit up *Sterett* for *Hiei*'s gunners and they sent new salvos of fourteen-inch shells after the fleeing American destroyer. Four of the 1-tonners missed, but two of them smashed the mid-quarter number three and number four handling rooms, killing everybody in both compartments; a dozen men.

Still, Ensign Pete Hall and his fire control crews brought the flames under control. USS *Sterett* remained afloat; but she had power, and limited steering. Two minutes later, she had finally escaped *Hiei*, leaving the battleship in the darkness behind her, and escaping the fate of USS *Cushing* and USS *Laffey*.

By 0230 hours, Ensign Hall had reached the bridge. "We've got things pretty well under control, sir, but we can't do a thing. Every gun is out except for the forward turret, main deck."

Coward sighed. "Let's hope we can make Tulagi."

Ensign Pete Hall nodded.

Meanwhile, as *Sterett* escaped, Lt. Cmdr. Hiroshi Yokumo and his fire control crews aboard *Hiei* fought the fires caused by the pesky American destroyers, who had popped away at the huge battleship with five-inch, 20mm, and even machine gun fire. Captain Nashida, *Hiei*'s commander, picked up a JV and talked to Yokumo, who told the battleship's skipper they were doing well.

However, Yokumo could not say when he would have all fires out. And in fact, they would not get fires out before yet another U.S. destroyer challenged *Hiei*.

A brisk wind had now begun to sweep over Ironbottom, whipping up small breakers, while broken clouds drifted overhead. Several minutes before *Sterett*'s skipper, Lt. Cmdr. Coward, had steamed away in the darkness, the USS *O'Bannon* had come about. At about 0154 hours, Lt. Cmdr. Ed Wilkinson stood on *O'Bannon*'s bridge and peered hard through his binoculars. He saw only burning ships in the distance, with no idea which ships were American and which were Japanese. Further, since the TG 67.4 armada had scattered in all directions, Wilkinson had no idea where the other American ships were. The *O'Bannon* commander prowled cautiously about Ironbottom Sound. He had sailed westerly about two minutes when he saw blinking lights off the port bow. Wilkinson carefully closed on the lights and then gaped. The blinking lights had been the exchange of gunfire between *Hiei* and *Sterett*, and now *O'Bannon* had found herself almost on top of *Hiei*, now moderately aflame from five-inch hits.

"Hard to port! Hard to port!" Wilkinson yelled to his helmsman.

*O'Bannon* veered left and soon came broadside of *Hiei*, lying off the battleship's starboard at a mere 1200 yards. The men aboard USS *O'Bannon* peered in horror, ogling at the hundreds of white shapes, Japanese sailors, who scurried about *Hiei*'s deck like white ants.

"Torpedoes! Launch torpedoes with short fuse!" Wilkinson yelled.

*Hiei* was still engaged with *Sterett*, when at about 0156 hours, a spread of *O'Bannon* torpedoes sped towards the big battleship. Most of them either failed to charge or they skidded up the hull of the battleship and slid off, despite the short fuses. However, two of the missiles exploded on *Hiei*'s stern, igniting a magazine. The big battleship shuddered from the ensuing blasts, and hot debris exploded, popped, convulsed, flashed, smoldered, zooming upwards like an exploding fireworks warehouse. Lt. Yokumo and his fire control crews stood aghast. The huge fires lit *Hiei* so brightly she could even be seen by U.S. marine spectators who had lined the shore of Guadalcanal to see the bloody Friday brawl.

The shudder and fires had also grasped the attention of *Hiei*'s gunners, allowing burning *Sterett* to get away.

On the flag of the battleship, both Capt. Masao Nashida and Admiral Hiroaki Abe reacted in horror. The huge stern fire would draw every naval gun in Ironbottom Sound. Captain Nashida screamed into a JV.

"We must douse the fires; we must douse the fires!" Then, Captain Nashida scowled at the silhouette of *O'Bannon*. The brazen destroyer had put his battleship in serious danger. "Open fire to port!"

But, even as the big fourteen-inch guns turned left, Lt. Cmdr. Ed Wilkinson aimed every one of his five-inch guns at burning *Hiei* and pummeled the big battleship with a barrage of shells. Several shots battered *Hiei*'s forecastle; more five-inch shells tore a hole in the forward conning tower.

Then, a searchlight beam caught *O'Bannon* and Wilkinson found himself in a precarious position. Cruiser *Nagara*, despite fires, had turned to and steamed full ahead to aid *Hiei*. Now, the cruiser sent six-inch shells at *O'Bannon*, all of which missed. Destroyers *Akatsuki* and *Inazuma* also plowed from their screen position off *Hiei*'s starboard and lobbed five-inch shells at USS *O'Bannon*. But, the barrage of shells, zooming around Ironbottom like huge, berserk Roman candles, missed their target and merely sent up dozens of shuddering geysers in the small patch of sea between *Hiei* and the American destroyer. Then, even battleship *Kirishima* came up from her rear position behind *Hiei* and tossed a volley of fourteen-inch shells at *O'Bannon*.

Two of *Kirishima*'s 1-tonners, near misses, bounced the little American destroyer out of the water, and one of the shells tore the forward torpedo rack from its deck mooring, tossing the rack and exploding torpedoes into the sea where the torpedo explosions shot up fragments of shrapnel, metal, and sea water in grotesque skyward geysers.

Next, the skippers of *Inazuma* and *Akatsuki*

unleashed spreads of torpedoes. But the Japanese torpedo crews fired too anxiously and from too far away. Seven of the torpedoes missed by a wide margin. However, one missile caught one of *O'Bannon*'s propellers and exploded, shaking the stern violently, and lifting *O'Bannon*'s aft out of the water before slamming the aft of the American destroyer on the surface again.

Lt. Cmdr. Ed Wilkinson yelled into a JV to the engine room. "Give us all you can. We've got to get the hell out of here."

"Aye aye, sir."

USS *O'Bannon*, zigzagged at top speed, sometimes leaning precariously to port and then to starboard. But, she escaped *Nagara*'s searchlight and scooted eastward, away from the closing Japanese cruiser and destroyers. Enemy shells and torpedoes followed escaping *O'Bannon*, but the shells fell short, and the lookout successfully directed the helmsman to comb the torpedo wakes. Thus, at about 0159 hours, after a furious three minutes of fire from two battleships, a cruiser, and two destroyers, USS *O'Bannon* escaped with minor damage and no casualties, while causing the worst damage yet to battleship *Hiei*. *O'Bannon* had surely enjoyed the luck of the Irish.

But then, suddenly, out of the dark sea, burning *Sterett* came almost perfectly abeam of *O'Bannon*, since both ships were escaping from *Hiei* at about the same time. However, *Sterett* had been running south while *O'Bannon* was running west. *Sterett*'s helmsman, rattled by the raging fires aboard his destroyer, had been slicing through the blackness as fast as he could to find safety. He did not even see *O'Bannon* cross his bow. Luckily, the fires aboard *Sterett* gave *O'Bannon*'s helmsman a clear view.

"Dead ahead, sir, a burning ship," the helmsman told Lt. Cmdr. Wilkinson. "Looks like one of ours."

Wilkinson peered through his binoculars and then turned to his helmsman. "Hard left!"

"Aye, sir."

*O'Bannon* veered to port in plenty of time to avoid a collision with *Sterett*. Then Wilkinson reduced speed and sailed parallel to *Sterett*. Sailors aboard *O'Bannon* hurried to the starboard decks to ogle at the burning fellow destroyer.

"Can we help out?" Wilkinson called *Sterett* with blinker signals.

"We're okay," Lt. Comdr. Jesse Coward answered with his own blinker light.

Soon, burning *Sterett* disappeared off *O'Bannon*'s stern and a few minutes later, *O'Bannon*'s sailors saw another ominous sight: a couple dozen American sailors floundering in the water. They were USS *Laffey* survivors. Lt. Cmdr. Wilkinson ordered reduced spped and he then spoke over a PA.

"Stand by to heave life preservers."

"Take us aboard," somebody yelled from the murky water.

"We can't stop for that; too dangerous,"

Wilkinson answered. "But we'll radio your position and help will come your way."

Wilkinson's refusal to pick up these fellow Americans demonstrated one of the strange ironies of the Pacific War. The Americans, who purportedly placed a high premium on human life, rarely plucked anybody out of the sea during the height of battle. Conversely, the Japanese, who treated life cheaply, supposedly, always attempted to rescue their floundering sailors, regardless of any danger to themselves.

The crew of *O'Bannon* merely tossed about twenty doughnut-shaped life preservers into the dark water, and the men in the sea swam frantically to retrieve them. The *O'Bannon* crew had barely mulled over this woeful sight of floundering fellow sailors when they met still another perturbing scene, this time off their starboard. Wilkinson again ordered reduced speed as his destroyer now closed on burning, listing *Cushing*, still belching fires and explosions. The *O'Bannon* sailors saw in the water nearby more sailors on the surface of Ironbottom, the survivors of lifeboats that had been riddled or sunk from the Japanese shellfire at the burning and abandoned USS *Cushing*.

Lt. Cmdr. Ed Wilkinson again shouted from the bridge. "We can't pick you up, but we'll report your position."

Soon, the crews of *O'Bannon* threw more life preservers overboard to the dozen or so sailors in the water.

Wilkinson then checked with his navigation

officer. "What's our position?"

"9.15 south by 157.5 east," the officer answered.

"Call Tulagi. Find out if they can send out Higgins boats or a minesweeper for these *Cushing* and *Laffey* survivors."

The navigation officer nodded before he called Task One Shore Headquarters in Tulagi. The Task One OD officer said that minesweeper USS *Bobolink* was getting ready to leave the harbor at first light. The OD officer would relay the 9.15 south by 157.5 east location to the minesweeper and hopefully the ship would rescue these men. However, the OD said, *Bobolink* would be so busy, nobody was certain how many sailors the minesweeper could rescue.

Then, at about 0200 hours, a flight of PBYs dropped a bouquet of aircraft flares over Ironbottom Sound and brightened a huge patch of sea. The flares blatantly exposed a number of ships, all steering about the sea in haphazard confusion within 3,000 yards of each other. The sight of so many close quarter enemy vessels stirred both American and Japanese gunners in their gun turrets.

In the brief moments of pseudo-daylight, a thunder of gunfire spewed across Ironbottom Sound, probably the heaviest ever seen or heard in naval warfare. Even barrages of long range 155mm American artillery fire from Tulagi and Pistol Pete Japanese artillery from Guadalcanal joined the heavy naval gunfire.

The numbing din and blinding flashes of gunfire spewing over Sealark Channel rattled the sailors on the sea, as well as the American marines and the Japanese troops in the Solomons war zone. The barrage of fire shuddered the murky waters of Sealark Channel, already littered with floating dead, debris, oil slicks, floundering sailors, and crowded lifeboats.

When one 155mm shell barely missed *San Francisco,* Adm. Daniel Callaghan angrily called Tulagi. "Stop that firing before you hit us!"

The marine artillery fire abruptly stopped only one minute after it began. But, whizzing shells from naval ships continued to fly from every direction, churning up waters as though convulsing volcanoes had erupted from the ocean floor. An uncontrolled maelstrom now prevailed over the entire area. Boiling wakes erupted from engine screws as vessels maneuvered swiftly into fire positions or zigzagged to avoid hits from errant turret shells. Red tracers, smoking explosions, shattering balls of fire, and spewing geysers of water heaved over Ironbottom Sound. Ships were hit, sailors were blown away, vessels belched sudden flames.

Then, the flares died and Ironbottom reverted to total darkness. Still, the unchecked salvos of five-inch to fourteen-inch gunfire continued to bolt over Ironbottom.

Japanese destroyer *Akatsuki* had abandoned

its screen position next to *Hiei* and skimmed wildly about the sea, her five-inch guns blazing while her lookout sought a target. He found burning *Cushing*, and *Akatsuki* gunners shelled the American destroyer, adding more fires to this already furiously burning ship. Unaware they were beating a dead horse, the *Akatsuki* gunners cheered with each hit. "Banzai!" However, *Akatsuki*'s keen-eyed sailors had also spotted burning *Atlanta* and sent two torpedoes towards the cripped American cruiser. Both hit, adding more woes to the flaming American warship. But repair crews, despite intense heat, successfully sealed off two compartments to stem a flood of sea water.

The Japanese sailors aboard *Akatsuki* also cheered these torpedo hits, "Banzai! Banzai!" But, in the midst of these successes during the nightmarish bloody Friday brawl, the Japanese destroyer was suddenly caught in a cross fire between *San Francisco* and the American destroyer *Aaron Ward*. A barrage of eight-inch and five-inch shells came from two directions.

The American shellfire smashed *Akatsuki*'s superstructure. The torpedo station exploded, sending missiles flying skyward before the ignited torpedoes plopped into the sea. *Akatsuki*'s conning tower collapsed, carrying the pilot house and staff with it. The number four and number five turrets crumpled in a mass of twisted metal from two eight-inch hits. The antiaircraft pits warped into piles of debris from two five-inch hits from *Aaron Ward*.

Even burning *Sterett* got in a few punches from the two forward guns still in operation. The hits blasted *Akatsuki*'s depth charge pit and left her stern in a ball of fire.

The Japanese destroyer tried desperately to escape the cross fire, finally running left and scooting northward where she caught another eight-inch hit—this one from her own cruiser *Nagara*.

"Fools! Fools!" the commander of *Akatsuki* yelled into a UHR (ultra high radio). "Stop firing! You are striking your own vessel."

*Nagara* abruptly ceased fire, and when Admiral Abe learned of the hits on his destroyer from his own cruiser, he too yelled into the UHR. "All units, cease fire! Cease fire! We will withdraw to the northward to reorganize. All units will withdraw to reorganize." Then, at 0202 hours, Abe ordered *Hiei* to retire. The helmsman brought the big battleship about and steered burning *Hiei* up the darkened Slot.

Abe got an immediate call from the ever zealous Capt. Tameichi Hara. "I beg you, admiral, we should not withdraw. We are winning this fight."

But the Raiding Force Two commander would not listen. His fleet was in utter confusion and he did not believe they could dispose of the Americans unless they merged themselves into some kind of orderly attack pattern. Thus, all Japanese ship commanders would retire.

Adm. Daniel Callaghan got a call from USS

*Atlanta* at about the same moment that Abe had ordered his ships to retire for regrouping. The call came from Lt. Hank Bell, *Atlanta*'s surviving senior officer.

"Goddamn it, admiral, what the hell's going on? I think a couple of *San Francisco* shells hit us. We're barely afloat and we don't need hits from our own guys."

The angry words from the lowly gunnery officer brought no reprimand. Callaghan knew well enough that his ships were in disarray after the short, furious, disorganized clash. He cried into his TBS. "All ships cease fire! Cease fire! We will withdraw to reform column."

The confused battle in Ironbottom had raged for a mere few minutes, but during that time American destroyer *Barton* had been sunk, *Cushing, Laffey*, and *Monssen* were severely disabled. Cruiser *Atlanta* was badly crippled, and other American ships were damaged. On the Japanese side, destroyers *Ikazuki, Yudachi,* and *Akatsuki* were battered, with two of them not expected to survive. Cruiser *Nagara* and battleship *Hiei* were aflame, and both ships would be large, tempting targets for American guns.

Thus, at 0203 hours, after both Admiral Abe and Admiral Callaghan ordered a cease fire to reorganize their battered fleets, a sudden silence settled over Sealark Channel. But the serenity would be only temporary. A few minutes later, the two wounded armadas would turn on each

*Admiral William Halsey, commander of Allied South Pacific Forces drew up plan to reinforce Guadalcanal—Operation Orange.*

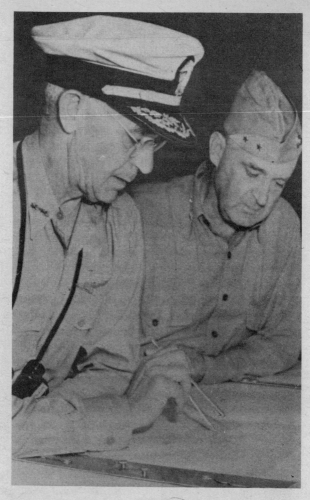

*Admiral Richmond Turner (L) and General Alex Vandegrift (R) were responsible for carrying out Operation Orange.*

*Admiral Daniel Callaghan was trapped in the awesome responsibility of trying to stop a Japanese battleship with his TG 67.4 cruiser fleet.*

Admiral Norman Scott commanded the second support fleet for Operation Orange from Cruiser USS Atlanta. He was killed in opening minute of battle.

Colonel Leverne Saunders, CO of USAF 11th Bomb Group, scored first blow in the Bloody Friday brawl when he led B-17's north to destroy Japanese air base at Buin.

*Captain Cassin Young (L) and Lt. Cmdr Don Ross (R) were Captain and gunnery officer respectively on the TG 67.4 flagship, USS San Francisco.*

Lt. Cmdr Ron Schonland (L) was damage repair officer of San Francisco, and Cmdr. Bruce McCandles (R) was communications officer. Because of battle casualties, McCandles inherited the awesome job of directing the TG 67.4 U.S. fleet.

Cmdr Bill Cole of U.S. destroyer USS Fletcher led his destroyer in the final minutes of battle that prompted the Japanese fleet to withdraw.

Lt. Cmdr Ed Parker commander destroyer USS Cushing. His ship took the brunt of Japanese attack in the opening minutes of battle.

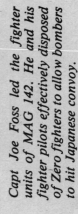

Capt Joe Foss led the fighter units of MAG 142. He and his fighter pilots effectively disposed of Zero fighters to allow bombers to hit Japanese convoy.

Major Robert Richards of Marine Air Group 142 led the air attacks that finished off the Japanese plans to reinforce Guadalcanal.

*Captain Joe Sailer led Dauntless unit on murderous
attacks against the Japanese reinforcement convoy.
The air attacks wiped out 10 of the Jap transports.*

*Admiral Thomas Kinkaid got in last shots of the Naval Battle off Guadalcanal when his TF 16 fleet sunk Japanese battleship Hirishima.*

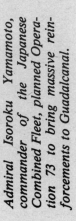

Admiral Isoroku Yamamoto, commander of the Japanese Combined Fleet, planned Operation 73 to bring massive reinforcements to Guadalcanal.

Admiral Gunichi Mikawa, commander of Japanese 8th Fleet, was responsible for carrying out Operation 73.

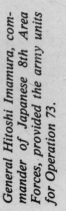

Colonel Kiyonao Ichiki led the first ground counterattack against marines on Guadalcanal. His unit was wiped out and Ichiki committed suicide.

General Hitoshi Imamura, commander of Japanese 8th Area Forces, provided the army units for Operation 73.

Admiral Nobutake Kondo commanded the Main Attack Force that was supposed to destroy Henderson Field. He tried, but he was unsuccessful.

Admiral Jinichi Kusaka commanded the 11th Air Fleet. He promised plenty of air support for Operation 73, but he never delivered.

*Admira Raizo Tanaka, knicknamed Tanaka the Tenacious by the Americans because the success of his Tokyo Express to bring reinforcements to Guadalcanal. However, in the biggest run of all, he failed because of American air strikes.*

*Admiral Hiroaki Abe (seated C) with his staff of Raiding Group II. He engaged in vicious Blood Friday fight off Guadalcanal with U.S. TG 67.4 fleet.*

*Admiral Susumu Kimura was Abe's chief of staff. He was flabbergasted when Abe gave an order to withdraw from battle.*

*Captain Hideo Shoji, lower right, with some of his pilots of 26th Air Flotilla at Buin. He never got a chance to use his flotilla because B-17's destroyed his airbase the day before the Friday the 13th battle.*

*The staff of the Reinforcement Group II transport unit. Admiral Tanaka is fifth from right, first row.*

*lt. Cmdr. Kiyoshi Kikkawa when a young cadet trainee. He lost his destroyer Yudachi in the Bloody Friday fight off Guadalcanal.*

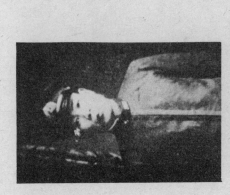

*Captain Tameichi Hara, commander of Japanese Desron 10 in the bloody battle, was infuriated when Admiral Abe made the decision to withdraw.*

*American marines on Guadalcanal move inland after invasion of this island on 7 August 1942.*

*Wreckage on Guadalcanal: Japanese naval units came off shore almost nightly to bombard U.S. marine positions on the island.*

*Henderson Field: Japanese were determined to destroy this American air base on Guadalcanal.*

*Japanese Pistol Pete artillery bombards Henderson Field from positions in the Guadalcanal jungles.*

*Scattered dead of the Ichiki Detachment. They failed completely in their banzai charges against U.S. Marine positions.*

*Two Japanese planes hit Ironbottom Sound after being shot down on the afternoon of 12 November 1942, when planes attacked American ships.*

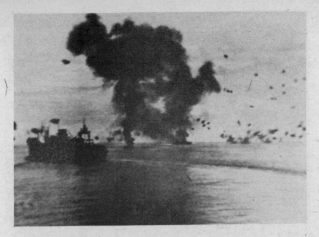

*American ships in Ironbottom Sound shot down more Japanese planes during the afternoon air attacks on 12 November. Transport USS President Adams at left.*

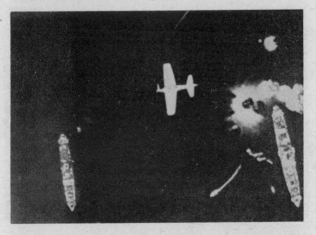

*Japanese scout plane flies over Japanese ships during battle on 13 November. American shells land close to Japanese crusier Nagara at right.*

*Thunderous exchange of gunfire between Americans and Japanese flash across Ironbottom Sound during Bloody Friday battle.*

*A Japanese searchlight catches American cruiser before Japanese open up on the U.S. warship.*

*Rattling fire spews across Ironbottom shoreline near Guadalcanal at height of the night action in Bloody Friday battle.*

*Japanese cruiser Nagara flees north after heavy hits by American warships.*

*Battered Japanese battleship Hiei tries to escape the combat zone. She was finished off day after the night battle by American aircraft.*

*Tanaka's transports burn on the shoreline of Cape Esperance in Guadalcanal. Only four of his 11 marus reached island and they too were destroyed.*

*End of Operation 73. Japanese transport, sunk on the beach, is grim evidence of Japanese failure to reinforce Guadalcanal.*

*Success of Operation Orange: U.S. Marine troops land on Guadalcanal after the Bloody Friday battle off Guadalcanal.*

other again in this bloody Friday clash off Guadalcanal island, and the armadas would clash with even more ferocity than before.

# Chapter Ten

Only fifteen minutes had elapsed since *Amat-sukaze* opened the vicious Friday the thirteenth sea fight at 0148 hours. Now, Adm. Hiroaki Abe ordered battleship *Hiei* on an east by northeast course and directed his other ships to join him. Meanwhile, Adm. Daniel Callaghan, attempting to reorganize his own scattered vessels, led all U.S. ships to the eastward, almost paralleling Raiding Force Two. Capt. Cassin Young took *San Francisco* on a straight easterly course. Abe was sure the Americans had retired south, while Callaghan was certain Raiding Force Two had withdrawn to the north. But, in a few minutes, TG 67.4 and Raiding Force Two would meet each other again.

Callaghan called for a rendezvous point at 161.1 degrees east by 9.8 degrees south, but many of his ships could not join him. *Atlanta* was a battered wreck, and several American destroyers had been sunk, abandoned, or left burning. From the open deck beyond the flag bridge of *San Francisco*, Callaghan scanned the empty seas to the north, unaware that Abe was sailing in the same direction as TG 67.4, although a few miles to the rear. After Captain Young instructed his helmsman, he retired to the navigation room to consult with his navigation officer, Lt. Cmdr. Rae Arison. Young and Arison plotted a course for 161.1 east by 9.8 south, at 18 knots.

On the deck above, in the signal room, Cmdr. Bruce McCandles remained alert for any instructions that might come from Admiral Callaghan. McCandles scanned murky Ironbottom Sound through binoculars and saw blinking lights in the distance, apparently a shipboard fire. He did not know if this ship was American or Japanese; nor did he care. He welcomed this moment of quiet after the mind-boggling din of recent gunfire, torpedoes, and explosions. McCandles, perhaps like every other American or Japanese sailor in the numbing engagement, was content to avoid further battle. At their instrument stations on the signal bridge, the bluejacket enlisted men also sat with a measure of relief, gratified by the silent calm that now prevailed over the surface of Ironbottom Sound.

Then, McCandles got a call from Admiral Callaghan.

"Send another message to all units."

"Aye, sir."

"On re-forming, we will maintain a course at 032, at 18 knots—and ask all units to report damage."

"Yes sir," McCandles said.

At about 0205 hours, replies began filtering back to *San Francisco*. Lt. Hank Bell, the gunnery officer aboard *Atlanta*, told Callaghan that Admiral Scott and most of the ship's officers had been killed. The ship's commander, Capt. Sam Jenkins, was injured. Lt. Bell himself was trying to move southeast to make Tulagi, but *Atlanta* was burning and without power.

Lt. Cmdr. Jesse Coward of *Sterett* came in with the next report. "We're burning and we have no lights or gun control. We're trying to make Lunga Point."

Lt. Cmdr. Ed Wilkinson had been taking his slightly damaged *O'Bannon* toward Guadalcanal when he received Callaghan's call to reform into the B-1 column. "We'll come about at once, sir, and fall into column as soon as possible."

The skippers of unscathed destroyers *Aaron Ward* and *Fletcher* reported little or no damage and they quickly altered course to rejoin *San Francisco*.

No replies came from destroyers *Laffey*, *Cushing*, and *Monssen*, whose survivors were in the process of abandoning ship. And, of course, no answer came from the so quickly sunk USS *Barton*.

The other cruisers of TG 67.4 had yet to suffer any real damage, so the skippers of *Portland, Helena*, and *Juneau* quickly acknowledged Callaghan's request and steamed swiftly to fall into column at the designated 161.1 east by 9.8 south rendezvous point.

Callaghan now issued specific instructions to the commanders of his two able destroyers, first calling *Aaron Ward*.

"Commander McGregor?"

"Aye, sir," the *Aaron Ward* commander answered.

"From what I understand," Callaghan said, "*Aaron Ward* and *Fletcher* are still able among our destroyers. We'll need some eyes for our cruisers, so I'd like you to put *Aaron Ward* at full ahead and assume the forward picket position of our column."

"Yes sir," Lt. Cmdr. Orville McGregor answered before he ordered *Aaron Ward* to top speed. When *Aaron Ward* got about 800 yards ahead of the cruisers, Callaghan called McGregor again.

"Okay, commander, far enough. Reduce to 18 knots."

"Yes sir," McGregor answered. "We'll have both visual lookout and a radar man on full alert."

"Good," Callaghan said before he called Lt. Cmdr. Bill Cole of the USS *Fletcher*. "Commander, I've sent *Aaron Ward* ahead of our column as a scout picket. I want you to fall in behind the cruisers as rear picket."

"Aye, sir."

"And stay alert. I expect *O'Bannon* to join. Don't mistake her for an enemy vessel."

"We'll stay alert, sir," Lt. Cmdr. Cole promised.

Then, Callaghan picked up his binoculars and stared again into the murky darkness around him. It was now 0206 hours. The lull had prevailed about three minutes, and TG 67.4, what was left of it, had begun to jell into a renewed B-1 formation.

The Japanese, meanwhile, were also reforming. Adm. Hiroaki Abe called the other ships over his UHR, the equivalent of the American TBS ship-to-ship communications. Abe had held a quick conference with his staff aboard *Hiei* and the Raiding Force Two staff had decided to regroup to the eastward at a 161.0 east by 9.7 south rendezvous, with the battleships and cruiser in column and screened by destroyers. After Abe issued the order to form column, he asked for damage reports from his various ships, even as fire control officer Tokumo and his crews worked frantically to put out fires on *Hiei*.

Capt. Hara answered first. "We have suffered little damage, despite our heavy engagement, but we are quite distant from the proposed rendezvous area. We will move swiftly to join at the rear of the column. I have ordered *Harusame, Yudachi, Teruzuki,* and *Akatsuki* to take station as the starboard screen. I will join this screen with *Amatsukaze* as soon as possible. I will order destroyers

*Murasame, Asugumo, Ikazuchi, Inazume*, and *Yukikaze* to take stations as the port screen to the north."

"Fine," Abe answered. He then called Capt. Masakane Suzuki of *Nagara*. "You will assume position behind flagship *Hiei*. Can you do this?"

"Yes, admiral," Suzuki answered. "We are fighting many fires, but our crews are making headway."

By the same 0206 hours, most of the Japanese vessels had reached their respective positions and steamed on their east by northeast course at about 15 knots. At the slower speed, they had fallen somewhat behind the American column that was steaming to the south on a near parallel course at 18 knots.

Both Admiral Callaghan and Admiral Abe were content to end the vicious battle right here. Never in naval history had two surface fleets caused so much damage to each other in the course of a few minutes. Admiral Abe had suffered heavy damage to *Hiei*, *Nagara*, and two destroyers, with slight damage to a third destroyer. Since Abe was conservative by nature, the Japanese admiral was disinclined to chance losing his battleship, or even his damaged cruiser. Admiral Callaghan had seemingly thwarted Raiding Force Two's attempt to bombard Henderson Field, and the American admiral would have been fully satisfied to break off further action, especially if the Japanese were retiring to the north.

Neither side had seen its enemy for the past few minutes and indeed, the night action might have been over—except for a few stray torpedoes.

By 0207 hours, the American fleet was on its easterly course. Callaghan would cross Ironbottom Sound, and if he found no sign of the Japanese, or if scout planes verified the withdrawal of the Japanese fleet, Callaghan would make a wide sweep back to Guadalcanal. Destroyer *Aaron Ward* led the way, followed by cruisers *San Francisco*, *Portland, Helena*, and *Juneau*. Behind the cruisers came destroyer *Fletcher* and slightly damaged *O'Bannon* that had caught up to the column.

As the American ships steamed easterly, a lookout aboard *San Francisco* saw white wakes streaking towards the American cruiser. "Torpedoes off port bow! Off port bow!"

Capt. Cassin Young and Adm. Daniel Callaghan hurried to the port upper deck and peered into the distance. When Young saw the wakes, he yelled into his JV to the helmsman. "Hard left!"

"Aye aye, sir."

The helmsman spun the wheel and the American cruiser arched into a sweep straight north. The vessel had made a 90-degree turn before Captain Young watched the parade of white streaks skim harmlessly off the port quarter.

"They came from the north," Young told the admiral.

Callaghan nodded. "That means they *have* retired up The Slot. Some enemy ship must have unloaded a parting spread of torpedoes. We haven't seen any sign of the Japanese anyway. We may as well reverse course and go back to Lunga Point."

Captain Cassin Young nodded and ordered the *San Francisco* helmsman to make another 90-degree turn left and head back to Lunga Point. The trailing American cruisers and two destroyers simply made the turns in column under the assumption that Callaghan had ordered a course change. Scout destroyer *Aaron Ward*, however, continued eastward and soon left the rest of the TG 67.4 armada far to the northwest.

By 0209 hours, no American lookout had yet seen a sign of the Japanese fleet, and Callaghan was convinced that he had made the right decision to return to Lunga Point. Callaghan was certain the Japanese fleet had indeed left Sealark Channel and was now steaming northward up The Slot.

The TG 67.4 commander called Bruce McCandles. "Notify all ships we'll assume an 092 course, south by southwest, for retirement to Lunga Point. We will maintain an 18 knot speed."

"Aye aye, sir," McCandles answered.

When news of the retirement reached the other ships of TG 67.4, no American sailor complained. They had had enough battle. Little did they know they were now sailing directly into the Japanese fleet that was sailing eastward.

After making its second left turn within three minutes, the *San Francisco* continued westward, followed by *Portland, Helena, Juneau, Fletcher,* and *O'Bannon*. When Lt. Cmdr. Orville McGregor of the forward picket *Aaron Ward* heard Callaghan's order to assume the 092 westerly course, McGregor put his destroyer at full ahead into a 170-degree turn and sped westward to join the rest of the TG 67.4 column.

Meanwhile, USS *Atlanta*, dead in the water and unable to go anywhere, was already to the west and she would soon find herself again exposed to booming shells and skimming torpedoes from both sides. Destroyers *Cushing, Laffey,* and *Monssen* were burning wrecks off to the southeast and none of these vessels nor their survivors would participate in the resumption of battle. USS *Barton*, of course, was already on the bottom of Ironbottom Sound.

Raiding Force Two, steaming on its northeast by east course, was still maintaining its 15 knot speed. Destroyers *Yudachi* and *Akatsuki*, despite heavy fires, had generated enough power to rejoin Raiding Force Two's column. Damaged *Ikazuchi* also managed to reach and assume its position behind *Kirishima*. *Harusame*, burning *Yudachi*, flaming *Akatsuki*, and able *Terutsuki* jelled into its starboard screen south of the *Nagara, Hiei, Kirishima* screen. Destroyers *Marasame,*

*Asugumo*, damaged *Ikazuchi, Inazume*, and *Yukakaze* held its port screen to the north. Burning *Nagara*, flaming *Hiei*, and undamaged *Kirishima* sailed in the middle.

*Amatsukaze* soon caught up. Captain Hara's flag destroyer of Desron 10 had been involved in so much action, and she had covered so much area, that she had come far out of position when Admiral Abe ordered his units to reform. But on full ahead, Hara brought his destroyer into the tail position of the south destroyer screen.

Thus, the entire complement of Japanese ships, except for *Samidare*, had joined in some semblance of order. However, the calm would not last long, for Raiding Force Two was sailing eastward and, unwittingly, closing on the American TG 67.4 that was now sailing west to return to Lunga Point.

By 0209 hours, six minutes after Abe and Callaghan had broken off action, neither admiral was aware that their fleets were on a collision course. Both admirals thought the other's flotilla had sailed away from him. At 0210 hours, unwittingly, *San Francisco* came straight into the patch of sea separating the heavy Japanese ships from its starboard south destroyer screen. The first inkling of this naval mesh came when a lookout aboard the TG 67.4 flagship saw blinking lights off to the northeast. He had sighted burning *Nagara* and *Hiei*, and he quickly called the bridge.

"Captain, sir," he said to Captain Young, "I think there's a couple of burning enemy ships off our starboard bow."

Captain Young hurried to the port deck, with Admiral Callaghan on his heels. Both men stared at the blinking lights through binoculars and recognized a battleship and the smaller cruiser. Callaghan was utterly astonished.

"What the hell is this? I thought they were off to the north and out of Sealark Channel."

Captain Young shook his head. "Maybe they're a couple of cripples who couldn't get out of the channel. In this confusion who could tell?"

Callaghan again peered at the burning battleship. "Is that the monster we ran into earlier?"

"It must be," Captain Young said.

And while the two officers conjectured on the port deck of *San Francisco*, Cmdr. Bruce McCandles frantically called Captain Young over a JV. McCandles had received a call from the skipper of USS *Aaron Ward*. "Captain, sir," McCandles told Young, "we've got a communication from Lt. Cmdr. McGregor. His radar screen has picked up a horde of blips off our port bow, between 5,000 and 10,000 yards off."

"A horde?"

"Yes sir," McCandles answered. "McGregor thinks there may be at least a half dozen ships, small ones; probably destroyers."

Callaghan who had heard McCandles report to Young, licked his lips nervously. "What do you think, Cassin?"

"Apparently they don't know we're here," Young said. "We'd have seen gun flashes or torpedo wakes by this time."

Callaghan blinked his eyes to temper the spray of salt water mist on his face from *San Francisco*'s forward wash. The Japanese column was moving eastward. Was this column retreating from Ironbottom or were they reorganizing to resume action? If they were retiring, Callaghan had no worries—Henderson Field was safe. But, if the Japanese ships had come about in battle formation, they apparently intended to carry out their bombardment of Henderson Field. And something else worried Callaghan. All reports said there had been two battleships in the enemy fleet that came down from the north. Where was the other battleship? Was there another column of Japanese ships nearby?

Callaghan wrestled with his thoughts. Should he retire his battered task group or should he engage the enemy to stop a possible bombardment of Henderson Field on Guadalcanal.

"Admiral, sir," another call came from Bruce McCandles, "what are we going to do? What kind of message shall I send to the rest of the column?"

Callaghan took a deep breath. Then, at 0211 hours, he answered. "Maintain formation and prepare for battle. Odd ships will fire at starboard targets and even ships will fire at port targets. Our *San Francisco* and *Helena* will fire to the right, while cruisers *Portland* and *Juneau* will fire at targets to the left. Destroyers will fire at targets of opportunity."

"Aye aye, sir," McCandles answered.

"We want the big ones, get the big ones," Callaghan told Captain Young.

"Yes sir, admiral," Young said. The *San Francisco* commander then ordered star shells, and in seconds falling lights blossomed over both *Hiei* and *Nagara*. Young then ordered commence fire and the forward turret trained its barrels on the burning battleship that had been set afire only a quarter of an hour ago. Several heavy salvos from *San Francisco* sped towards the Japanese warship and some of the eight-inchers scored. Part of *Hiei*'s conning tower collapsed from one hit and her mid-ship torpedo quarter disappeared from a second hit.

Next, the aft eight-inch *San Francisco* guns loosened a barrage of shells at flaming *Nagara*, with several shells hitting the superstructure. *Nagara*'s pilot house collapsed, the conning tower toppled over, and the aft handling room exploded, adding more woes to the damaged Japanese cruiser.

Then, in quick succession, two more salvos of eight-inch shells spewed towards damaged *Hiei*. Most of the shells fell short, but two shells knocked out one of the forward secondary turrets and chopped another chunk of the conning tower away. Adm. Hiroaki Abe gaped in astonishment while he cowered from the *San Francisco* hits. He picked up a JV and screamed into the mouthpiece.

"Is every sailor in this fleet blind? Do they all sleep? Why has no one reported these enemy vessels? Why? We must respond. We must respond at once!"

"Yes, Honorable Abe," gunnery officer Hideo Sekino said, "at once."

Aboard *Nagara*, Capt. Masakane Suzuki also yelled instructions into a JV. "Answer the enemy fire; answer immediately!"

"Yes, captain, immediately."

But the gunners aboard the two ships found difficulty in adjusting their fire because of raging flames. Both Lt. Sekino on *Hiei* and Captain Suzuki on *Nagara* found their turret gunners torn between duty and the flames and smoke creeping ever closer to their stations.

Two more near miss salvos from *San Francisco* shot up sprays of water off the burning *Hiei*'s port quarter. Then the *San Francisco* gunners loosened a barrage of five-inch shells from their secondary turrets within 2,200 yards of the flaming *Hiei*, three of which struck the midsection and tore away chunks of deck and superstructure. Callaghan, aboard *San Francisco*, watched the hits with satisfaction. The two big Japanese warships had not responded and Callaghan had rightly guessed that flames and smoke on the enemy vessels had restricted their gunners, thus hampering their ability to strike back.

But another frantic call suddenly came from Bruce McCandles. "Sir, another report from

Lt. Cmdr. McGregor."

"Yes?"

"*Aaron Ward* picked up another big one—maybe another Japanese battleship. It's only 5,000 yards off and closing."

Callaghan gasped. There *was* a second battleship. But even more horrifying, Callaghan now realized that he had led his depleted column between two Japanese battleships and a cruiser on the right, with a screen of enemy destroyers on the left. He must extricate himself and his ships from this precarious position, or his column of ships could be caught in a devastating crossfire. Callaghan hurried to the flag bridge to consult with his staff while Captain Young rushed to the navigation room to plot a possible safe route out of this dilemma.

But, before Callaghan or Young did anything, their worst fears materialized. A powerful searchlight beam from less than 4,000 yards struck the starboard quarter of *San Francisco*, wavering for a few seconds and then settling on the cruiser's superstructure. The beam had come from battleship *Kirishima*. Callaghan blinked from the powerful light before he and his staff peered off the starboard quarter. In the signal house above the pilot house, Bruce McCandles also stared into the powerful searchlight beam. Even Lt. Cmdr. Herb Shonland, from his small damage control room on the main deck, rushed to starboard and squinted at the light.

Meanwhile, Captain Cassin Young, now in

the navigation room with Cmdr. Rae Arison, his navigation officer, quickly called the pilot house and ordered a hard left turn at full ahead to escape the searchlight. But too late: seconds after the powerful beam fell on USS *San Francisco*, a salvo of fourteen-inch shells from *Kirishima* rumbled towards the TG 67.4 flagship. Two shells fell short and sent up geysers of sea water that sprayed the deck. A second salvo of fourteen-inchers also missed, sending more geysers of water over the *San Francisco*'s decks. The twin salvos, even though they had missed, had given a respite to damaged *Hiei* and burning *Nagara*.

Then, two more searchlight beams, one from destroyer *Harusame* and another from *Kirishima* further brightened the superstructure of *San Francisco*.

Now, a third salvo of fourteen-inch shells spewed from *Kirishima* and this time four of the 1-ton monsters hit home. The first fourteen-incher struck the *San Francisco*'s flag bridge, turning the area into a twisted wreck while instantly killing Adm. Daniel Callaghan and his entire TG 67.4 staff. In seconds, at 0212 hours, 13 November 1942, the group of busy flag officers had become masses of bloody, shattered flesh, mixed with metal debris.

The next fourteen-inch hit battered the ship's steering, once more leaving the ship drifting erratically out of control. The third *Kirishima* shell knocked out the aft engine room; rupturing pipes, unleashing a heavy hiss of steam, killing half the engine crew, and scalding the others. The fourth hit knocked out the navigation room, turning this quarter into a metal junk heap. The navigation officer, Cmdr. Rae Arison, his assistant, and two bluejackets died instantly in the concussioning blast. The explosion blew Arison off the bridge and dropped him 15 feet below where he fell draped over the barrel of an antiaircraft gun. Capt. Cassin Young lay bleeding and unconscious under a heap of debris.

Cmdr. Bruce McCandles was in the communication center when another shell hit the conning tower less than a yard above the slit through which the officer peered. The concussion threw him backwards, slammed him against a bulwark and knocked him unconscious. He awoke a minute later, his head bleeding, and he stumbled about the bridge area to check damage and casualties.

Before McCandles could fathom the sudden destruction to *San Francisco* and the sudden death of almost all brass aboard the ship, destroyers *Harusame* and *Asugumo* veered from their positions in the Japanese column and closed swiftly on *San Francisco*. The gunners from the American cruiser sent salvos of five-inch shells from secondary turrets, but none hit the enemy. The Japanese destroyers, in turn, pumped round after round of five-inch shells into *San Francisco*. The pepepring fire tore away metal plates from the main and secondary decks, knocked out bulkheads from a variety of quarters, and toppled away the conning tower antenna. One five-incher short-circuited the wiring system and another ruptured a five-inch secondary turret. More five-inchers ignited the number 411 magazine, destroyed one of the handling rooms, and opened holes in a second magazine room to begin flooding.

Herb Shonland frantically called the bridge, but he got no response from the flag section, navigation room, or pilot house. Everybody in these areas was dead or badly wounded. Finally, Shonland called Bruce McCandles in the signal house. "Bruce, what the hell's going on up there?"

"I don't know," McCandles answered. "We were hit bad. I think a couple of fourteen-inch shells tore the bridge apart and killed everybody there, including the captain and the admiral."

"The captain and the admiral?" Shonland hissed.

"I think so," McCandles said again. "I'll go below for a look. How's the damage?"

"There's flooding in number 401 magazine and fire in number 411 magazine, but we can take care of it," Shonland said. "We got a couple of other fires, too. The worst is the steering. It's out. We're floundering. We may have to switch to manual."

"Okay, Herb, I'll check out the bridge and get back to you as soon as I know something."

Bruce McCandles left the slightly damaged signal house, warning his two bluejackets to call him in the event they got any communications. McCandles then scampered down a ladder to the main bridge deck and found the entire ship control area a mass of twisted, smoldering wreckage. McCandles threaded his way through the mess to reach the flag bridge. He peered into the rubble that looked weird and eerie in the intermittent light from gunfire.

McCandles saw helmeted and life jacketed torsos and limbs scattered about the ruptured decks. The siren was moaning, as though whimpering a dirge of death over the shattered corpses. Bruce McCandles also felt water dripping from a ruptured water cooling system above on the forward 1.1-inch quad. McCandles studied the littered flag bridge again and squeezed his face in horror. On the starboard side of the deck lay the bodies of seven dead: Callaghan, the flag secretary, the flag lieutenant, flag relay officer, assistant operations officer, and two bluejacket aides. The heap of broken bodies was saturated with blood and scattered amidst the debris. A sickening odor of scalding steel and burning flesh stung McCandles' nostrils.

The communications officer stumbled through the wreckage to the navigation room. Here he found two bluejackets dead in contorted pulps of flesh while Cmdr. Arison was missing. McCandles did not know that the navigation officer had been blown 15 feet below and his body draped over the barrel of an ack-ack gun. McCandles found the *San Francisco* skipper still breathing, although unconscious and half-covered with an array of debris. McCandles straightened and looked about until he found a dangling JV phone. He quickly called the dispensary.

"Pharmacist, this is Cmdr. McCandles. Bring a stretcher to the navigation room. On the double!"

"Aye aye, sir."

Painfully but cautiously, McCandles hoisted the loose debris away from Capt. Cassin Young, and when he finished the chore he looked up to see two pharmacists and two volunteers who had arrived with a stretcher. When McCandles gestured, the men gingerly laid the unconscious Young on the stretcher and then weaved out of the battered navigation room.

When the medics were gone, Bruce McCandles worked his way into the shattered pilot house. He found the helmsman and and another bluejacket enlisted man lying wounded while a third bluejacket and the deck officer were dead. A shell had struck the area and spread deadly shrapnel. McCandles looked at the wheel now turning erratically left and then right at the whim of the sea. McCandles quickly shifted steering control to Battle Two manual and took the wheel. Then, he called Herb Shonland.

"Herb, it's a disaster up here. Everybody's

dead except the captain and a couple of enlisted men, including the helmsman. I just sent Captain Young down to dispensary. Get those pharmacists back up here and send me a new helmsman along with a radio man."

"There's noboby left, Bruce, nobody?" Shonland asked in astonishment.

"Nobody except me."

"Then you're it, Bruce."

"What the hell do you mean, I'm it?"

"You're the last surviving senior officer. You'll have to con this flagship; she's yours. In fact, since we've lost outside communication, the whole column is yours. We know that Admiral Scott and his staff were also killed."

"What am I supposed to do?"

"I'll send up the pharmacists and the helmsman, and radio man," Herb Shonland said. "Beyond that, you'll have to do whatever you think is right. If you need anything, call me. I'll be directing damage control."

"Okay, Herb."

Cmdr. Bruce McCandles felt his body grow numb from the sudden responsibility thrust upon him. He stared about the damaged pilot house, then at the burning *Hiei* and *Nagara* off the starboard quarter. Never in a thousand dreams had the 30-year-old Bruce McCandles seen himself in command of an American ship column in the most bloody surface to surface ship engagement since the Battle of Jutland in World War II.

## Chapter Eleven

A pause in the Japanese gunfire gave Cmdr. Bruce McCandles a moment to concentrate on this unexpected responsibility. The round-faced, hefty-built officer, standing rigidly in the shattered pilot house of USS *San Francisco*, could not raise anybody on the TBS, verifying Shonland's statement that his intership radio communication had apparently been disrupted by enemy shell fire. McCandles knew that Admiral Scott and his staff had been killed aboard USS *Atlanta*, leaving a lieutenant in charge of the ship. He had no way to determine if the captains of the other American cruisers were stable, and he had no way to contact them. And, since *San Francisco* led the column, Mc-Candles did indeed need to assume command.

At 0214 hours, Bruce McCandles straightened, composed himself, and then made his decision. He believed he could not veer *San Francisco* left or right into the jaws of Japanese screen destroyers with their long lance torpedoes. The other American ships of TG 67.4 would follow him and the entire American flotilla might find itself in a crossing of the T position to invite total disaster. No, he must continue to run through the Japanese gauntlet, bombarding his way through. They might suffer, sure; but not as badly as veering off to escape the enemy.

McCandles picked up a JV and called Herb Shonland. "Herb, how about that helmsman and radio man?"

"They're on the way."

"Good." Then, McCandles called the gunnery officer, Lt. Cmdr. Don Ross. "How's our firepower?"

"Most of our turrets are okay," Ross said.

"Get our guns to starboard and let's hope the cruisers behind us follow the original OTC instructions, odds to starboard and even on port."

"What are we going to do?"

"We'll continue our run through the enemy formations."

"My God, Bruce, can we make it?" Ross asked. "Is that what the admiral and Captain Young want us to do?"

"They're gone, Don," McCandles said soberly. "The entire flag staff and con staff are dead, except for Captain Young. He's badly hurt and unconscious. I'm conning the ship."

Lt. Cmdr. Ross remained silent for several seconds before he answered.

"You're the last senior officer in the con area?"

"Yes," McCandles answered. "I don't think we've got any choice. We'll have to continue through the Japanese column. Maybe we can do enough damage to run them off."

"Okay, Bruce," Ross sighed. "I'll do whatever you want."

Then, a half dozen men suddenly came into the battered pilothouse: a helmsman, a radio man, and four pharmacists. The medics immediately took away the unconscious helmsman and the dead pilot house officer. They promised to remove the others as soon as possible. The new helmsman took the wheel, while the radio man cleared away some rubble, sat at the rear, and put on earphones.

"Can you raise anybody?" McCandles asked.

"The TBS seems dead, sir," the radio man said, "but the intercom is okay."

McCandles nodded, picked up a JV, and flipped on the PS. "All crew, here this; now hear this," the communications officer said. "This is Cmdr. Bruce McCandles. All flag officers and con officers aboard San Francisco are dead or disabled, and I will assume command. We will continue the OTC strategy and sail through enemy formation. Cruisers San Francisco and Helena will concentrate fire on starboard targets; Portland and Juneau will concentrate to port. Destroyers will attack targets of opportunity." Then, McCandles called the bluejackets in the signal house. "Release star shells to port, about 4,000 yards, to illuminate targets for trailing cruisers."

Seconds later, bright lights fell over burning *Akatsuki* and *Yudachi*, along with destroyer *Teruzuki*. *Portland*, behind *San Francisco*, quickly unleashed salvos of eight-inch shells on the three targets. One shell hit the damaged *Yudachi* to knock out another chunk of her superstructure, but none of the *Portland* shells hit *Akatsuki* or *Teruzuki*. Then a staccato of eight-inch shells from *Helena* began exploding on *Hiei*'s decks. McCandles felt elated. The other American cruisers were following OTC orders.

Almost simultaneously with salvos from *Portland* and *Helena*, Lt. Cmdr. Don Ross directed new salvos of *San Francisco* shells at both *Nagara* and *Hiei*. One shell erupted a new fire on *Nagara* and prompted Captain Suzuki to take his cruiser to the northeast where he would again seek to put out flames before returning to battle. Another eight-incher ripped into the starboard quarter of *Hiei*, seemingly bouncing harmlessly off the thick armor plate. In reality, however, the pounding by *Helena* and *San Francisco* began to loosen plates on *Hiei*'s upper and main decks.

Bruce McCandles peered through his field glasses and no longer saw *Nagara* but he noticed something peculiar on *Hiei*, only 3,000 yards off. The midsection of the ship appeared warped from the array of hits that had struck

*Hiei* from American cruisers and destroyers. He called Lt. Cmdr. Ross.

"Don, concentrate your fire on that battleship's midsection. I think if you hit her hard enough and long enough, you might rupture her armor plating."

A new barrage of eight-inch shells tore into the midsection of damaged *Hiei*. Now, at a range of less than 1500 yards, the eight-inch shells brought dire problems to the Japanese flagship. Shells tore away more of the deck plates and knocked apart the upper four-inch armor section. One shell wrecked one of the huge smoke stacks, emitting a spew of heavy smoke and hot steam. Another salvo of *San Francisco* shells completely destroyed the aft conning tower along with a midship six-inch gun turret. More shells pounded the eight-inch thick hull to loosen more breast plates. Within a minute, the *San Francisco* gunners had pumped more than twenty rounds into *Hiei* at close range and most of them struck home at the midsection. McCandles thought the huge 32,000-ton vessel now sagged in the midquarter, even while fires raged throughout the battleship.

Aboard *Hiei*, an irritated Admiral Abe cowered on the flag bridge while Captain Nashida spoke frantically into a JV. "Silence those enemy guns. You must silence them."

"We are having difficulty, Honorable Nashida," Cmdr. Hideo Sekino said. "The enemy vessel is too close and we cannot depress turrets low enough to fire into her. Also, fire and smoke threaten the gunners in the gunpits."

"Then use secondary batteries."

"They have been put out of commission, captain," Cmdr. Sekino said.

"Launch torpedoes."

"My regrets, captain; the torpedo launchers have been destroyed."

Capt. Masao Nashida scowled and peered at *San Francisco* through his binoculars. With the magnification of the cruiser at close proximity, Nashida could see the extensive damage on the American cruiser along with fires. Still, this pesky cruiser was able to shoot rapid eight-inch shellfire, while he could not respond. Nashida felt frustrated. Just one salvo of fourteen-inch shells from this close range would surely finish off *San Francisco*. But, as gunnery officer Sekino said, the close range presented the ironic problem of an inability to depress guns and strike.

And, as Nashida grumbled, more eight-inch shells from *San Francisco* and *Helena* struck the battleship behind the forward conning tower. Another hit tore apart the navigation room, killing the entire staff and toppling the communications antennae. But most of the shells continued to hit the precariously cracked midsection of the battleship. The skipper of *Helena*, Capt. Gilbert Hoover, had apparently noted the same mid-quarter sag on the Japanese battleship and he too was concentrating fire on this sensitive area. The strategy from the two cruiser commanders apparently paid off, for an ominous call reached Captain Nashida from *Hiei*'s damage control officer.

"Honorable Captain," the officer said grimly, "our vessel is in serious condition. The countless enemy shells have badly damaged the mid-ship. Our hull is cracked and this vessel now sags. I fear that more such hits will rupture the hull and flood our vessel like a tidal wave with no possibility to seal such flooding."

Admiral Abe also heard the report and he squeezed his face. "This is indeed a grim report, captain."

"Yes, admiral," Nashida said.

"I suggest we retire at once to avoid further damage."

"Retire?" Captain Nashida gasped. "But is such a strategy fitting at this time? We have trapped the enemy cruisers between our battleships and destroyers. Our fire power is far superior. With accurate marksmanship we can easily dispose of these cruisers."

"Already, we have stopped one and badly damaged the one that has taken us under fire," Capt. Susumu Kimura, Abe's aide, said to the admiral. "A few good hits can surely finish our enemy."

"We must reverse course and retire," Abe insisted.

Those others on the bridge were astonished. The staff officers were not reckless men, but, like Nashida and Kimura, they saw a rare opportunity for Raiding Force Two. They had already pulverized a half dozen American destroyers and a couple of cruisers, and there was no evidence that the Americans had battleships in their fleet. The gods had favored them by sending the rest of the American ships into a potentially fatal crossfire, with no means of escape. The Americans must (as Bruce McCandles knew) continue through the Japanese columns, and the fourteen-inch guns of the battleships alone could tear the American ships to shreds before they cleared the gauntlet. If *Hiei* could not strike burning *San Francisco*, she could surely lash out at the cruisers to the rear. The dozen destroyers or so in the Japanese columns could certainly launch enough torpedoes to make every square yard of sea a death trap for the American ships.

Capt. Masao Nashida peered down at the gun crews in the forward turrets, crews who stared back at the conning tower, obviously awaiting orders to resume fire, despite nearby flames and smoke. Nashida's sailors, like the Japanese sailors throughout Raiding Force Two, knew full well the risk that came with combat. They were willing to take their chances in this opportunity to destroy an American flotilla. The sailors were not eager for death, but they had fully prepared themselves to die if it became necessary to accomplish their mission.

Nashida turned away from the turrets and glanced at the staff officers before he turned to the Raiding Force Two commander. "Honorable Abe, I do not desire the destruction of my ship. But if we must lose this vessel to accomplish our mission, then I and my sailors are prepared to die with her. We have a duty to Admiral Tanaka and the 15,000 men of the Hiroshima Division who even now sail towards Cape Esperance. If we do not destroy the enemy airfield, disaster from American air power will descend on the thousands of Japanese sailors and soldiers of Reinforcement Group Two."

"*Nagara* has been forced to retire," Abe said, "and this cruiser appears incapable of further combat."

"You must excuse my interruption, Honorable Abe," Captain Kimura spoke, "but Captain Suzuki has assured us he will return to combat as soon as he contains the flames aboard his cruiser. Further, we understand that *Kirishima* has suffered but the slightest damage. She alone can destroy the American airfield. We need only dispose of the American cruisers, a task that seems firmly within out grasp."

"As for ourselves," Captain Nashida spoke again, "we are willing to fight so long as one gun turret can still shoot at our enemies."

Adm. Hiroaki Abe looked at the others on the bridge. He then licked his lips and lowered his head. "I shamefully apologize, captain," he told the *Hiei* commander. "In my concern for the safety of the brave sailors aboard this vessel, my heart clouded logical thinking." He sighed. "Continue the fight."

"Yes, admiral," Captain Nashida answered, grinning. He called the communications officer. "Release star shells over the enemy cruiser. This vessel will take under fire the cruiser that trails the American lead cruiser."

Abe nodded and turned to Captain Kimura. "You will notify *Hirishima* to take under fire this lead enemy cruiser. You will also notify all destroyers to close on the enemy for torpedo launches."

"Yes, captain," the Raiding Force Two chief of staff answered elatedly. Capt. Susumu Kimura now issued orders at a rapid pace to staff members of the Japanese fleet and the officers moved quickly to fulfill instructions. Still, Abe's hesitancy would foreshadow sad tidings for the big battleship *Hiei* and the repercussions would be heard all the way to Tokyo.

*San Francisco* had been opening distance on retiring *Nagara* and burning *Hiei*, with her turrets well trained on the battleship. Now, aft turrets barked, and eight-inch shells slammed into *Hiei*'s conning tower, knocking out the observation post and tower. More shells from *Helena* smashed into the midsection of *Hiei* and opened another crack in the armor plating. Water poured into the battleship hull on the port side and damage control crews worked feverishly to seal the ruptures.

The next and last salvo of shells from Don Ross's *San Francisco* gunners was the worst.

Two shells hit the steering mechanism, knocking the equipment to pieces and leaving *Hiei* dead and rudderless in the water, without power of steering. When Admiral Abe heard this, he quickly called damage control.

"Honorable Abe, we have suffered badly from the last two enemy salvos," the damage control officer said. "Our tower is battered and the navigation room has been destroyed. We can make no further gun plots, and steering is disrupted. But worst of all, the midship is now flooding."

"Can you contain this flooding?"

"Perhaps, admiral, but I fear that another hit will surely unleash a flood that would make all efforts useless."

Abe now turned to Captain Nashida. "I had conceded to your wishes, but it is now obvious that this battleship is in mortal danger. We must simply retire. We cannot lose this vessel and its thousands of men foolishly. Alter course and retire. We will try to join *Nagara*."

Captain Nashida knew it was senseless to argue further. "Yes, admiral."

Thus, at 0216 hours, the lucky gunners aboard damaged *San Francisco*, with help from USS *Helena*, had forced *Hiei* to turn tail. McCandles and the *San Francisco* crew could well feel proud of themselves. The retirement of the battleship left a huge gap in the Japanese firepower. Now, as McCandles watched the burning *Hiei* sail into the northern darkness, the *San Francisco* continued eastward. Soon, burning *Akatsuki*, fourth vessel in the south destroyer screen, loomed into view. Cmdr. Bruce McCandles peered avidly at the destroyer before he spoke into a JV.

"Don," he told the gunnery officer, "off port bow—a burning Japanese destroyer. Maybe we can finish her off."

"We'll try," Don Ross said.

A salvo of eight-inch shells from a forward *San Francisco* turret spewed towards *Akatsuki*, but all missed. Don Ross quickly altered range and sent a new salvo after *Akatsuki* and this time the eight-inchers walloped the destroyer's superstructure in a series of concussions, knocking apart a five-inch gun turret, a 40mm gunpit, a depth charge rack, and a magazine compartment. Now, belching flames erupted, hampering the Japanese fire crews who were already fighting fires aboard *Akatsuki*.

"Return fire, return fire!" Cmdr. Atimino Koki, *Akatsuki*'s skipper, cried.

Before the gunners could respond, however, a hail of five-inch shells erupted on the port side of harassed *Akatsuki*. American destroyer *Aaron Ward* had finally reached the battle scene, hurried towards the starboard quarter of the Japanese destroyer, and unleashed a salvo of shells. *Akatsuki*'s gunners hurriedly responded with five-inch salvos of her own, both to starboard and to port. Those off starboard failed to hit *Aaron Ward* and those off port failed to hit *San Francisco*.

However, at about 0217 hours, star shells

from somewhere fell over *Aaron Ward* and lit her up like a gaudy showboat. Now, *Akatsuki* enjoyed a clear view of the American destroyer, and Cmdr. Koki ordered another salvo. Several five-inch shells whacked *Aaron Ward*'s superstructure, knocking away a closet locker, a whaleboat, and the stern rudder control that left the ship without steering.

"Torpedoes! Launch torpedoes!" Lt. Cmdr. Orville McGregor yelled. The *Aaron Ward* skipper needed to chase off the enemy.

A spread of torpedoes whooshed off the deck of the American destroyer, and seconds later, *Akatsuki* rocked from two heavy explosions. One torpedo wrecked the engine room and the second struck an aft magazine compartment, almost tearing the stern apart in the concussioning explosion. Sea water suddenly poured into the bowels of the Japanese destroyer.

"We cannot contain flooding," the damage control officer told Cmdr. Koki.

"You must, you must," Koki answered.

But, within the next minute a new salvo of eight-inch shells from *San Francisco* and another salvo of five-inch shells from *Aaron Ward* spewed towards *Akatsuki*. The heavy crossfire blistered Cmdr. Atimino Koki's ship from stern to bow: the navigation room, pilot house (earlier hit by *Atlanta*), control room, ready room, and a half dozen other compartments. All disintegrated from the heavy bombardment. New fires erupted on her decks and stern, and *Akatsuki* began to settle aft under the murky waters of Ironbottom Sound.

"We are lost, Honorable Koki," the damage control officer yelled over a JV.

Atimino Koki felt frustrated. He and his crew had put a stubborn fight since the opening moments of battle, ever since the American cruiser *Atlanta* first set the Japanese destroyer aflame. At one point, Koki had almost rammed an American destroyer, foiling any attempt for the enemy to get off shellfire or torpedoes. On another occasion, he had been on a parallel course with *Juneau*, inviting a heavy salvo from that cruiser that had missed. The shelling had forced Cmdr. Koki to scoot away. *Akatsuki*, in fact, had spent her minutes of battle like a wounded deer, ever running from a pack of pursuing wolves. But the predators had finally caught up with her and Cmdr. Koki's destroyer was finished.

At 0217 hours, Koki yelled into a JV. "Abandon ship! Abandon ship!"

More than half of *Akatsuki*'s crew was dead from the battering by *San Francisco*, *Aaron Ward*, and earlier by *Atlanta*. The other sailors quickly lowered lifeboats, helping the wounded over the side with them. By 0230 hours, thirteen minutes after the order to abandon ship, Cmdr. Atimino Koki would be standing in a life raft, sadly watching his ship sink, stern first, to the bottom of Ironbottom Sound. Luckily, destroyer *Yukikaze* would find him and his surviving crews within the next hour to rescue them.

After the successful shelling of *Akatsuki* and *Hiei*, both *San Francisco* and *Aaron Ward* paid dearly for their triumph. Japanese destroyers *Teruzuki* and damaged *Ikazuchi* quickly closed on *San Francisco* from opposite directions and launched torpedo spreads. Bruce McCandles successfully avoided the wakes. However, a new searchlight beam, again from *Kirishima*, suddenly fastened itself on *San Francisco*'s starboard quarter before the big fourteen-inch turrets swung right and pointed at the American cruiser.

One of the wonders of this bloody Friday battle off Guadalcanal would transpire in the next minute. *San Francisco* would suffer thirty-seven hits, including thirteen fourteen-inch hits and twenty-three five-inch hits from *Kirishima*, *Hiei*, *Teruzuki*, and *Ikazuchi*. The American cruiser would be a flaming wreck, but miraculously, she would remain afloat and would still navigate.

At 0218 hours, three fourteen-inch shells from *Kirishima*'s first salvo struck *San Francisco*'s starboard. One shell twisted the armor plates on the forward, tearing loose the number thirty-four stringer plate and scorching the cables underneath. Another fourteen inch shell struck behind the number one turret, ripping out the number thirty-two plate along with the turret room and number three magazine. A third shell struck under the forward number two turret, blowing away the last of the deck along with a gun turret. Several holes, some 6 to 10 feet square pocked the forward deck. Fires erupted from broken cables and smashed wiring until the forward deck became a mass of smoke and flames. Bruce McCandles could see nothing from the pilot house except raging fires and scurrying sailors who tried to put out the flames.

"Get more men on damage control, more men," McCandles yelled into a JV.

"We're doing the best we can, Bruce," Lt. Cmdr. Herb Shonland answered. "Just con this ship the hell out of here."

But the Japanese were not finished. A skyfull of five-inch shells from destroyers *Teruzuki* and *Ikazuchi* mangled the superstructure of *San Francisco*. The shells knocked out searchlights, blinker lights, and fighting lights. The shells also demolished the 40mm gunpits and the 20mm machine gun decks, along with Battle Two manual steering gear. Metal fragments and portions of the decimated conning tower tumbled to the main deck with clanging thuds and cascading fires.

Then, another fourteen-inch shell struck the number four magazine beneath the forward stack, disintegrating number six handler room. Ammunition exploded and shot skyward in streaking whooshes of fire. One shell from the next battleship salvo slammed into the rear con house, killing everybody there, while a second shell smashed the lower bridge behind the number two turret, causing increased fires. More ammunition exploded and more water

214

poured into the ruptured handling rooms. Lt. Commander Herb Shonland mustered every man he could to contain damage.

*San Francisco* repair crews were soon fighting twenty-five fires raging throughout the cruiser. Then, abruptly, another deluge of five-inch hits from *Teruzuki* and *Ikazuchi* ironically snuffed out a half dozen of these fires when the shells exploded along the forward quarter. However, the explosions also killed a dozen American sailors fighting fires. A final fourteen-inch hit from *Kirishima* hit the hull at mid-quarter and opened a breach that quickly drew a flood control crew.

Then, in a final irony, retreating *Hiei* loosened two salvos at burning *San Francisco*. Four hits opened holes in the hull, two below the aft stack and one below the rear wardroom, and one on the stern. Two more of the same from *Hiei* tore to smithereens the rear deck behind the number three turret.

Only smoldering ruins and macerated, burned corpses were visible when the smoke cleared along *San Francisco*'s decks. By 0219 every gun pit on the cruiser had been knocked out, all central power was gone, every quarter topside lay in wreckage. All uninjured sailors were commandeered to fight flooding and the conflagrations throughout the cruiser.

Fortunately, none of the thirty-seven hits, most of them on topside, had left McCandles without means of navigation and power. When a hit knocked out emergency Battle Two manual steering, McCandles switched to the last emergency steering, Battle Three. And, by 0220 hours, *San Francisco* had cleared the guns of the big *Kirishima* and the two enemy destroyers. The crews worked feverishly under the direction of Lt. Cmdr. Herb Shonland to successfully kill fires and seal flooding.

Now, with no guns, no electricity, and a smashed superstructure, McCandles continued eastward until he cleared the Japanese column.

"We're pretty well under control," Herb Shonland called the pilot house.

"Good," McCandles answered. "What about our crew?"

"We've counted a hundred dead so far," Shonland answered, "a miracle, considering the shape we're in."

Bruce McCandles called the dispensary. "Get as many people as you can through the ship to retrieve dead and wounded. We'll try to make Lunga Point."

"Aye aye, sir," the chief pharmacist mate answered McCandles.

McCandles squinted to the rear and he could see the faint outline of USS *Portland* behind him, some 800 yards distant. He hoped the other American cruisers could get *Kirishima* as *San Francisco* had forced *Hiei* and *Nagara* out of the battle. If this second battleship disengaged, the Japanese fleet would surely retire without bombarding Henderson Field.

Now, McCandles saw only a dark, empty horizon ahead of him, and he was certain he had cleared the battle area.

Meanwhile, the Japanese had turned on *Aaron Ward*. She was damaged on topside, using substandard steering, and wallowing on the surface of Ironbottom Sound, when the American destroyer got caught in a searchlight from *Kirishima*.

"Open fire, open fire!" Lt. Cmdr. McGregor cried desperately. "Torpedoes! Launch torpedoes!"

McGregor's men responded quickly, launching a spread of torpedoes and loosening a salvo of five-inch shells at *Kirishima*, some 5,000 yards off starboard. But, the torpedoes skimmed far wide of the mark and the shells fell short.

Unfortunately, *Kirishima*'s gunners were more accurate, scoring with nine heavy shell hits. At 0225 hours, a barrage of fourteen-inch shells boomed towards *Aaron Ward* and within seconds the American destroyer lay in shambles. One hit almost yanked her out of the water before bouncing her on the surface again. Another hit wrecked the destroyer's direction system, necessitating a shift to local gun control. The next 1-tonner opened the hull on the starboard aft quarter, flooding the engine room. Repair crews worked frantically to stem the heavy gush of sea water as the destroyer quickly listed to starboard. Another fourteen-inch hit brought down the destroyer's mast and radar, also killing fifteen men and wounding another fifty-seven.

"We can't contain damage," the damage control officer called McGregor.

McGregor called the engine room. "Let's get the hell out of here."

"Can't do much, Sir," the engine room chief replied. "We're trying to move on a single auxiliary engine.

Lt. Cmdr. Orville McGregor scowled, but he ordered a parting salvo at *Kirishima*. This time two of the five-inchers hit the big battleship's midsection and opened two cracks on the main deck; minor damage, certainly, but the beginning of more for the huge, 32,000-ton *Kirishima*.

The engine room crew of *Aaron Ward* finally worked up enough power to move the destroyer out of harm's way. However, flood waters soon snuffed out the auxiliary engine and repair crews sealed off the entire main and auxiliary engine rooms. By 0227 hours, *Aaron Ward* was dead in the water. McGregor called Task Two but the port officer told him he must wait until daylight for a tow. He should call back about 0700 hours to report his position and Tulagi would send *Bobolink* or a Higgins boat to tow in the battered destroyer.

Meanwhile, as *San Francisco* steamed eastward, *Amatsukaze* was steering hard to catch the Japanese formation, and the destroyer inadvertently neared retreating *San Francisco*. Capt. Tameichi Hara had seen the flashes of gunfire and he had heard the shuddering booms of exploding shells to the east.

However, he could not raise *Hiei* because the battleship's UHR was out.

At 0215 hours, Hara scowled. "*Hiei* must be in trouble," he told pilot Kijuro Matsumoto. "We will attempt to help her, perhaps with torpedo launches. Maintain full ahead at our 213 course."

The helmsman steered *Amatsukaze* a few hundred yards when a huge hulk, totally dark, eerily quiet, and with smoke rising from its hull like black phantoms, loomed out of the darkness. As Captain Hara watched the big ship draw closer, he dared not flash recognition lights for he could not tell if the black silhouette was friend or foe.

"Who can she be?" Lt. Matsumoto wondered.

"A mystery," Captain Hara answered the pilot.

Soon, the two ships passed each other off each other's port, less than 500 yards apart. Hara saw no activity aboard the seemingly phantom ship and he saw no gun turrets, only the wisp of smoke rising throughout the superstructure. Could this shadow be the fuel tender *Jingei Maru?* If so, why had she come so far south into the battle zone? But then, Captain Hara suspected he was passing an enemy cruiser whose topside had been demolished.

And indeed, Hara had guessed correctly. *San Francisco*'s wrecked topside was deserted because every man but the pilot house crew was working feverishly below deck to care for wounded and to seal flooding. Hara had not recognized any gun turrets because every turret had been smashed beyond recognition. And, Hara had seen no lights because all the cruiser's power had been knocked out, save for engine and steering.

"Ready torpedoes!" Hara cried.

"Ready!" answered Lt. Miyoshi, the torpedo officer.

But Hara faltered. Suppose the ship was not an American cruiser, but cruiser *Nagara*? He ordered a searchlight on the silhouetted specter and the illumination of the mystery ship quickly identified her as an enemy cruiser. Hara ordered the torpedo launch as well as shell fire at 0220 hours and two salvos of five-inch shells along with a spread of torpedoes spewed towards *San Francisco*'s mangled superstructure. Seven shells scored, but the hits did little more than rearrange the rubble already prevalent on the cruiser's decks. The ship's personnel, safely in the bowels of the ship, had suffered no further injuries since the five-inch shells had not penetrated the armor plates.

Twenty seconds after the eight torpedoes flew off the deck of *Amatsukaze*, no explosions followed and the shadowy hulk continued on. Hara cursed, for he realized that his torpedoes' safety devices would prevent detonation within 500 meters of launch position, and *San Francisco* had been well within this 500 meter range. Thus, the torpedoes had struck the battered

American cruiser before they were set to explode.

Captain Hara watched the *San Francisco* disappear into the western darkness, the cruiser now picking up speed to more than 20 knots. The Desron 10 commander did not pursue. Instead, he continued eastward to help *Hiei* or to find another enemy target to harass as he had already flailed several of the American ships in the TG 67.4 flotilla.

But within seconds Hara would need plenty of help himself.

## Chapter Twelve

Next in line behind *San Francisco* came the cruiser USS *Portland*, Sweet Pea as her crew called her. She had already fired a salvo at Japanese destroyers off the port forward, causing damage to *Yudachi*. From the bridge, Capt. Larry DuBose, Sweet Pea's skipper, had seen and heard plenty of gun fire in front of him, particulary the exchange between *San Francisco* and *Hiei*. At about 0214 hours, after a salvo to port, Captain DuBose looked at his executive officer.

"Are we still together?"

"We're still on the 092 course at 18 knots as instructed by the flag," the executive officer answered, "and the other ships are behind us."

Captain DuBose then squinted to the southwest through binoculars, hoping to get another glimpse at flaming *Akatsuki* or burning *Yudachi* or pesky *Teruzuki* so he could get off another salvo. These ships had earlier been exposed by the star shells from *San Francisco*, but the burning shells had now flared out. DuBose now withheld fire until he was sure he could identify the enemy ships once more. *Portland*'s captain checked with his navigation officer and learned that they were now at a 9.18 south by 159.5 east position, only slightly east of the original rendezvous point. If he could be certain the other TG 67.4 ships were in column, DuBose would waste no more time before he resumed fire. He ordered star shells of his own and then got a call from the signal house.

"Captain, we've seen those burning destroyers off port, and the big ship, probably the battleship, is off to our right."

DuBose acknowledged the call, but he had barely hung up the JV phone when a searchlight beam from burning *Ikazuchi* suddenly fell on *Portland*'s bow. DuBose yelled into a JV. "Take that burning destroyer under fire with forward turret and get the aft turret on the big one off starboard; the hell with this odd and even crap."

"Aye aye, sir," the gunnery officer said.

Almost at once, at 0215 hours, while *San Francisco* and *Helena* were plastering *Hiei*, *Portland*'s gunners sent salvos of eight-inch shells at burning *Yudachi*, burning *Ikazuchi*, and battleship *Kirishima*. Cmdr. Miyoshi Kikkawa of *Yudachi* jerked when a *Portland* shell hit his superstructure for the second time. He immediately ordered return gunfire and a torpedo launch in the direction of the gun flashes. However, the five-inch shells fell short and the torpedoes swished too far off course, missing the American cruiser by several hundred yards. *Portland*'s shells had also missed all targets, except for the shell hit on *Yudachi*.

A relative calm prevailed for a few minutes while the crew of USS *Portland* watched in horror while *Kirishima* and the Japanese destroyers battered *San Francisco* with their thirty-plus hits. Not until *San Francisco* had disappeared into the western darkness at 0219 hours did Capt. Larry DuBose act again.

DuBose ordered another salvo of eight-inch shells at *Yudachi*, with several hits. The eight-inchers knocked out *Yudachi*'s 20mm gunpit, aft handling room, and two lockers, tearing asunder the compartments and erupting new fires. *Yudachi*'s repair crews scurried to fight fires and to seal flooding.

"Return fire!" Cmdr. Kikkawa cried.

"Yes, Honorable Kikkawa," somebody answered.

A new barrage of five-inch shells zoomed towards *Portland*, but the shells again fell short. Meanwhile, *Portland*'s forward eight-inch turret again sent accurate fire into *Yudachi*. One hit tore away the main deck aft turret and threw the gunpit and its crew into the sea. A second shell hit the mid-ship depth charge rack and shocked *Yudachi* with new convulsions before more fires belched from her topside decks. Finally, two shells hit the aft and mid-quarter magazines and rocked the destroyer in numbing concussions. More than half of the crew died in the deafening explosions.

"We are lost! We are lost!" the damage control officer cried into a JV.

"We must abandon ship, commander," the executive officer said.

Cmdr. Miyoshi Kikkawa nodded. And at 0218 hours, *Yudachi* survivors, only 20 percent of her crew, began scrambling over the side of the listing, blazing destroyer.

Meanwhile, more star shells blossomed over *Kirishima* at about 0219 hours, just after the Japanese battleship had finished with *San Francisco*. *Portland*'s gunners sent a quick salvo of eight-inch shells at the battleship. All fell short except one that struck *Kirishima*'s superstructure and started a small fire. The same explosion also warped one of the second deck platforms and killed a dozen sailors.

*Kirishima*'s commander cowered from the shell burst before he peered at the gunfire flashes from *Portland*. "The enemy cruiser is some 5,000 meters off, 240 degrees. Respond immediately."

"Yes, captain," somebody answered the battleship commander.

A salvo of fourteen-inch shells spewed toward *Portland*, with two hits. One of the 1-tonners knocked out the number twelve wardroom of the American cruiser and started flooding. A second shell destroyed the number two pressure turbine and ripped up several hundred feet of electrical ground cables. Twelve Sweet Pea sailors died in the numbing blasts.

The worst damage, however, came from the Japanese destroyers, whom Admiral Abe had ordered to cover the patch of sea with torpedoes before the Raiding Force Two commander had departed with battered *Hiei*. Destroyers *Asugumo, Marasame*, and *Teruzuki* steered quickly towards Sweet Pea after *Kirishima* got a new searchlight beam on the American cruiser. Within a minute a dozen torpedoes swished towards USS *Portland* from the three destroyers.

*Portland*'s lookout gaped in astonishment. "Torpedoes! All over! Starboard bow, starboard quarter, and port aft!"

Captain DuBose scanned the sea and ogled at the wakes. "Hard left!"

"Aye, sir."

The helmsman swung the big cruiser into a sharp turn and successfully avoided two of the torpedo columns, but he could not avoid the third. Two torpedoes exploded in *Portland*'s stern and tore a gash in the aft. The hits ripped away hull plates, knocked out the cruiser's steering, and also sheared the number two and number three propellers. The hits also jammed the rudders and bent a structure plate so that the damaged plate became an unwanted auxiliary rudder that froze the steering at 10 degrees. *Portland* could only steam in circles.

226

"Damn it," DuBose cursed. He yelled into a JV. "Can we do something about steering?" he asked the damage control officer.

"We'll try, sir."

And, while *Portland* remained in this precarious circle, Captain DuBose ordered his gunners to fire at anything that moved, port or starboard. He assumed that Japanese destroyers were all around him.

But the blind gunfire hit nothing. However, the gun flashes gave Japanese destroyer commanders intermittent views of *Portland*'s location on the dark waters of Ironbottom Sound so they sent more torpedoes after the American cruiser. Fortunately, the Japanese were unaware that *Portland* now steamed in circles and the Nippon commanders had set torpedoes to strike ahead. Still, one of the torpedoes hit Sweet Pea's number 134 frame on starboard, knocking out all compartments between frames 125 and 139. Repair crews luckily sealed off these compartments to prevent flooding.

But now, five-inch shells also spewed forth from the Japanese destroyers. Most of the shells missed, but three hit. One shell shattered Portland's number 3 gun turret, killing three and wounding three of the gun crew. Another shell chopped away the number 202 and number 203 plates on the second deck, while a third shell ripped apart the motor room on the second deck.

Still, Captain DuBose's gunners fired away with eight-inch salvos in all directions. One shell chopped part of *Marasame*'s bow, another eight-incher nearly bounced *Asugumo* out of the water with a near miss, and a third *Portland* shell blew away *Teruzuki*'s pilot house, killing the helmsman and radio man. The heavy salvos discouraged the three destroyers and the vessels steered away from the Americans. But from a safe distance, the Japanese tin cans launched more torpedoes, although none hit Sweet Pea. By 0220 hours, after a mere few minutes of combat, *Portland* was finished for the night and steering in its involuntary circle.

*Helena*, meanwhile, had also sailed on its 092 course. "Helen's" commander, Capt. Gilbert Hoover, had urged his gunners to fire furiously at *Hiei* and *Nagara*. As Hoover continued westward, he lost sight first of *Nagara* and then of *Hiei*. After both Japanese ships had disappeared into the darkness, Captain Hoover peered into the darkness to seek another target. He saw nothing, so he called his radar room.

"What have you got?"

"Blips on the screen, sir, but they're all 10,000 to 12,000 yards off and we can't tell if they're friend or foe."

"Damn it," Hoover scowled. He peered once more over Ironbottom Sound, but still he saw nothing. He sailed on through the murky night for another five minutes and he then got a call from his radar room.

"Captain, an enemy destroyer off starboard bow, maybe 3,000 yards."

Seconds later, *Helena*'s lookout yelled into a JV. "Enemy destroyer ahead!"

Capt. Tameichi Hara's gunners aboard *Amatsukaze* had been firing at *San Francisco* like a group of men gone shell drunk. The seven five-inch hits had merely altered *San Francisco*'s battered superstructure, but had failed to hit engines or steering. So, the phantom cruiser had merely wobbled on. But the gun flashes from the Japanese destroyer had revealed her position to *Helena*'s lookout and Captain Hoover ordered immediate fire.

At 0221 hours, while Captain Hara watched *San Francisco* disappear into the darkness, two sudden explosions erupted off his port aft and sent tons of sea water over *Amatsukaze*'s stern. Hara jerked, fearing for a moment that the vanishing phantom to the west had answered the destroyer's five-inch salvos.

"She had no turrets," Lt. Matsumoto said. "She could not attack us."

"Then who?" Hara asked, puzzled.

But suddenly, another barrage of shells came toward *Amatsukaze* and sent new geysers of water washing over her decks with near misses. Hara frowned and peered to the east, squinting, until he got a call from W/O Shigeru Iwata, the officer in the destroyer's observation station.

"Captain, an enemy cruiser comes towards our starboard."

Captain Hara whirled and then peered hard through binoculars until he saw the misty black outline of a ship coming towards him. He yelled into a JV. "Douse searchlights! Stop shelling; make smoke!"

All too late. A new six-inch salvo from *Helena* screamed into *Amatsukaze*. This time, two shells exploded on the bridge complex, knocking Hara off his feet in the wheelhouse with a deafening concussion. When Hara regained his feet, sluggishly, he quickly felt his body, but found no wounds. He looked about him and saw that his staff officers were still alive. However, a shell had wrecked the observation post above the wheelhouse and killed Sigeru Iwata, whose body now lay draped over the twisted range finder gear, blood dripping from his head, neck, and chest.

Before Hara could react to this tragedy, more six-inch shells slammed into *Amatsukaze*. Another burst tore apart the fire direction post and killed everybody in the quarter. A third shell blew away the main forward deck turret, including gunner officer Dima Shimizu and every man in the number one gunpit. The next *Helena* shell exploded in the radio room, killing all occupants. Hara turned frantically to the helmsman but cowered when another shell wrecked the main hydraulic system and started electrical fires.

"Turn left, turn left!" Hara cried. "We must escape these shells."

But the helmsman said alarmingly, "I cannot, captain. There is no response. Our navigation system is dead."

"Then we must fight," Hara stiffened proudly.

However, the damage control officer gave Hara a shocking report. "Captain, the damaged hydraulic system has affected gun control. The turrets will not move and the rudders have failed. Only engines are undamaged and fortunately the fuel has not caught fire."

"What of Lt. Shimizu?"

"He was blown away from the number one gunpit. Only a leg was left behind."

"Damn it," Hara cursed.

Thus, in a single minute, 0221 to 0222 hours, USS *Helena* had left Captain Hara's *Amatsukaze* a battered wreck.

And while Tameichi Hara's ship lay in this perilous position, the looming American cruiser off starboard loosened still another salvo of six-inch shells at *Amatsukaze*. Near misses shook the destroyer violently, while two hits erupted more flames on the superstructure. Fire fighters worked desperately to put out flames, but Hara and his crew felt trapped and hopeless. Most of his turrets were out, he had no more torpedoes, and *Helena* was still closing.

Hara stood rigidly on the bridge as did his subordinate officers. They had been eager to mix with American warships and Hara himself had helped to persuade Abe not to abandon the fight. But, in a single minute, Hara, his officers, and his crew fell into a near state of shock, suffering themselves the same array of punches they had administered on American sailors. The avid appetite for battle that had swept through the *Amatsukaze* crew had soured to bitter doubt. Hara now feared the worst: he, his crew, and his destroyer would soon be on the bottom of Sealark Channel, for he saw no way to avoid further destruction.

Still, Captain Hara straightened resolutely. "We still have one turret and we shall fight to our last breath."

"Yes, captain," Lt. Matsumoto said.

But fortune shone on Captain Hara, even in this dark, dreadful night.

*Helena*'s gunners, who had been merrily pelting *Amatsukaze*, were suddenly besieged by three Japanese destroyers, using *Helena*'s gun flashes as beckoning lights. *Asugumo, Marasame,* and *Harusame* closed towards *Helena* just as Captain Hoover ordered another salvo at harassed *Amatsukaze*. The destroyers opened on USS *Helena* with a barrage of five-inch shells. Most of the shells fell short, erupting cascades of sea water around the American cruiser. However, one shell shattered *Helena*'s portside supply house. Another five-inch shell disintegrated a whaleboat, and a third shell warped the aft deck in front of a six-inch gun.

Capt. Gilbert Hoover scoured the sea anxiously, but he saw nothing except the blinking gun flashes some 3,000 to 4,000 yards off both his starboard and port quarters. He called the radar room. "Where are those enemy ships?"

"One is off port quarter, sir, about 3,000

yards. The other two are off starboard aft, maybe 4,000 yards."

"Okay, keep a fix on them and let me know if they make a sudden move."

"Yes sir."

Captain Hoover then called the signal room. "Give me star shells, one about 3,000 yards off port and a couple at 4,000 yards off starboard aft."

"Yes sir."

Seconds later star shells zoomed into the darkness and exploded in brilliant lights in the sky. However, the experienced Japanese destroyer commanders quickly scooted away from the descending light and the shells fell over an empty patch of sea. And worse, the delay caused by the Japanese shell fire gave Capt. Hara an opportunity to zigzag his near crippled *Amatsukaze* away from *Helena*'s six-inch guns.

Captain Hoover peered again into the dark sea, but he saw nothing. However, three destroyers closed again on *Helena* like determined canines who persistently returned to the odor of sizzling meat after being shooed away. They unloaded new salvos of five-inch shells. Most of them missed, but three hit *Helena*'s topside, knocking out an observation station, rupturing the number 134 second deck plate, and ripping out some topside vents. The damage was minor, but another shell struck the aft and knocked away two plates.

Captain Hoover had enough from the pesky

trio of phantom destroyers. In any event, the Americans had already chased the big ships, *Hiei* and *Nagara*, out of the battle, while *Helena* had personally pummeled and put to flight a Japanese destroyer. Hoover was satisfied. These other Japanese destroyers, the only ships now active, could not hurt Henderson Field.

"All ahead full," Hoover yelled into a JV to the engine room. Then to the helmsman: "Maintain the 092 course and find the rest of our ships."

"Aye aye, sir," the helmsman answered.

At about 0216 hours, USS *Juneau*, the last cruiser in the American TG 67.4 column, entered the patch of sea that would become the graveyard of nine ships. Capt. Lyman Swenson, *Juneau*'s captain, had also seen the burning vessels and seen the thundering gunfire whooshing all over Sealark Channel. Swenson had no idea who was hitting whom, as he had been unable to raise flagship *San Francisco*. Swenson had simply remained on the 092 course at 18 knots as instructed by OTC. He had no knowledge of Adm. Daniel Callaghan's death. *Juneau*'s commander suspected that the battle had again turned into a confused melee, with perhaps both sides often firing at their own vessels in the obscure darkness. So, Swenson ordered his ship slowed to 14 knots while he searched the sea.

"Maybe we should try star shells," Lt. Ed Wilkes, the deck officer, said.

"Where would we drop them?" Swenson said. "Those Japanese ships were in nice formation a few minutes ago, but everything is in confusion again."

"How about *Fletcher* behind us?" Lt. Wilkes said. "Maybe she can get something on her radar."

Capt. Lyman Swenson nodded. "Call her."

*Juneau*'s deck officer contacted *Fletcher*'s executive officer, Lt. Jim Wylie. "Have you got any radar blips?"

"We have a few," Lt. Wylie answered, "but the blips have been jumping all over the screen. The last reading showed a couple of small ones off port bow, probably destroyers. They must be right off your port quarter, maybe 3,000 yards or so. We also have a big one at about 8,000 yards off your starboard bow; might be a battleship."

"Okay, lieutenant, thanks," Ed Wilkes said. The *Juneau* deck officer relayed the information to Captain Swenson who immediately ordered star shells. Seconds later, blooming lights fell over huge *Kirishima*, the third time she had been brightened by star shells in the past few minutes. The battleship was several miles to the east of *Juneau*. Other star shells from the American cruiser fell on *Yukikaze* and *Marasame* who were now far to the southward.

"Let's get the monster," Captain Swenson said.

"Okay," Lt. Wilkes answered. He picked up

a JV and called the forward gunnery officer. "Open fire on the big one off to the northeast."

Also for the third time, American cruiser shells spewed towards *Kirishima*. The five Sullivan brothers, who had all joined the same ship as gunners, were on the forward guns and they unleashed a salvo of six-inchers that fell short and erupted geysers of water in front of the big battleship. The shells from the second salvo, however, hit home. One shell struck *Kirishima*'s port quarter to scorch a supply locker, starting fires. From the relatively long distance, the six-inch shells could not do much damage against the eight and six inch armor plating. The gunners on the American cruisers needed a vital hit to hurt *Kirishima*. Unfortunately, neither the Sullivan brothers nor any other of *Juneau*'s gunners would ever get the chance.

Destroyers *Yukikaze* and *Marasame* quickly took advantage of the gun flashes from *Juneau*. The flashes gave the Japanese commanders a good idea of the cruiser's location. Both destroyers quickly swept the dark waters of Ironbottom Sound with searchlight beams until two rays fell on the starboard side of the American cruiser. Ironically, even with radar, *Juneau*'s star shells had failed to bloom over the two destroyers as her star shells had bloomed over *Kirishima*.

At 0221 hours, only ten minutes after the vicious fighting resumed, two torpedoes from the Japanese spreads struck *Juneau*'s forward quarter with a shock that shuddered the 6,000-ton cruiser. The shock knocked Captain Swenson off his feet and onto the hard deck. Before he arose, two more long lances smacked the underside of the American cruiser, broke the forward keel, flooded the prow, and sent *Juneau* into a ten degree bow list.

Damage control crews quickly descended into the bowels of USS *Juneau*'s forward section and worked speedily to seal off the forward keel section to prevent the bow from sinking under the waters of Ironbottom.

"We've got her under control," the damage control officer soon told Swenson.

Lt. Ed Wilkes, meanwhile, had hurried to the wheelhouse to join the helmsman. "Let's get this ship the hell out of here," he called the engine room. "Full ahead! Full ahead!"

"Aye, sir."

But, the Japanese destroyers were not finished with *Juneau*. A long lance torpedo now wallopped the stern section of the American cruiser to rip up the aft deck and two propeller shafts. *Juneau*, moving at 25 knots, stopped abruptly, dead in the water, and pitching hundreds of her American sailors forward.

The helmsman turned frantically to Lt. Wilkes. "We can't move."

Wilkes called damage control. "What can you do?"

"Two shafts gone. We'll have to go on one propeller."

"Hell, that means we can't move any faster than a snail."

"Yes sir."

Lt. Ed Wilkes had barely relayed this bad news to Captain Swenson when two fourteen-inch shells from *Kirishima* smashed into *Juneau*'s superstructure and toppled the crows nest along with the signal house. Fortunately, no fires erupted and no more 1-tonners hit the cruiser. And most luckily, no more torpedoes from the pesky Japanese destroyers struck *Juneau*. Still, the American cruiser was finished and Captain Swenson and his crew now directed their energies to steering the ship out of harm's way. *Juneau* soon disappeared slowly into the west. She was safe for the moment, but in several hours she would suffer one of the most horrifying fates of World War II.

Thus, at about 0222 hours, the Japanese formation and the single American column were again in total disarray. The battered Japanese battleship *Hiei*, without power and rudder, had drifted off to the northwest, joining sluggish *Nagara* that was still afire. *Kirishima*, somewhat to the north with slight damage, waited for instructions from Admiral Abe. *Yudachi* floundered in flames, her crew abandoning ship; *Akatsuki* would soon be down, *Ikazuchi* fought fires, *Inazuma* worked on her minor damage, and *Amatsukaze*, battered and crippled, plodded aimlessly about the sea with a smashed superstructure.

On the American side, shattered *San Fran-*

*cisco* plied off to the west; *Portland* steered in circles, wondering how to get away; *Atlanta* lay battered and dead in the water, fearing some Japanese ship might finish her off. *Helena* sped westward, trying to find the rest of TG 67.4, while *Juneau* struggled over Ironbottom at a dangerously reduced speed. Among the destroyers, battered *Aaron Ward* flitted about the sea with damaged steering, hoping to find a friend and praying to avoid a foe. Flaming *Cushing* and battered *Monssen* were being abandoned. *Laffey* and *Barton* were already down. *Sterett* was heavily damaged and brightly ablaze, hoping to avoid further punishment.

Like *Kirishima*, six Japanese destroyers, *Marasame*, *Asugumo*, *Yukikaze*, *Teruzuki*, *Harusame*, and *Inazume* were very slightly damaged and fully able to continue the fight. They zigzagged about Ironbottom Sound, waiting for more orders from flagship *Hiei*.

Among the Americans, only USS *Fletcher* and slightly damaged USS *O'Bannon* were still able to fight to full capacity. The two U.S. destroyers moved cautiously into the diabolical patch of Ironbottom Sound that had bedeviled a horde of ships and hundreds of sailors within the past twenty-five minutes.

Tactically, the Americans had seemingly lost the battle, for two destroyers were very poor odds against a battleship and six destroyers. Even though Admiral Abe had wavered, the Japanese were in excellent position to complete their bombardment mission against Guadalcanal's Henderson Field. No American ship was really in a position to stop huge *Kirishima* from barreling into Guadalcanal where she could bombard the American airfield for half the night if she so chose. Six Japanese destroyers could screen her and they could easily deal with USS *O'Bannon* and USS *Fletcher*.

But a strange turn would occur in the last few minutes of this bloody Friday night action on the surface of Ironbottom Sound.

## Chapter Thirteen

Aboard *San Francisco*, Cmdr. Bruce Mc-
Candles sat with gunnery officer Don Ross and
damage control officer Herb Shonland in a battered ward room. In a preliminary survey they
found that twenty-five fires had raged
throughout the ship during her brief moments
of combat. They had lost all firepower.

"Every last gun is out, Bruce," Don Ross
said. "I'm not sure we have a machine gun in
working order."

"There's more than thirty holes in the upper
deck alone," Herb Shonland said, "and half
the superstructure is still smoldering. I don't
know about steering."

"We switched to Battle Three manual, the
last auxiliary," McCandles said. "But if we get
another serious hit, we'll likely be dead in the
water. How about casualties?"

"Bad," Shonland squeezed his face. "We've
got about 200 men dead, wounded, or

missing." Then Herb Shonland looked hard at Bruce McCandles, a tinge of admiration beaming from his blue eyes. "Bruce, you did a hell of a job," he said softly. "You ran that gauntlet and scattered the Japanese pretty good. I'd guess that big battleship and that burning cruiser are out of it. Maybe the Japanese can't make Henderson Field to work over the place."

"Maybe," McCandles nodded. "Anyway, I've got some bluejackets in the navigation room plotting a course to Lunga Point."

"What about the other ships?" Don Ross asked.

McCandles shook his head. "We can't raise anybody. I'd guess it's everybody for himself."

And as *San Francisco* groped its way over the Ironbottom darkness during the depths of night, officers on other American ships also took stock.

At 0222 hours, *Atlanta* still lay dead in the water, with her skipper, Capt. Sam Jenkins, still lying unconscious in the ship's abandoned dispensary. Lt. Hank Bell tried to raise Guadalcanal for a tow into Lunga Point or Tulagi. But he could do nothing until radio maintenance men repaired the damaged TBS system. Meanwhile, pharmacists and other able men worked on the wounded, medicating and comforting them. Fortunately, the melee had scattered all ships and no enemy vessels were threatening *Atlanta* at the moment.

Aboard *Portland*, Capt. Larry DuBose urged

repair crews to work harder on the damaged steering system. He felt an utter frustration as his ship simply wandered in circles on the surface of Ironbottom Sound. But, repair crews could not loosen the damaged rudder, remove the damaged props, or chop away the warped plate that had thrown *Portland* into her involuntary circle.

"We need dry dock welding torches," the damage control officer told Captain DuBose. "Can we get a tow from the minesweeper?"

"I'll call them." At 0223 hours, the *Portland* skipper contacted Tulagi, but the Task Two port officer told DuBose the same thing he had told the skipper of *Aaron Ward*. Help could not come until daylight. DuBose should call back at about 0700 hours and report his position. Captain DuBose grimaced irritably, but he could do nothing but curse and wait.

Aboard *Helena*, Capt. Gilbert Hoover, the last able senior officer of the TG 67.4 armada, successfully weaved the cruiser through the array of damaged and sinking ships. *Helena* had only sustained minor damage, although her SG radar had been knocked out. Hoover now followed on the heels of *San Francisco*, but at a faster pace, and he soon came next to the TG 67.4 flagship.

At 0225 hours, the lookout on *Helena* spotted a smoldering, darkened ship and Captain Hoover ordered gun turrets trained on the shadowy hulk. As *Helena* closed on the unidentified vessel, Hoover called over the TBS, but the ship did not respond. DuBose ordered a strong blinker message.

"This is Captain Hoover of *Helena*. Please identify yourself or take fire."

McCandles flashed back a reply: "We are USS *San Francisco*."

Hoover sent back a reply: "To Admiral Callaghan: *Helena* still on our 092 course. Are we retiring? Please acknowledge."

"All flag and con officers of *San Francisco* dead or disabled," came a blinker reply. "Cmdr. Bruce McCandles has conned this vessel. We cannot make more than 15 or 20 knots because of extensive damage. Captain Hoover, you are now apparent senior officer of this task force. Any instructions?"

When Hoover read the message from the flagship, he gaped in astonishment. A subordinate commander had led the American armada through the Japanese ships, scattered the enemy, and driven off at least two big enemy ships. Hoover was flabbergasted by this McCandles' daring leadership. He vowed to meet personally with the man at the first opportunity. But *Helena*'s captain now understood that he was in command and he quickly flashed a response to *San Francisco*.

"This is Capt. Gilbert Hoover: congratulations Cmdr. McCandles for job well done. I will assume command of task force. We will maintain a ten knot speed, 092 bearing, and return to Espiritu Sancto."

"Acknowledged," The *San Francisco* flashed back.

The fifth American cruiser, *Juneau*, had suffered severe damage, including a bow list and the loss of two propellers. The men aboard were not sure they could make Espiritu Sancto. The five Sullivan brothers, Joseph, Francis, Albert, Madison, and George, loitered tensely aboard listing *Juneau* with hundreds of other sailors, hoping they met no new enemy attacks. Captain Swenson, meanwhile, managed to bring his damaged cruiser westward, and soon he got a call from Captain Hoover, who had brought his own *Helena* behind *San Francisco*.

"We can't move very fast, captain," Swenson said.

"Neither can the rest of us," Hoover answered. "We'll slow down until you catch up."

As for the American destroyers, they were all out of action but *O'Bannon* and *Fletcher* who were just getting into the battle area again and who were unaware that Capt. Gilbert Hoover was re-forming column to sail south.

On the Japanese side, Adm. Hiroaki Abe stood on the bridge of *Hiei* with a worried look on his face. His 32,000-ton flagship was dangerously depressed in the mid-quarter from the terrible pounding by *San Francisco* and *Helena*, and the American destroyers. *Hiei*'s pagoda mast lay in shambles from a multitude of hits, her engines were damaged, her rudder jammed, and her torpedo launchers wrecked. Fires blazed along her huge decks and the ship could barely move.

Only moments earlier, fire control officer Horishi Yokumo had sent the admiral a message: "We have received eighty-five hits, Honorable Abe. Our middle is badly cracked and every available man now labors to stem flooding throughout the hull. Fires still rage, and should the flames reach a magazine, our vessel will surely explode and sink. In such an event, we will most certainly lose most of our crew."

"Eight-five hits," Abe scowled. "Even the most powerful vessel cannot take such punishment."

Only *Hiei*'s main gun batteries still worked and Captain Nashida could at least defend his crippled ship if necessary.

The cruiser *Nagara* had been a victim of numerous hits, and flames still rose from her superstructure while Captain Suzuki nursed his wounds inside a damaged con room. However the fire fighters were slowly putting out the flames and there was little prospect of losing the ship. Further, *Nagara*'s power was still intact and most of her guns were still operating. Thus, the 5,200-ton cruiser still had plenty of fight in her for offensive or defensive action.

Among Abe's smaller ships, *Akatsuki* was gone, ready to sink under Sealark Channel, with Cmdr. Atimino Koki and survivors of his crew abandoning the destroyer at that very moment. *Yudachi* burned furiously and her skipper, Cmdr. Kiyoshi Kikkawa, doubted that he could save her. Aboard *Ikazuchi*, Cmdr. Naka

Ikeda and his crew, furiously repairing damage and containing fires, were in no condition to fight at the moment. Finally, Capt. Tameichi Hara's *Amatsukaze*, whose crew had caused havoc to a multitude of American vessels, was now herself a near cripple, with forty-three dead and scores wounded. Captain Hara and all surviving hands fought fires and tended wounded. Fortunately, Lt. Matsumoto had led *Amatsukaze* away from further American naval guns.

Of the still able American destroyers, USS *O'Bannon* now came into the renewed battle area. At about 0224 hours, the U.S. destroyer had been steaming behind *Juneau* in the renewed American column. *O'Bannon* had earlier administered serious damage to *Hiei* when one of her hits ignited a magazine on the battleship. Another five-incher from the American destroyer had knocked out part of *Hiei*'s forecastle and a third had begun heavy fires on *Yudachi*. Lucky *O'Bannon*, despite her heavy engagement with the enemy, had managed to wiggle away with minor damage, destruction of a forward torpedo rack. When the battle resumed at 0210 hours, with staccato gun flashes and deafening booms of gunfire, Lt. Cmdr. Ed Wilkinson had ordered *O'Bannon* on almost full ahead, more than 30 knots, to reenter the fray. However, by the time Wilkinson had led his ship into the blistering battle area again, he saw nothing but burning vessels in the distance.

"We'll stay on our 092 course and see what happens," Wilkinson said.

"Aye aye, sir," the helmsman answered.

Now, at 0225 hours, a lookout on *O'Bannon* called Wilkinson. "There's a listing ship ahead, about 3,000 yards."

Lt. Cmdr. Ed Wilkinson peered through his binoculars, and then grinned. The vessel, down in the bow and battered in the stern, was struggling to move. She appeared to be crippled. "All ahead full," Wilkinson yelled into a JV to the engine room. "Let's get the bastard." Then to his gunnery officer: "Aim those forward turrets at the ship ahead. We'll close for some good shots."

USS *O'Bannon* increased and came within 7,000 yards of the ship. But Wilkinson got a frantic blinker message from the listing vessel: "*Juneau!* This is *Juneau!* Hold fire!"

Wilkinson frowned. Then, at 0226 hours, he got a TBS call from *Helena* that had now pulled ahead of *San Francisco*. "This is Captain Hoover," the skipper of *Helena* said. "I have assumed command of column. Fall in behind *Juneau* to protect her rear. We will remain on the 092 course for retirement to Espiritu Sancto."

"But sir, there may be more enemy ships around."

"That's an order!" Hoover barked. "Now fall in!'

"Aye aye, sir," Wilkinson answered.

Both Ed Wilkinson and his crew were disappointed. They had charged forward to resume fighting, but instead, they were out of the battle. By 0235 hours, *O'Bannon* had fallen in behind *Juneau* and all four vessels headed south out of Sealark Channel.

Meanwhile, USS *Fletcher* had been tail-end-Charlie in the original B-1 formation of TG 67.4. She would have been tail-end-Charlie again in the re-formed American column at 0210 hours, save for the fact that *Aaron Ward* had to catch up to them. Until 0226 hours, *Fletcher* and her crew had been mere witnesses to the furious twenty minutes of surface action, with the seven minute respite in between. *Fletcher*'s only contribution thus far had been her radar reports on the location of enemy ships. Cmdr. Bill Cole and his *Fletcher* crew had spent the rest of the time simply gaping at the gun flashes and wincing from heavy concussions.

Only three minutes still remained in the night action segment of the naval battle off Guadalcanal. More than two dozen warships and thousands of sailors had engaged each other since 0148 hours. But now, a single American ship would engage the enemy for a mere two minutes and prompt Adm. Hiroaki Abe to make a fatal decision.

USS *Fletcher* enjoyed two advantages: the first was the grace of god which had thus far spared her and which she would certainly need to engage a battleship and three destroyers for 120 seconds; *Fletcher*'s other advantage was her modern SG radar equipment that could pinpoint and identify a ship within 15,000 yards. Thus, while other ships in this bloody Friday donnybrook were containing damage, fighting fires, or sailing away, *Fletcher* was fresh and ready for action.

Cmdr. Bruce McCandles had done an excellent job in leading the American ships through the Japanese formation, while inflicting considerable damage on the enemy and forcing *Hiei* and *Nagara* out of the fight. But Japanese ships still prowled Ironbottom. The Americans had no assurances that Admiral Abe might not yet send his slightly damaged *Kirishima* and cruiser *Nagara* into Guadalcanal to bombard Henderson Field. Abe had plenty of undamaged destroyers to protect these larger ships. Further, Captain Yashide Setoyama was still barreling north to rejoin the Japanese fleet, and Setoyama might well discover the retreating TG 67.4 fleet. A report of this American withdrawal might easily have swayed Admiral Abe to fulfill the bombardment mission.

But as McCandles had put Admiral Abe in doubt with *San Francisco*'s daring run and blistering shells, Cmdr. Bill Cole and his destroyer crew would contribute the straw that would break the camel's back.

At 0226 hours, the radar man on *Fletcher* gave Cmdr. Cole an up to date report. "A large enemy vessel, 7,000 yards off starboard; two smaller blips off port quarter."

Bill Cole, a rugged, square-faced man with a gravel deep voice, carefully heard the report and then ordered torpedo and gun crews to prepare for battle. Lt. Jim Davenport, *Fletcher*'s gunnery officer, had a thorough knowledge of his radar controlled five-inch guns, and Lt. Bob Scott, the plotting room officer, possessed an adept ability to set firing range from radar reports. *Fletcher* was plowing across Ironbottom at 22 knots, so both Lt. Davenport and Lt. Scott had taken this speed into consideration as they prepared to open fire.

At 0227, with radar control, a twin spread of ten torpedoes flew off the decks of *Fletcher*'s starboard and skimmed on a three and one-half mile run towards the big target. Two torpedoes hit *Kirishima*'s port midsection, shuddering the vessel and sending huge orange glows skyward. The torpedoes had twisted two hull plates, and water oozed into *Kirishima*'s bowels. Repair crews quickly sealed the breach, but the hull plates remained loose as *Aaron Ward* had loosened a deck plate only moments earlier.

Meanwhile, again with radar help, Lt. Jim Davenport loosened two salvos of five-inch shells to port in the direction of the smaller radar targets. Some of the shells fell short, but some found their targets. One five-incher knocked out the forward boiler room of *Marasame*. Another shell shattered the forecastle of the Japanese destroyer *Ikazuchi*, already damaged by other American ships.

The Japanese responded. Searchlights from *Kirishima, Marasame*, and *Ikazuchi* swept across Ironbottom Sound until the beams fell on *Fletcher* and illuminated her like a Christmas window display. Immediately, a barrage of five-inch shells from *Marasame* and *Ikazuchi* spewed towards the American destroyer while *Kirishima* unleashed a salvo of fourteen-inch shells. But *Fletcher*, under the apparent grace of god, successfully zigzagged all over the sea to avoid the rain of shells and a sudden school of torpedoes from the Japanese destroyers. One of the fourteen-inch bursts nearly bounced *Fletcher* out of the water, but caused no damage.

The frustrated Japanese destroyer commanders now unleashed their last torpedoes after plucky *Fletcher*, but once more the American destroyer darted out of harm's way. And to add insult to the Japanese efforts, Cmdr. Bill Cole ordered another attack against the three enemy warships.

Once more, using radar readings, gunnery officer Jim Davenport sent three salvos of five-inch shells outward, one off starboard and two off port. One shell hit *Kirishima* again, bending another main deck plate. Another shell hit *Marasame*, knocking out her plotting room and killing the plotting room staff. Two of *Fletcher*'s five-inchers struck *Ikazuchi* and started huge fires on the aft deck. The Japanese destroyer commanders, frustrated by the accurate fire from the American warship, now closed on *Fletcher* for a close quarter slugfest. Then, a new searchlight beam, this one from *Teruzuki*, fell on *Fletcher*'s port quarter.

"This new enemy destroyer is only 3,000 yards off port," the radar man told Cmdr. Cole.

"We can send out more salvos," Lt. Davenport told the *Fletcher* skipper, "but four-to-one odds aren't very good, even with radar."

"Okay," the gravel-voiced Cole sighed. "Let's get the hell out of here."

Thus, at 0229 hours, after a mere two minutes of action, Cmdr. Bill Cole ordered full ahead on the 092 course. Within seconds, *Fletcher* was dashing away from her stalkers whose salvos of five-inch shells, incredibly, were now zooming towards each other. When a searchlight beam from burning *Ikazuchi* fell on *Teruzuki*, Cmdr. Naka Ikeda, skipper of *Ikazuchi*, gasped in horror. He recognized the illuminated ship as one of his fellow destroyers.

"Cease fire! Cease fire!" he yelled into a JV. Then he screamed to his radio man. "Call other vessels to cease fire at once!"

"Yes, Honorable Ikeda," the communications officer answered.

When all firing stopped, Cmdr. Ikeda scanned the dark sea, but he saw no sign of the American destroyer. *Fletcher* had slipped away. Fortunately, none of the shells from the Japanese destroyers had hit each other.

By 0230 hours, USS *Fletcher* was steaming full ahead to catch up with the retiring TG 67.4 column.

Aboard *Hiei*, Admiral Abe received continual reports, all discouraging. Destroyer *Akatsuki* was sinking with only 20 percent of her crew still alive and now floundering in the sound. *Yudachi* was burning furiously and Cmdr. Kikkawa saw little chance of saving her. Then came the reports from *Ikazuchi* and *Marasame*, reporting their damage during the brief minutes of battle with USS *Fletcher*. Abe squeezed his face irritably and peered at burning *Nagara* that plodded alongside *Hiei*. Two of Abe's big ships were out of action along with several destroyers. Then, Abe got a report from *Kirishima*.

"A few of the midsection hull plates have ruptured from shell fire and two torpedo hits," the *Kirishima* captain told Abe. "There has been some flooding but we are sealing these breaches."

Admiral Abe paled. The near destruction of flagship *Hiei* had begun with ruptured hull and deck plates. Now, *Hiei* sagged badly in the middle and she was in danger of sinking. Enemy guns and torpedoes had similarly ruptured the armor plates of *Kirishima*. Suppose enemy fire did further damage to *Kirishima?* She too would be in danger of sinking. For a full minute, Admiral Abe remained stiff on the bridge of *Hiei*, his face sober, his eyes reflecting deep meditation.

Capt. Masao Nashida, Capt. Susumu Kimura, and other staff officers watched the admiral intently but said nothing. Finally, at

0231 hours, Abe turned and looked at Admiral Kimura. "Notify all vessels that we shall retire to Truk on a 174 course at 25 knots."

"Retire, admiral?" Captain Kimur asked.

"Yes," Admiral Abe answered softly. "Admiral Kondo is sailing down the Solomon Strait with Main Attack Group. He will be able to carry out this mission where we have failed."

Captain Kimura and other officers on *Hiei*'s bridge were stunned. Both the *Kirishima* and *Nagara* were fit to fight, with several undamaged destroyers to screen them. The enemy fleet had been sunk or scattered. Surely, the remnants of Raiding Force Two should continue on to bombard the enemy airfield.

"Please, admiral, reconsider," Captain Kimura pleaded. "The Honorable Kondo has no fourteen-inch guns as has *Kirishima*."

"We will retire," Abe said adamantly, "and leave the mission to the Main Attack Group. Six cruisers with dozens of eight-inch guns will cause considerable damage."

When Capt. Tameichi Hara, the Desron 10 commander, got the order to retire, he was shocked. True, USS *Helena* had badly damaged his destroyer and *Amatsukaze* was in poor condition to fight. Still, Hara had personally caused serious damage to many of the American surface ships and Hara had seen some of them retire. There were plenty of Japanese ships to protect *Kirishima* while the big battleship laced the enemy airfield with her fourteen-inch guns. Hara was certain the

Americans had nothing left but a few destroyers to challenge them, and *Kirishima* could spend several hours during the night to unleash her shells. Captain Hara called the Raiding Force Two commander.

"Please, admiral, we must continue this mission. We must!"

"We will retire, captain," Abe said.

"I say again," Hara persisted, "you will bring shame on us and desecration on those who gave their lives in this vicious battle."

"Your own destroyer is in no position to fight any longer."

"Nonetheless, we will fight to the last man if necessary," Hara said.

"I have heard enough, captain," Abe said angrily, "you will obey my orders."

"Yes, admiral," Hara answered softly. Then, he turned to pilot Matsumoto. "We will follow the admiral's order. Alter course to a 174-degree bearing."

The pilot nodded.

Hara now walked to the open deck of the bridge and scanned the dark sea as *Amatsukaze* made a sweeping 90-degree turn and sailed north. The Desron 10 commander felt angry and frustrated. Abe had elected to quit just before victory was in their grasp. Hara promised himself he would pen a scathing report when they returned to Truk, even if he suffered a court martial for severely criticizing his flag commander.

And in truth, Abe's decision to withdraw

would prove disastrous.

Miles to the southeast, Capt. Gilbert Hoover stood soberly on the bridge of *Helena*, wondering himself if he had done the right thing to withdraw the TG 67.4 ships out of Ironbottom and out of battle. Yet, Hoover believed they were no longer capable of continuing the fight, especially against battleships. He hoped that Admiral Kinkaid's Task Force 16 would somehow reach Guadalcanal soon enough to attack the Japanese battleship, should these Japanese warships still attempt to bombard Henderson Field.

Hoover did not know that the efforts of USS *Fletcher* in the final minutes of the bloody night action had prompted the Japanese fleet commander to retire. By 0235 hours, Ironbottom Sound had settled again to darkness and silence. But, Ironbottom would not stay quiet long. Adm. Thomas Kinkaid's TF 16 battleship-carrier force was on the way north, and Adm. Nobutake Kondo's Main Attack Group of six cruisers and six destroyers was coming into Sealark Channel.


Adm. Nobutake Kondo, commander of the Main Attack Group had carefully read the reports of the night action just over that had reduced both Raiding Force Two and the American cruiser fleet. He had quickly agreed to Admiral Abe's request to carry out the mission himself—bombarding Henderson Field.

Admiral Kondo had been a favorite with the

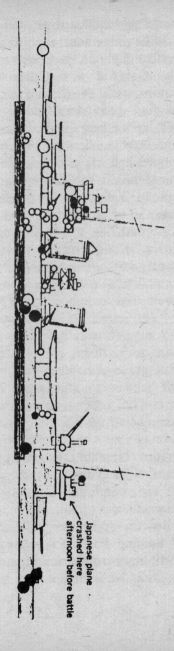

Diagram showing hits of various calibers on U.S.S. San Francisco in night action of November 12, 1942. Large circles show hits estimated as 8 in. or over. Small holes are 6 in., 5.5 in. and 5 in. Black—port side. White—starboard. Most of major caliber hits were estimated by Navy inspectors as 8 in. However, as no Japanese heavy (8-in. gun) cruiser was present, it is likely that these "8 in." were from 14" bombardment projectiles with reduced burning charges. Not shown are many hits by automatic weapons and shell fragments.

Japanese plane crashed here afternoon before battle

Japanese brass, a man often compared to the British gentleman: sophisticated, immaculate, perfect manners, and ever amiable. Kondo was also a scholar with a thorough knowledge of history, world events, and military theory. When he had been commandant of the Japanese military academy, he had capably instilled pride and determination in his cadets. All these attributes had left in others a sense of awe for the round-faced, roly-poly Kondo. Thus, Adm. Isoroku Yamamoto had welcomed the opportunity to offer Kondo a combat command.

Aboard flag cruiser *Chokai* of Main Attack Group, Kondo turned to his chief of staff, Capt. Shinto Hashimoto. "Order battleship *Kirishima* and whatever destroyers remain of Abe's fleet to join our task force at once."

"Yes, admiral," Hashimoto answered.

Kondo then called Capt. Shoji Nishimura, commander of his group's Crudiv Seven. "We have asked *Kirishima* to join. The battleship will help us to engage any enemy fleet while your Crudiv Seven bombards the enemy airfield. My own Cardiv Four will lay in the channel where we can intercept any American surface craft that may attempt to interfere with Admiral Tanaka's transport group."

"Yes, admiral," Captain Shoji Nishimura answered.

But the destroyers and battleship *Hirishima* of Raiding Force Two were already steaming north away from Ironbottom and heading back to Truk. None of the commanders of Raiding

Force Two even got the message to join Admiral Kondo's Main Attack Force, so they never arrived to aid the force.

Still, at 0330 hours, only sixty minutes after the bloody Friday melee, Captain Nishimura arrived off Lunga Point, with his Crudiv Seven of three cruisers and three destroyers. A moment later, a Japanese float plane dropped star shells over the Henderson Field complex. And, at 0335 hours, Nishimura gave the order to his Crudiv Seven commanders. "Commence fire!"

Eight- and five-inch turrets swung to starboard and the incendiary bombardment began, rattling the patch of coastal plain with concussioning explosions. No American fleet waited now in Ironbottom Sound to challenge, and the men at Henderson Field cowered from the bombardment. For a half hour, the Japanese cruisers and destroyers fired 200 rounds, destroying a dozen parked aircraft and damaging another thirty planes. Nishimura had intended to bombard Henderson for several hours, until he had wrecked the airstrip and every American plane sheltered here.

But, at 0405 hours, the Crudiv Seven commander received a shocking report from his communications officer. "Captain, an American fleet is sailing through the indispensable strait towards Sealark Channel. The force includes at least two battleships and a carrier. They are expected to reach here within a few hours."

A Japanese scout plane had spotted Admiral

Kinkaid's TF 16 with carrier USS *Enterprise*, two battleships, cruisers, and screening destroyers. Adm. Bill Halsey had no choice but to send Kinkaid north with the report of Japanese fleets coming south towards Guadalcanal.

Nishimura had barely digested this report when he got a call from Admiral Kondo. "Captain, our cruisers and destroyers are no match for battleships and carrier planes, especially during daylight hours. We must retire from Sealark Channel at once. We must be far up the Solomon Strait by daylight or we will surely suffer disaster from this enemy fleet and its aircraft."

"Yes, Honorable Kondo," Nishimura answered.

Captain Shoji Nishimura might have unloaded a few farewell salvos, but a squadron of American PT boats, six of them, sortied out of Tulagi and loosened a dozen torpedoes at the Japanese ships. All missed and the Japanese destroyers quickly scattered the boats. However, like bees after honey, the PT boats returned and launched more torpedoes. Once more destroyers chased off the pesky boats, but this minor harassment prompted Captain Nishimura to depart Sealark Channel at once.

Thus, at 0410 hours, a mere thirty-five minutes after the bombardment began, Nishimura prematurely broke off his attack and Crudiv Seven steamed out of Ironbottom at a speedy 30 knots, following on the heels of

Kondo's own Crudiv Four. Incredibly, none of the sailors of the Main Attack Group had seen any of the flotsam or wallowing sailors in Ironbottom Sound.

By 0415 hours, surprised Americans crawled out of their foxholes on Guadalcanal, puzzled by the short bombardment. But, Maj. Bob Richards, commander of the Marine Air Group 142, was elated. He quickly took stock of his aircraft and found that he still had thirty available planes, those undamaged in the bombardment.

"I want every man working on these planes for the rest of the night," Major Richards told his line chief. "We suspect that Japanese transport group will try to reach Cape Esperance sometime tomorrow, and we want to start after them at first light."

"They'll be ready, sir," the line chief promised.

"What about the *Enterprise* planes?" Capt. Joe Foss asked.

"They'll be here by morning, too," Major Richards answered.

## Chapter Fourteen

Thus passed the night so foul, till morning fair
Came forth with pilgrim steps in amice gray,
Who with her radiant finger stilled the roar
of thunder, chased the clouds, and laid the winds
On grisly spectres, which the fiend had raised . . .

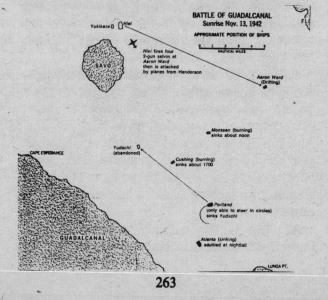

BATTLE OF GUADALCANAL
Sunrise Nov. 13, 1942

APPROXIMATE POSITION OF SHIPS

0 1 2 3 4 5
NAUTICAL MILES

Yukikaze · Hiei

FL

Hiei fires four
2-gun salvos at
Aaron Ward
then is attacked
by planes from Henderson

SAVO

Aaron Ward
(Drifting)

Monssen (burning)
sinks about noon

CAPE ESPERANCE

Yudachi
(abandoned)

Cushing (burning)
sinks about 1700

Portland
(only able to steer in circles)
sinks Yudachi

GUADALCANAL

Atlanta (sinking)
scuttled at nightfall

LUNGA PT.

263

John Milton penned the lines above in *Paradise Regained* almost three centuries before the Guadalcanal campaign. The stanza aptly described Ironbottom Sound when daylight emerged over Sealark Channel. As the mountains of Guadalcanal changed from a silhouetted black to deep purple and then to lush green in full daylight, both the Americans at Lunga Point and the Japanese at Cape Esperance ogled at the scene beyond Guadalcanal. The skies had cleared over Ironbottom and the landlubbers, perhaps with the aid of binoculars, could see one able and seven crippled ships.

Five of the ships were American: unsteerable *Portland*, shattered *Atlantic*, immobile *Aaron Ward*, abandoned *Cushing*, and deserted *Monssen*. Three were Japanese: listing *Hiei*, abandoned *Yudachi*, and able *Yukikaze* that stood by the big battleship. Already on the bottom of Ironbottom Sound were USS *Laffey*, USS *Barton*, and Japanese *Akatsuki*.

And if the landlubbers looked hard enough, they also saw floating flotsam and heavy debris on oily patches of sea, or the heads of swimming sailors, or the blots of burned corpses. And finally, the shoreline spectators no doubt saw the Higgins boats skimming over Ironbottom like morning water bugs as the boats searched for survivors from last night's holocaust.

At 0630 hours, battered *Hiei*, rudderless, burning, and without steering, wallowed on the calm gray sea a mile northeast of Savo Island. She had barely made four knots since the guns went silent at 0230 hours. Destroyer *Yukikaze* carrying her own crew plus the survivors from *Akatsuki*, stood by to take off survivors or to defend *Hiei* if necessary. Adm. Hiroaki Abe sipped tea for breakfast, but ate nothing, for his insides foamed with apprehension. He called Lt. Cmdr. Hiroshi Yokumo, the battleship's fire and damage control officer.

"What is the situation?"

"Our efforts seem futile, Honorable Abe," Yokumo answered. "As soon as we control one fire, another erupts on some other section of the vessel. As soon as we stop one breach, flooding begins elsewhere."

"What about repairs?"

"Regretfully, our steering is gone, and we have little power. I do not believe we can move far without help."

"I see," Abe answered. He squinted into the daylight and then turned to Captain Kimura. "Perhaps *Kirishima* can take us in tow. I believe we should retire as swiftly as possible for the enemy will surely send out aircraft before long. Call *Kirishima*. Give them our position and ask them to come at once to take us in tow."

"Yes, admiral," Captain Kimura said.

Nine miles due south of *Hiei* and some seven miles directly east of Cape Esperance, the sinking and burning *Yudachi* drifted in the middle of Sealark Channel: her gun turrets a mass of rubble, her engine rooms mangled wrecks, her topside warped and battered, her bowels taking on water from a magazine explosion. A mile south, Cmdr. Kikkawa peered from a life raft at the wreck that had once been his proud destroyer.

Kikkawa next stared about the sea and scowled. Japanese destroyers were noted for quick rescue of survivors from fellow warships, but no one had picked up him or his sailors. Then Kikkawa squinted at the outline of Guadalcanal to the west.

"Is that not Cape Esperance in the distance?" he asked a fellow officer in his life raft.

"Yes, commander, Cape Esperance and safety," the officer said. "We should make the shoreline within several hours."

Kikkawa nodded and studied the life rafts scattered in the distance. He hoped the rafts held the rest of his crew who had survived *Yudachi*, and he prayed they would all reach the safety of a Japanese encampment on Cape Esperance.

Then, suddenly, the sea under Kikkawa shuddered violently as a barrage of shells exploded atop and around burning *Yudachi*. The shells had come from 12,000 yards off to the southeast, out of the still working turret barrels of USS *Portland*. Capt. Larry DuBose, even though his cruiser had steered unmanageably in circles throughout the night, decided to get in a few final punches when he saw the listing

Japanese destroyer in the daylight. Two of the eight-inch shells struck a third magazine on *Yudachi* and the subsequent explosions literally blew the destroyer to pieces. The fragments of the Japanese destroyer sank quickly to the bottom of Ironbottom Sound and *Portland*'s crew cheered. However, the American sailors did not know they had sunk a derelict.

Cmdr. Kiyoshi Kikkawa and his surviving sailors merely stared passively at the dazzling fireworks and the final demise of *Yudachi*. Perhaps a quick death from gunfire was apropos for the proud destroyer that had carried a fighting crew through several sea battles in the past six months.

After sinking *Yudachi*, Captain DuBose returned to his frustrating problem—getting *Portland* safely out of Ironbottom Sound. At 0700 hours, he again called Task Two port headquarters at Tulagi.

"When the hell are we going to get that tow?"

"We're sending out some Higgins boats now," a base dispatcher said.

"Higgins boats!" DuBose cried. "What can they do? We're drifting to the southwest and we may drift right into Cape Esperance and a whole Japanese army."

"All we've got is *Bobolink* and she's scheduled to help *Atlanta*. That cruiser is worse off than you."

"Goddamn it, lieutenant," Captain DuBose cursed, "if we're not out of here soon, we'll come under fire from Japanese shore batteries."

"The Higgins boats will do what they can. If they can't move you, you'll need to abandon your vessel and the boats will take on your crew."

"Ah, hell," DuBose cursed again and then angrily snapped off the TBS.

Less than three miles south of *Portland*, USS *Atlanta*—battered, beaten, and dead in the water—still remained miraculously afloat. She now drifted towards the Guadalcanal coastline, two miles away. Lt. Hank Bell had contained most of *Atlanta*'s fires, but repair crews could not stop the widespread flooding in the deepest holds of the cruiser. Further, a large number of the crew had been stacking some 200 *Atlanta* dead in one of the battered mess halls, while other crew members medicated some 200 wounded. At 0730 hours, Lt. Bell made another frantic call to the Task Two headquarters in Tulagi.

"Where the hell is the minesweeper?"

"*Bobolink* is gearing up now," the base dispatcher answered. "She should be out there in a couple of hours."

"A couple of hours! Christ, with our list, we may be on the floor of Sealark Channel in a couple of hours."

"It's the best we can do."

"Goddamn it," the *Atlanta* gunnery officer cursed before he too snapped off the TBS.

Five miles northeast of Guadalcanal, Cmdr.

Ed Parker and executive officer Tom Stokes were among the 45 percent of *Cushing*'s crew still alive when daylight emerged over Sealark Channel. The *Cushing* survivors had been paddling their rafts and whaleboats throughout the night in the hope of seeing tugs or LCIs come to their rescue. But no rescuers would find Parker and his men, and a full day would pass before they finally reached the Guadalcanal shoreline to work their way through coastline jungles to Lunga Point.

Almost in the middle of Ironbottom Sound, Lt. Cmdr. Charlie McCombs and the survivors of *Monssen* sat in near exhaustion. They too had been paddling rafts and lifeboats for five hours, with burning *Monssen* drifting after them. 40 percent of *Monssen*'s crew had abandoned ship, many of the men badly wounded or seriously burned. Throughout the night, many of these casualties had died and the *Monssen* survivors had suffered the further ordeal of continually tossing these dead overboard.

At daylight, Lt. Cmdr. McCombs allowed three sailors to reboard *Monssen* to rescue eight helplessly wounded men, and by 0800 hours, the trio of bluejackets had completed the dangerous chore. Lt. Cmdr. McCombs had watched the rescue tensely for he knew the ship could have blown up at any moment.

"If we ever get rescued," McCombs told the daring bluejackets, "I'm putting all three of you in for Navy Crosses."

At 0900 hours, 13 November, rescue came when a Higgins boat spotted the burning *Monssen* survivors. By 0930, the sailors had arrived safely in Guadalcanal. Skipper McCombs would get the opportunity to recommend Navy Crosses for the three heroic sailors: M/M 1st Gary Storey, G/M 2nd Leon Sturgeon, and M/M 1st Jim Hughes.

Luckily for the floundering survivors of *Laffey* and *Cushing*, those who were tossed life-jackets by *Sterett* sailors, Task Two had correctly received their location. A few had drowned during the night, but a Higgins boat had picked up the rest of them shortly after dawn. Another Higgins boat had found and picked up a half dozen survivors of *Barton* by about 1030 hours, while two *Barton* survivors were picked up by *Portland*, and two more miraculously swam to shore, where Melanesian natives found and brought them to Henderson Field. The other *Laffey* survivors, those in lifeboats, reached Guadalcanal about noon of 13 November and worked their way through the jungle to Henderson Field.

Some three miles off the Florida Islands, *Aaron Ward* lay dead in the water, her steering and power gone. Still, her sailors had successfully doused most of her fires and repair crews had sealed most of her flooding, particularly in the engine room. Now, Cmdr. Orville McGregor sat in a wardroom and ate breakfast of toast and coffee. At 0700 hours, the executive officer came into the wardroom with a broad grin on his face.

"Two Higgins boats are on the way to push us into Tulagi."

"Thank God for small favors," McGregor said. "Sit down; have some coffee."

The executive officer nodded and sat next to the *Aaron Ward* skipper.

But then *Aaron Ward* suddenly shook violently from two near miss explosions. Both officers gaped, stunned. McGregor looked at his watch: 0702. Then an anxious bluejacket hurried into the wardroom.

"Commander, sir, we're under attack by the big one—battleship shells!"

"W—what?" McGregor hissed. He rushed out to the deck just as a new salvo of fourteen-inch shells again rattled *Aaron Ward* with near misses. The concussions nearly threw McGregor off his feet.

"Son of a bitch!" Son of a bitch!" he cursed. "I thought this goddamn fight was over."

As Capt. Larry DuBose had spotted *Yudachi*, so too had Capt. Masao Nashida spotted *Aaron Ward* in the morning daylight. So, even while *Hiei* struggled with her damage, the battleship's gunners had opened fire on the American destroyer with a salvo of fourteen-inch shells. Fortunately for *Aaron Ward*, a savior would come to her rescue before *Hiei* got off another salvo.

On this same 13 November morning, other American sailors would find salvation.

Minesweeper *Bobolink* would push *Atlanta* to Kukum Bay in Tulagi, but seabees would be unable to save her, and at 1400 hours, *Atlanta*'s crew would scuttle the ship. Higgins boats would manage to push *Portland* to Tulagi Harbor where emergency repair crews would patch the cruiser's steering so *Portland* could return to the the United States for an overhaul. On the same morning, Higgins boats would push *Aaron Ward* into Kukum Bay and safety. However, nobody could save destroyers *Monssen* and *Cushing*. They would burn and flood through most of the day and finally explode, sinking to the bottom of Ironbottom at 1400 and 1600 respectively.

Meanwhile, by daylight of 13 November, the other ships of TG 67.4 had cleared Ironbottom Sound and were now sailing southward towards Espiritu Sancto.

The remainder of Raiding Group Two, meanwhile, was already 100 miles north of the Solomons on the open sea, steaming back to Truk, thus dispelling any chance for *Kirishima* to take *Hiei* into tow. *Nagara*'s fire fighters had snuffed out most of the cruiser's flames and repair crews had stopped all flooding. Behind *Nagara* sailed *Kirishima*, while in front of the cruiser sailed undamaged *Asugumo*. To the flanks of the larger ships plied undamaged *Harusame* off port and slightly damaged *Inazuma* off starboard. Behind *Kirishima* limped burning *Ikazuchi*, battered *Amatsukaze*, and damaged *Marasame*.

Aboard *Amatsukaze*, Captain Hara ate breakfast of tea and biscuits in glum dejection. Daylight and a course back to Truk had confirmed defeat for the Desron 10 commander. He had lost forty-three men killed on his shattered destroyer and a depressing nausea boiled in the pit of his stomach. So, he merely nibbled at his biscuits.

"You must eat, captain," Lt. Matsumoto said.

"I am weary and discouraged, Kijuro," Hara answered the pilot softly. "We have failed in our mission."

Lt. Matsumoto smiled. "I would hardly call this a defeat. We battered the enemy fleet and word has reached us that Admiral Kondo's Main Attack Force has destroyed the enemy airfield. Admiral Tanaka's Reinforcement Group Two will surely reach Cape Esperance before another day has passed."

"Perhaps," Captain Hara answered. But a doubt clung to the captain's mind when he scanned the bright horizon behind him.

Far to the southeast, Captain Gilbert Hoover led his reduced column of TG 67.4 towards Espiritu Sancto. By the same morning daylight, Hoover had come more than 150 miles south of Guadalcanal. Now, *Helena, San Francisco, Portland, Juneau,* and trailing destroyers *O'Bannon, Sterett,* and *Fletcher* zigzagged at 18 knots southeast of San Cristobal. *San Francisco, Juneau,* and *Sterett* were badly damaged and could barely keep up.

Aboard *San Francisco*, Cmdr. Bruce Mc-Candles peered from the smashed wheelhouse at the bright morning, thinking about the other seven ships of TG 67.4 and wondering if Henderson Field had come under Japanese attack. During the night he had taken count of *San Francisco*'s casualties: fourteen officers and sixty-three enlisted men killed; seven officers and ninety-seven enlisted men wounded; and one officer and six enlisted men missing.

By daylight, Capt. Cassin Young had died of his serious wounds. Pharmacists had medicated and treated the skipper all night, but loss of blood and gangrene poisoning had been too severe, and Young had passed away at 0600. His death had depressed McCandles for he had found Captain Young a fair man and a capable ship commander, a credit to the U.S. Navy.

McCandles sipped a cup of coffee, feeling miserable, when Lt. Cmdr. Herb Shonland joined him. "We've got everything pretty much under control, Bruce. Don't look so down. You did a hell of a job."

"But they finished us. Who's going to protect Henderson Field?"

Shonland grinned. "We finished them, too. You saw the battleship and cruiser retire. Anyway, even before that donnybrook started last night, Admiral Turner called Halsey. I'd bet that Kinkaid started up north full ahead with *Enterprise* and his battleships last night and he might be around Ironbottom soon. He can stop anything that tries to hit Henderson Field."

"Maybe," McCandles nodded.

But the Japanese were not yet finished with TG 67.4. At about 1100 hours, just off San Cristobal, Cmdr. Minoru Yokoto of submarine I-26 spotted the American ships. He immediately launched torpedoes and a moment later McCandles saw the wakes skim past the stern of *San Francisco*. With no TBS communications, McCandles tried frantically to warn *Juneau* with blinker lights. But, he could not do so in time. A pair of torpedoes struck *Juneau* on the port side under the bridge and the explosions ignited magazines. McCandles almost fell over from the concussioning blasts a thousand yards away. He said later:

"*Juneau* didn't sink. She blew up with all the fury of an erupting volcano. There were terrific thunderclaps and plumes of water blotted out the sky. Then there were a couple more explosions and when the dark clouds of smoke lifted a moment later, there wasn't a sign of *Juneau* or her 700 man crew. It was the most awesome spectacle I had ever seen."

In fact, 600 American sailors went down with *Juneau*, including the five Sullivan brothers— Joseph, Francis, Albert, Madison, and George. This stunning loss of five members from one family later prompted the United States never to allow all men from the same family to again join the Armed Forces; nor would America ever again allow brothers to be assigned to the same military unit.

Miraculously, the explosions that blew

*Juneau* asunder also blew a hundred of her crew into the sea, although many were burned or lacerated. Captain Hoover reported the location of the survivors, but he refused to stop and rescue them for fear of more submarine attacks. However, the message, given to a B-17 reconn plane, never reached anybody and no one ever came for the *Juneau* sailors. They floundered on the open sea for several days, with sharks, the sea, and exposure claiming most of them. Only ten men finally reached shore and safety.

Then, by daylight of 13 November, while eight ships wallowed on Ironbottom and the other surviving ships from both sides limped back to Truk or Espiritu Sancto, a new element entered the battle—air power! What surface ship turrets and torpedoes could not accomplish during the vicious first hours of 13 November, air power would accomplish throughout the rest of Friday, 13 November 1942.

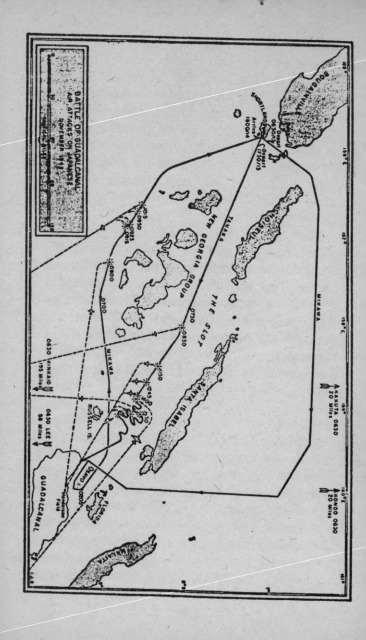

BATTLE OF GUADALCANAL
AIR ATTACKS ON JAPANESE
November 1942

## Chapter Fifteen

At dawn of 13 November, Adm. Thomas Kinkaid had come within 150 miles of Guadalcanal with his carrier-battleships TF 16. He prepared to launch planes from USS *Enterprise* to stop any further Japanese fleets from bombarding Henderson Field; or Kinkaid hoped to use the *Enterprise* planes to sink the transport marus of Admiral Tanaka's Reinforcement Group Two convoy.

At the same dawn hour, some forty-four aircraft of MAG 142 rolled out of their dispersal areas on Guadalcanal: twelve Dauntless dive bombers, eleven Avenger torpedo bombers, and twenty-one Wildcat fighter planes. Finally, far to the south, at Espiritu Sancto, the engines of a dozen B-17s from the Eleventh Bomb Group whined into the growing daylight like baying hounds howling at the emerging dawn.

Capt. Joe Sailer, a sober-faced, ten-year veteran of the Marine Air Corps, commanded the MAG 142's Dauntless dive bombers. He had slept only intermittently during the night of 12-13 November, anxious and uncertain over the outcome of the surface ship battle on Iron-bottom Sound and then rattled by the bombardment of Henderson Field by the Japanese Main Attack Force. Sailer ate breakfast with relief when daylight revealed Henderson Field still intact.

Captain Sailer had just finished breakfast when he heard aircraft engines warming up on the field. A scout plane had discovered floundering *Hiei* at about 0600 hours about five miles northeast of Savo Island and Maj. Bob Richards, the MAG 142 commander, had ordered the group's aircraft to get ready for a strike.

Sailer left the mess hall and hurried to MAG 142's operation tent to get details on the scout report.

"We've got another report besides that battleship, captain," the radio man told Joe Sailer. "There's an enemy cruiser force about 150 miles up The Slot, probably the Japanese fleet unit that hit Henderson last night. And there's an enemy transport group under destroyer escort about 200 miles to the north-west."

"Well, well," Sailer grinned, "looks like a busy day."

A moment later, Major Richards came into the operations tent where he spoke to Sailer. "I've called the Eleventh Bomb Group in Sancto. Colonel Saunders will locate those targets for us with B-17s and maybe make a strike himself. Meanwhile, Joe, you may as well take your Dauntlesses out after that crippled Japanese battleship."

"Right away," Captain Joe Sailer said.

The Dauntless squadron leader took off at 0620 hours with his twelve Dauntlesses. Ten minutes later, Sailer sighted the burning *Hiei*. A barrage of antiaircraft fire greeted his VBD crews, but the marine dive bombers dove through the screen of fire and attacked the big battleship with 1000-pound bombs. Two bombs struck the superstructure to start more fires, two bombs ruptured more deck plates to start more flooding, and two hits opened gaping holes in the aft that sent big *Hiei* into another heavy list.

Sailer's aerial attack diverted *Hiei*'s guns from *Aaron Ward*, and Cmdr. Orville McGregor expressed elated surprise when the fourteen-inch shells stopped bouncing his destroyer. A savior had come to his rescue in the form of MAG 142s Dauntlesses.

Meanwhile, Adm. Hiroaki Abe, cowering from the aerial attack, screamed into a JV. "Where are the Mitsubishi fighter escorts? Where?"

"They are on the way from carrier *Junyo*," somebody answered.

Only fifteen minutes after Sailer's attack, another group of bombers, twelve Dauntlesses, with a dozen Wildcat escorts, arrived over *Hiei*.

The interlopers were the AG Ten unit under Lt. Cmdr. James Lee from USS *Enterprise*. By 0650, Lee and his pilots scored another half dozen hits on *Hiei*'s superstructure and then Lee took his planes to Henderson Field. They could not return to *Enterprise* because the carrier's elevator still malfunctioned and the AG Ten unit could not land on the carrier's deck.

At 0710, Maj. Robert Richards arrived over *Hiei* with his MAG 142 Avenger dive bombers. This time, Zeros were waiting. However, escorting Wildcats under Capt. Joe Foss went after the Zeros. With confidence and determination, the American fighter pilots repeated their performance of yesterday afternoon over Ironbottom Sound. In a single minute, Captain Foss and his airmen shot down seven Zeros and scattered the rest, thus stopping any interference with the torpedo bomber attack on *Hiei*.

Thus, unmolested, the Avenger pilots unleashed skidding torpedoes that whooshed towards the crippled ship. Major Richards and a fellow Avenger pilot delivered the most telling blows with two torpedo hits. The twin explosions cracked a breast plate, shuddering the huge ship and opening the hull; water poured into the breaches in deluges and Lt. Cmdr. Horishi Yokumo could do nothing. After the U.S. Avenger attack, Admiral Abe was forced to give the sad order:

"Abandon ship!"

Thus, on 13 November, hundreds of

Japanese sailors scrambled over the side of *Hiei* and boarded *Yukikaze* and *Samidare*, that had finally arrived in Ironbottom Sound. Then, the big *Hiei* slowly capsized and by sunset she had sunk to the bottom of Sealark Channel, taking 450 of her crew with her. *Hiei* had thus earned the ignominious distinction of being the first Japanese battleship sunk by the enemy in World War II.

The elated marine and navy flyers enjoyed little respite. At 0800 hours, scout planes reported the location of Adm. Nobutake Kondo's Main Attack Group of six cruisers and six destroyers sailing up The Slot. The American scout planes had spotted the ships about 150 miles north of Guadalcanal, just due west of New Georgia. Crudiv Four was in the lead with cruisers *Chokai*, *Kinugasa*, and *Maya*; and destroyers *Asashio* and *Arashio*. Behind Crudiv Four came Crudiv Seven under Capt. Shoji Nishimura: cruisers *Suzuya*, *Tenryu*, and *Isuzu*, with destroyers *Makigumo*, *Yugumo*, *Kazagumo*, and *Michishio*.

Six Dauntlesses under Capt. Joe Sailer and six Avengers from *Enterprise* under Lt. Cmdr. James Lee dove at the Japanese ships, while Capt. Joe Foss and his Wildcat fighter pilots hovered at 12,000 feet to intercept any Japanese Zeros that might come down The Slot from carriers *Junyo* or *Hiyo* to attack the bombers. Captain Sailer now led his six Dauntlesses after cruiser *Mayo* while he dispatched Lee's Avengers after cruiser *Kinugasa*.

The Dauntlesses sent a half dozen 1000-pounders whistling towards *Maya*. Two hits blasted the superstructure on the port beam. The Avenger pilots skimmed into *Kinugasa* and loosened a half dozen torpedoes. Two hit the aft, erupting fires and flooding the Japanese warship.

Admiral Kondo tried to increase speed to the northeast. However, at 0915, Major Richards caught up with Kondo's ships with twelve Avengers. He split his torpedo bombers, leading six planes himself against *Kinugasa*, while six others pounced on cruiser *Chokai* and destroyer *Arashio*. Two of the torpedoes from Richards' unit slammed into *Kinugasa*, starting more fires, opening more holes, and sending the cruiser into an uncontrolled list to port. The other MAG 142 aircraft hit *Chokai* and flooded a boiler room, while the same aircraft slightly damaged *Arishio*.

Then, all 27 B-17s from the Eleventh Bomb Group, led by Col. LeVerne Saunders, suddenly appeared at 17,000 feet over Crudiv Four at 0923 hours and dumped fifty-six tons of bombs on the zigzagging cruiser force. Two bombs exploded atop *Kinugasa*, final death blows, and the big cruiser sank slowly to the bottom of The Slot. Other Flying Forts opened a huge hole on the deck of *Maya* and battered the superstructure of destroyer *Arashio*.

Mikawa's Crudiv Four under Admiral Kondo was hit again at 0950 and 1015 hours by more Dauntlesses and Avengers, but with little more damage, for the battered flotilla was now moving out of range.

The loss of *Kinugasa* and the damage to the other ships of Crudiv Four had rattled Admiral Kondo, but the determined Japanese admiral decided he would return to Guadalcanal on the evening of 14 November and bombard Henderson Field again. Adm. Gunichi Mikawa, commander of the Eighth Fleet, agreed with Kondo and promised to get the big battleship *Kirishima* back into Sealark Channel to aid Kondo's cruiser force.

Captain Nishimura was reluctant. "Admiral," he told Kondo, "will we not jeopardize our entire fleet if we return to Sealark Channel?"

"We must bombard the enemy airfield," Kondo answered soberly. "Think what will happen to Admiral Tanaka if aircraft attack his maru transports as these Yankee aircraft attacked us. No, we must destroy the enemy airfield, no matter what the cost to our Main Attack Force."

"Yes, admiral."

Thus, despite the battering air attacks on this 13 November morning that sent *Hiei* to the bottom and that had damaged Crudiv Four, the Japanese were determined to knock out Henderson Field.

Aboard flag destroyer *Hayashio* of the Reinforcement Group Two, Adm. Raizo Tanaka awoke early on the morning of 14 November.

He now stood on the bridge and peered through binoculars at the gray sea. Behind him, in twin columns sailed eleven transports that carried the reinforced Thirty-eighth Imperial Hiroshima Division. Four destroyers plied on both flanks of the eleven transports, while to the rear as trailing pickets sailed destroyers *Mochizuka* and *Amagiri*. Admiral Tanaka had been quite successful on his Tokyo Express runs; he and his sailors had delivered more Japanese reinforcements to Guadalcanal than all other reinforcement commanders combined.

However, on the bright morning, a soberness radiated from the dark eyes of the narrow faced admiral. Tanaka was a night owl, always delivering men and supplies just after dark and returning up The Slot before daylight to avoid a possible American air attack. Thus, he did not like the idea of sailing through several hours of daylight to reach Cape Esperance by mid-afternoon.

Admiral Mikawa had ordered Tanaka to delay his sail down The Slot after Admiral Abe ran into TG 67.4 during the first hours of Friday the thirteenth. By morning, Mikawa had ordered Tanaka to proceed, since Abe's raiding force had annihilated the enemy fleet. Mikawa had stopped Tanaka again, however, when American planes first sank *Hiei* and then battered Kondo's cruiser fleet. By dark, Mikawa ordered Tanaka again to proceed, but cautiously. Then, with the decision to bombard Henderson Field again, Tanaka had received a final order:

"All is clear, Admiral Tanaka," read the message from Eighth Fleet. "The capable Admiral Kondo will totally destroy the American airfield and its aircraft, as the Honorable Abe destroyed the American fleet. You should proceed with all speed to deliver our troops and supplies to Guadalcanal."

But Tanaka read this last order with skepticism before his communications officer, Cmdr. Tadashi Yamamoto, came next to the admiral.

"Honorable Tanaka, can we offer you breakfast? They have prepared tea, fish, and rolls for the bridge officers."

Tanaka nodded, but he did not alter the look on his somber face.

"You should not be apprehensive," Cmdr. Yamamoto grinned. "General Kawaguchi eagerly awaits our arrival so he can chase the enemy from the Solomons. All reports assure us the Americans cannot interfere with us."

Tanaka scowled at his aide. "There have always been assurances, commander, but too often Yankee ships and Yankee aircraft come from nowhere."

"But not this time," Yamamoto said. "Surely, Admiral Kondo will complete the destruction of the American airfield this evening."

Tanaka did not answer. He knew that many naval commanders often exaggerated their claims. He had always harbored a suspicion for Admiral Abe, who was overly cautious. And although he admired Admiral Kondo, he was not sure Kondo could reach Henderson Field again to complete a bombardment job he had failed to complete earlier.

Tanaka's suspicions grew when, at 0730 hours, a sailor came onto the bridge. "Please excuse this intrusion, Honorable Tanaka, but we have seen American scout planes over our convoy."

"They can be of no consequence," Cmdr. Yamamoto said. "Our mission will be completed before the Americans can send more aircraft from the south, after Admiral Kondo destroys the enemy airbase at Guadalcanal."

"Perhaps," Tanaka said. "Nonetheless, radio Admiral Mikawa and tell him to send us fighter plane cover from carrier *Junyo* to protect us."

"Yes, admiral."

The scout plane radioed both Henderson Field and *Enterprise* with the same message: "Now hear this, all you fly boys: a slew of fat cats, eleven of them, at 157.10 east by 8.55 south, moving at 15 knots on a 290-degree course. They're about 125 miles northeast of 'Canal."

A trio of SBD armed scout planes from *Enterprise* who heard the report zoomed straight north. At 0830 hours, they attacked, scoring a hit on one transport. However, a swarm of Zeros shot down two of them and damaged the third.

Tanaka's real danger lay at Henderson Field. Eleven army P-38s and nine P-40s of the Sixty-seventh Army Fighter Squadron had flown up from Espiritu Sancto during the night. Now, thirty Dauntlesses, nineteen Avengers, twenty-one Wildcats and twenty army air force planes were ready for action.

"We'll take off in units of twelve with fighter escorts," Major Richards told the mixed bag of airmen at a quick briefing. "As soon as one unit returns, the unit will immediately reload and refuel to go out again. If we work fast enough, we should hit that convoy four or five times. We'll call Espiritu Sancto and ask Colonel Saunders to send his B-17s to help out." Richards turned to his line chief. "Can your ground crews keep bombs, torpedoes, gas, and machine guns ready to reload and rearm at once to keep planes out continually?"

"Major," the ground chief grinned, "we got a few thousand ground troops who'll work around the clock. Nobody wants to see that convoy stopped more than the marines."

"Okay," Major Richards nodded. "Let's move it."

Thus began the Buzzard Patrol out of Henderson Field on Guadalcanal that would bring disaster to the Japanese Operation Seventy-three.

All day on 14 November, planes would zoom out of Henderson Field to hit Reinforcement Group Two. The continuous efforts of the marine, navy, and army aircraft would stop both Tanaka's transport group and Kondo's cruiser group.

At 1010 hours, the first planes left Henderson Field: six Avengers, eighteen Dauntlesses, and twelve Wildcats, two units. At 1150 Capt. Joe Sailer found Tanaka's convoy in the middle of The Slot between New Georgia and Santa Isabel. "Okay, boys," Sailer yelled into his TBS, "let's get 'em."

Twenty-four American aircraft streaked through a wall of antiaircraft fire in two waves. Twelve planes under Captain Sailer attacked transports *Canberra Maru* and *Nagara Maru*, and within seconds 1000-pound bombs and skimming torpedoes left both transports sinking. The next wave of aircraft, under Lt. Cmdr. James Lee, pounced on transport *Sado Maru*. Four torpedo hits shook the transport and started fires. By the time the American planes pulled away, *Canberra* and *Nagara* were settling under the surface of the sea, while Sado was listing and burning. Destroyers *Amagiri* and *Suzukaze* quickly jammed their decks with survivors, while *Amagari* headed north, escorting limping *Sado Maru* back to the Shortlands.

On the bridge of *Hayashio*, Cmdr. Tadashi Yamamoto stared in disbelief at the sudden destruction. "How can this be?"

"Another example of exaggerated claims," Admiral Tanaka answered bitterly.

"Perhaps we should retire, admiral," Yamamoto said.

"It is too late," Tanaka said. "We must continue on, maintain a smoke screen, and hope that fighter planes will arrive to protect us."

"Yes, admiral."

At 1245 hours, another unit of American Dauntlesses and Avengers reached the patch of sea to attack Tanaka's scattered convoy. The aircraft dropped a dozen 1000-pound bombs and loosened a half dozen torpedoes. Near misses ruptured the hull of two transports and two direct hits set afire *Shinanogawa Maru* and *Arizona Maru*. Two torpedoes hit the stern and starboard quarters of these two ships, leaving both transports listing and dead in the water.

Before repair crews could stem damage, B-17s under Col. LeVerne Saunders arrived over the convoy at 1400 hours. Within a minute, four bombs exploded on the decks of crippled *Shinanogawa* and *Arizona*, opening huge holes in the hull and starting flooding. Both marus quickly sank, taking most of the sailors and soldier passengers to the bottom with them.

Another B-17 1-ton bomb struck *Brisbane Maru* and ignited fires throughout her decks. American Fortress bombs also started fires aboard destroyer *Suzukaze*, already crammed with rescued troops and sailors. The destroyer was ordered back to the Shortlands.

Only a minute later, at 1401 hours, a flight of Avengers skimmed into the zigzagging *Naka Maru* and unleashed a spread of torpedoes that slammed into the aft and starboard quarters of the ship. When the smoke and debris cleared, the maru listed badly to starboard and began to sink.

Destroyers *Nagami, Makinami,* and *Michishio* hurried to the side of the three sinking maru transports and miraculously rescued most of the sailors and Thirty-eighth Division soldiers aboard the doomed *Shinanogawa, Arizona,* and *Naka.*

The battered Reinforcement Group Two enjoyed a mere hour and a half of respite, while a dozen Zeros arrived from carrier *Junyo* to cover the convoy. But at 1530 hours, eight Dauntlesses and twelve Wildcats arrived from *Enterprise* to hit the transports. Admiral Kinkaid had decided to "shoot the works," clearing his decks of all planes. The USS *Enterprise* Dauntlesses dropped sixteen 500-pound bombs. Two hit destroyer *Takanami* and started fires on the forward deck. Another bomb near missed flagship *Hayashio* and flooded a boiler room. The Zeros tried to intercept the Dauntlesses but the Wildcat escort pilots successfully knocked two of the Mitsubishis out of the air and drove off the rest. The American planes returned unscathed to Henderson Field, where they joined the rest of the Buzzard Patrol.

Meanwhile, a squadron of Zeros, twenty planes, had come down from carrier *Junyo* to give more cover to the battered convoy. They were circling at 18,000 feet when at about the same 1530 hours, the next swarm of Dauntlesses and Avengers from the American Buzzard Patrol reached the convoy with a dozen Wildcat escorts.

"There's a lot of Zekes upstairs," Major Richards radioed Captain Foss. "Can you handle them?"

"You get the fat cats," Foss answered. "We'll take care of the bandits."

And, while Captain Foss and his fighter pilots engaged the Zeros in a blistering dogfight, Major Richards led his Dauntlesses and Avengers of MAG 142 into the Japanese convoy. Despite a heavy curtain of ack-ack fire, the American planes scored several hits on the escorting destroyers and two near fatal hits on already damaged *Brisbane Maru*. Fires suddenly whooshed along the deck of the transport and the jammed soldiers and sailors scurried about the ship seeking safety.

By the time the American bombers zoomed away, Capt. Joe Foss and his fighter pilots had knocked eleven of the Zeros out of the air to a loss of three Wildcats. The surviving Zeros scurried back to carrier *Junyo*.

When the planes had gone and the smoke screen had lifted, Admiral Tanaka and Cmdr. Yamamoto stared in awe at the holocaust around them: burning, listing transports, battered topsides on two destroyers, men jumping overboard, and others floundering in a patch of flotsam-covered sea.

Then, at 1535 hours, came the last attack from the Buzzard Patrol. Lt. Cmdr. James Lee led a unit of Avengers, under escort by the P-40s and P-38s of the Sixty-seventh Army Fighter Squadron, into the convoy. Lee skimmed towards listing *Brisbane Maru* where he and his pilots scored four torpedo hits that blasted open the hull. The 7,000-ton transport quickly listed and began to sink, prompting hundreds of sailors and soldier passengers to scramble over the side and into the sea. For good measure, the P-40s and P-38s strafed the decks to hasten *Brisbane*'s plunge to the bottom of The Slot.

By late evening of the fourteenth, Adm. Raizo Tanaka limped into Cape Esperance with his four surviving transports and the remaining destroyers to unload whatever men and supplies he could. Meanwhile, Adm. Thomas Kinkaid's TG 16, with battleships *South Dakota* and *Washington*, had reached Sealark Channel shortly after midnight, 15 November. At the same hour, Adm. Nobutake Kondo had arrived in the channel with his five surviving cruisers, six destroyers, and the battleship *Kirishima*. The two fleets opened fire on each other a few miles south of Savo Island. Battleship shells exploded on the surface of Ironbottom like monstrous meteors. The one hour engagement sent *Kirishima* and a Japanese destroyer to the bottom, while Kinkaid lost four destroyers, suffered heavy damage to battleship *South Dakota*, and moderate damage to battleship *Washington*.

Admiral Kondo had really fared best in this second sea fight at night in two days. But, the Japanese had lost their appetite for battle after the bloody Friday donnybrook and the stunning air attacks by the Buzzard Patrol. Admiral Kondo simply retired his fleet up The Slot.

Of course, this nighttime battleship engagement in the early hours of 15 November 1942 was really anti-climactic. The failure of Admiral Abe to bombard Henderson Field on 13 November because of TG 67.4's efforts and the subsequent air attacks on Tanaka's transports had settled the issue.

At 0700 hours, 15 November 1942, flights of Avengers and Dauntlesses of the Buzzard Patrol appeared once more over Cape Esperance. Major Bob Richards and his pilots needed but a few minutes to utterly destroy Tanaka's remaining four transports with bombs and torpedoes. The planes also destroyed or set afire hundreds of tons of supplies stacked on the shoreline. By the time the American planes zoomed away, all four Japanese maru transports lay burning or sunk off the Cape Esperance beaches.

Cmdr. Tadashi Yamamoto could not believe that such a tragedy could befall sly Tanaka the Tenacious.

"It is over; we are lost," Admiral Tanaka softly told his aide.

Tanaka had accurately recognized the total failure of Operation Seventy-three. Less than 2,000 of the Thirty-eighth Division troops had landed on Guadalcanal, and only five tons of supplies, that included 1500 bags of rice and a mere 260 cases of ammunition. Gen. Kiyotake Kawaguchi would have little help to reinforce his ground troops. Conversely, the Americans successfully concluded Operation Orange when Adm. Richmond Turner returned to Lunga Point and unloaded the remainder of his American troops and hundreds of tons of arms and supplies.

More than 10,000 sailors from both sides died in the vicious Bloody Friday battle off Guadalcanal, most of them during the thirty minutes of action between Abe's Raiding Force Two and Callaghan's TG 67.4. The Japanese lost two battleships, a cruiser, three destroyers and ten maru transports. They had also lost nearly 100 planes between the Eleventh Bomb Group attack on Buin and their dogfights with Capt. Joe Foss and his Wildcat fighter pilots. The Americans lost two cruisers and seven destroyers, along with twenty-seven aircraft on the ground at Henderson Field and in the air over Tanaka's Reinforcement Group Two convoy.

And there were heroes and goats on both sides.

When the crippled Operation Seventy-three fleet reached Truk, Capt. Tameichi Hara and Capt. Masakane Suzuki received hero's welcomes for their efforts during the heavy night action. The commanders of Desron 10 and cruiser *Nagara* had administered almost half the damage on the 67.4 American fleet.

Tameichi Hara continued to lead Japanese squadrons throughout the war, finally leading a cruiser division. Hara's last engagement came in April of 1945 when he joined a Japanese suicide fleet that attempted to stop the American landings at Okinawa. Nearly 400 American carrier planes destroyed the convoy, including the mighty battleship *Yamato*, Hara's cruiser *Yahigi*, and several Japanese destroyers.

"We lost 3500 brave sailors that day," Captain Hara said later. "I floundered in the water, hanging on to a piece of driftwood with a fellow sailor. I expected to perish and I took consolation in the Song of the Samurai:

If I go to sea, I shall return a corpse awash,
   Thus for the sake of the Emperor
I shall not die peacefully at home."

But destroyer *Hatsushima* rescued Tameichi Hara and after the war he became an executive for a Japanese shipping firm.

Capt. Masakane Suzuki, shortly after the Bloody Friday battle of Guadalcanal, became an admiral. He led Japanese cruiser divisions for another year until he was badly wounded during the Battle of Kolombangara and his cruiser *Jintsu* went down with almost all hands. A destroyer rescued Suzuki and the admiral returned to Japan to command Crudiv Ten. In May of 1945, he became a vice admiral and directed the hydrograph bureau until war's end and retirement.

Adm. Nokutabe Kondo won praise from Adm. Isoroku Yamamoto for his determination to bombard Henderson Field at all costs and he received a new command. He continued to lead

Japanese cruiser divisions to war's end.

On the debit side, both Adm. Hiroaki Abe and Capt. Masao Nashida received severe reprimands from a court of inquiry for losing battleship *Hiei*, as if either of them had any control over the events that destroyed *Hiei*. But perhaps the inquiry board took stock in Captain Hara's scathing letter of protest to Admiral Yamamoto, in which Hara accused Abe of quitting the fight when victory was in their hands. Yamamoto did not court martial Hara for his criticism of a flag commander, but instead praised him for his concern.

The court "retired" both Abe and Nashida, almost the equivalent of an American dishonorable discharge. However, both officers were given pensions. Admiral Abe retired to his quiet village of Kamakura, north of Tokyo, where he lived quietly with his wife until his death in 1962. Captain Nashida returned to Tokyo and a civilian desk job which he held until the end of the war.

The heavy losses on both sides in this action left Admiral Isoroku Yamamoto full of remorse. He composed a Haiku poem to dedicate the Bloody Friday action on Ironbottom Sound:

> "I mourn the many sacrifices;
>    Beneath the moon
> Stretches a sea at whose bottom
>    Lie many ships."

Yamamoto himself, of course, lost his life when American P-38 pilots, on 18 April 1943, shot down a converted Betty bomber that was carrying the admiral to Bougainville. Japan still honors Yamamoto today and historians consider him one of the world's most noted military strategists.

To the credit of every Japanese officer and enlisted sailor in this naval battle off Guadalcanal, not one of them ever came under suspicion as a war criminal.

For the Americans, both Adm. Daniel Callaghan and Adm. Norman Scott received posthumous Congressional Medals of Honor: "For extraordinary achievement and conspicuous intrepidity above and beyond the call of duty against an enemy force off Salvo Island on the night of 12-13 November 1942." Lt. Cmdr. Ed Parker of USS *Cushing* received a Gold Star in lieu of a third Navy Cross for "Extraordinary achievement on the night of 12-13 November 1942." Parker rose to vice admiral and remained in the U.S. Navy until retirement in 1963.

Lt. Cmdr. Herb Shonland won the Navy Cross for "Conspicious gallantry and intrepidity as damage control officer of *San Francisco* on 13 November 1942." Unlike some of the others, Shonland left the navy after the war and he returned to private business in his native Nebraska.

The flyers of the Buzzard Patrol, Maj. Robert Richards, Cmdr. James Lee, and a host of others won Navy Crosses or Distinguished Flying Crosses for their continual two day effort to disperse the Main Attack Group and to destroy Tanaka's Reinforcement Two convoy.

The cornfed Joe Foss would shoot down twenty-six Japanese planes before he returned to the United States in February of 1943. For his efforts in the Solomons campaign, he became a third winner of a Congressional Medal of Honor for his courage in the naval battle off Guadalcanal.

Capt. Joe Sailer was the fourth American to win a Congressional Medal of Honor in the Friday the thirteenth melee. However, he never lived to receive it personally. On 7 December 1942, on the anniversary date of Pearl Harbor, Sailer led a flight of Dauntlesses against a Tokyo Express. Zero fighter planes shot down his bomber and he plunged into Ironbottom Sound to his death.

The fifth Congressional Medal of Honor winner for the Bloody Friday brawl off Guadalcanal was Cmdr. Bruce McCandles. The citation read:

"In the midst of violent night action, the fire of a desperate enemy seriously wounded Commander McCandles and rendered him unconscious; killed or wounded the admiral and his staff, the captain of the ship, the navigator, and all other personnel on the bridge. Faced with a lack of superior command upon his recovery, and displaying superb initiative, he promptly assumed command of the ship and ordered her course and gunfire against an over-whelmingly powerful enemy force. With his superiors in other vessels unaware of the loss of their admiral, and challenged by his great responsibility, Commander McCandles boldly continued to engage the enemy and to lead our column of following vessels to a great victory. Largely through his brilliant seamanship and great courage, the *San Francisco* was brought back to port and saved to fight another day."

McCandles later commanded destroyer USS *Gregory* during the battle of Okinawa where McCandles won a Silver Star for "Conspicious gallantry and intrepidity in action against the enemy in the vicinity of Okinawa between 1 April and 8 April 1945."

Bruce McCandles rose to the rank of admiral and retired in May of 1952. He died in Washington in 1968 at age fifty-six from multiple sclerosis.

On the debit side, Adm. Bill Halsey reprimanded Capt. Gilbert Hoover and relieved him of command, calling incredible Hoover's decision to abandon the *Juneau* survivors. Halsey agreed with a subordinate who said Hoover could at least have left a destroyer behind to pick up survivors. Halsey also criticized Task One port headquarters at Tulagi, because they delayed rescue of American sailors floundering in Ironbottom after the vicious night action. "The efforts of rescue teams was shocking," Halsey said later. "They allowed dozens of sailors to perish in a mere twenty mile width of Sealark Channel, where we controlled the coastline on both sides. Rescue boats should have gone after survivors the moment they got word of ship abandonments."

Thus, surprisingly, while the Americans' sluggish resuce efforts had cost dozens of lives, the Japanese rescued almost every soldier and sailor who went overboard. In fact, the Japanese had retrieved over 10,000 men of the Hiroshima Division alone, although few of them reached Guadalcanal.

The naval battle off Guadalcanal, or The Third Battle of Savo Island as the Japanese called it, became a fork in the road that favored the Americans.

Still, Tanaka the Tenacious would frustrate the Americans one more time. In the first week of February, 1943, Adm. Raizo Tanaka, under the very noses of American scout planes, successfully evacuated Gen. Kiyotake Kawaguchi and 11,706 men from Guadalcanal in several successful Tokyo Express runs.

Adm. Chester Nimitz said later: "Only Admiral Tanaka's skill in keeping his plans disguised, and his bold celerity in carrying them out, enabled the Japanese to withdraw the remnants of their Guadalcanal garrison."

But, Tanaka's cunning was in a defeated cause. With the Japanese evacuation of Guadalcanal, the vital supply line between the United States and Australia became safe and secure.

The Solomons campaign brought untold hardships and death to thousands of young Americans before the Japanese finally quit King Solomon's Isles. Was such agony on the humid, rancid islands worth the price?

When the Melanesian populace of the Solomon Islands received their freedom from England in 1978, many nations sent delegations to the independence ceremonies in Honiara on Malatia Island. As these delegations from thirty nations marched by the reviewing stand, they received protocol applause from the crowd. The American delegation consisted of a mere two sailors carrying the American flag. As they passed the reviewing stand, the Melanesians gave them a standing ovation that lasted for more than an hour and all but disrupted the ceremonies.

One of the two sailors stared for a moment at Ironbottom Sound beyond Honiara, the Sealark Channel that had been the graveyard of hundreds of U.S. bluejackets. "I guess this is one place where they still appreciate the American sacrifice in World War II," the American sailor told his companion.

True! The Melanesian natives of the Solomons are among the few people who at this late date still remember and love the United States for what American combat troops did for them in World War II.

# Bibliography

Books:

Blair, Clay. *Silent Victory*, Volume 1. J. P. Lippincott, Philadelphia, 1975.

Coggin, Jack. *The Campaign for Guadalcanal*. Doubleday & Co., Garden City, 1972.

Craven, Frank Wesley and James L. Gate. *The Army Air Forces in World War II*. Vol. 4, "The Pacific, Guadalcanal to Saipan." U. of Chicago Press, 1964.

Griffith, General Samuel B. *The Battle for Guadalcanal*. J. P. Lippincott, Philadelphia, 1963.

Harrington, Joseph D. *I-Boat Captain*. Major Books, Canoga Park, California, 1976.

Jablonski, Edward. *Air War, Outraged Skies*. Vol. 2. Doubleday and Co., 1971.

———*Flying Fortress*. Doubleday and Co., Garden City, L. I., 1965.

Miller, John Jr. *U.S. Army Forces in World War II*. Vol. II. *Guadalcanal, the First Offensive*. Chapt. 7, "Decision at Sea". Office of Military History, Washington, DC.

Morison, Samuel E. *The Struggle for Guadalcanal*. Little Brown & Co, Boston, 1964.

———*The Two Ocean War*. Little, Brown and Co., Boston 1963.

Pineau, Roger. *Japanese Destroyer Captain*, "As told by Tameichi Hara". Ballentine Books, New York City, 1961.

Poleston, Captain W. D. *Sea Power in World War II*. Chapt. 3, "The Solomons and Aleutians". Yale U. Press, New Haven, Conn., 1947.

Pratt, Fletcher. *The Marines' War*. New York City, Sloan Associates, 1949.

Reisenberg, Felix. *Sea War—The Story of the Merchant Marine in World War II*. Chapt. 2, "Pacific Lifeline". Rinehart & Co., New York City, 1956.

Shanenthe, Ted. *Heroes of the Pacific*. Chapt. 4, "The San Francisco" and Chapt. 5, "Cornfed Ace—Captain Joe Foss". Julian Messner, New York City, 1944.

Tregaskis, Richard. *Guadalcanal Diary*. Random House,

New York City, 1943.

Watts, Anthony. *Japanese Warships of World War II*. Ian Allen Ltd., London, 1966.

Wolfert, Ira. *Battle for the Solomons*. Houghton Mifflin, Boston, 1943.

Zimmerman, Major John L. *The Guadalcanal Campaign*. Historical Archives Division, Headquarters, USMC, Washington, DC.

National Archives:

Washington, DC. Naval Historical Center, Washington Navy Yard.

Reel #NRS, 1973-42, Battle of Guadalcanal, 11-15 November 1942.

Action Reports:

ComDesdiv (*Cushing*) (no serial #), 15 Nov. 1942.

*LAFFEY*, (no serial #) 14 Nov. 1942.

*O'BANNON*, Ser. #0134, 17 Nov. 1942.

*STERETT*, Ser. #005, 20 Nov. 1942.

*HELENA* (including *JUNEAU*), Ser. #008, 15 Nov. 1942. (Lt. Roger W. O'Neil USNR).

*PORTLAND*, Ser. #073, 21 Nov. 1942.

*FLETCHER*, Ser. #S-1, 15 Nov. 1942.

ComDESRON 12 (*AARON WARD*), Ser. #0033, 27 Nov. 1942.

*BARTON*, (no serial #), 26 Nov. 1942.

*SAN FRANCISCO*, Ser. #067, 16 Nov. 1942.

*AARON WARD*, Ser. #007, 30 Dec. 1942 and Ser. #003, 20 Nov. 1942.

*MONSSEN* (no serial #), 12 Nov. 1942.

VB 10 (Ens. J.H. Carroum USNR) Ser. #82, 4 Nov. 1942.

Reel #1976-22, Reports Relating to Battle of Guadalcanal, 11-15 Nov. 1942.

Action Reports:

CINCPAC, Ser. #03772, 25 Dec. 1942.

CINCPAC, Ser. #03763, 24 Dec. 1942.

McCAWLEY, Ser. #023, 23 Nov. 1942.

Navy Record Documents:

Commander Task Force 16. Ser. #0032, Operation Order #1-42, Operation Watchtower, 28 July 1942.

Halsey, William F. Admiral. "Narrative Account of the South Pacific Campaign, 20 April 1945 to 15 June 1944." Navy History Division, SSUSA.

Report of Operations of Task Force 67 and Task Force 62.4. Reinforcement of Guadalcanal, 8–15 Nov. 1942, and summary of Third Battle of Savo Island (renamed Battle of Guadalcanal), Ser. #00469.

Report of Operation for the Reinforcement of Guadalcanal Island by 7th Marines. Ser. #00195, 27 Sept. 1942.

Naval History Biographies:
Callaghan, Daniel Rear Admiral, USN, (deceased).
McCandles, Bruce Rear Admiral, USN, (deceased).
Parker, Edward N. Vice Admiral, USN, (retired).
Scott, Norman Rear Admiral, USN (deceased).
Shonland, H.E. Captain, USN (retired).
Japanese Flag officers;
Abe, Hiroaki Admiral. Trans. #202, 5 June 1945.
Kimura, Susumu Admiral. Trans. #204, 5 June 1945.

ATIS Documents (Allied Translator and Interpretation Section of Japanese Reports):
Note: Japanese referred to this engagement as "Third Battle of Savo Island"
US NAVY:
#15931, prepared by Lt. Cmdr. Henry Solomon, "Third Battle of Savo Island."
#851-100, prepared by Lt. Roger Pineau, "Southwest Pacific Naval Operation #1."
02    #161-709, Lt. Roger Pineau, "Atis Board of Ment Report.
#0268, prepared by Lt. Roger Pineau, "War Diary, 8th Fleet, Advance Force Battle Report No. 12."
#065, S-063, translator, Lt. Cmdr. Henry Solomon, "Report of *KINUGASA* Sinking."
#1-141, Atis Report, interrogation of Lt. Cmdr. Horishi Yokono, *HIEI* fire control officer.
#1-418, Atis Report, interrogation of Cmdr. Tadashi Yamamoto, communications officer to Adm. Raizo Tanaka.
U.S. MARINES: American Division Records, inter-

rogation of 17th Army officers

Lt. Gen. Harukichi Hyakutaka, former CG, 17th Army.

Maj. Gen. Shuicho Miyazaki, former Chief of Staff, 17th Army.

Col. Shigetaka Obara, former commander of 29th Infantry.

Col. Yoshitsugu Sakai, former commander of 16th Infantry.

Maj. Gen. Harukazu Tamaki, former Chief of Staff, 2nd Division.

Annapolis, Md. U.S. Naval Institute Documents, accounts of Japanese naval officers:

Hara, Tameichi, Captain, Commander of Desron 10, "The Tokyo Express."

Ohmae, T., Captain, Admiral Isoroku Yamamoto's Chief of Staff, "Third Battle of Savo Island."

Tanaka, Raizo, Admiral, "The Battle for Guadalcanal."

## PHOTOGRAPHS AND CHARTS:

Washington, D.C. U.S. Navy Photographic Center.

Washington, D.C. U.S. Marine Corps Photo Center.

U.S. Army Map Service

The author wishes to extend his personal thanks to Mr. D.C. Allard, head of Naval Historical Center's Operational Archives Branch for all his help in aiding me to compile information for this book, Operation Friday The 13th.

## NAVAL BATTLE OFF GUADALCANAL
### 12–15 November 1942

### American Units and Participants

COMSOPAC: Noumea, New Caledonia, Adm. William Halsey, Commander in Chief.

Task Force 67—Adm. Richmond Turner

TG 67.4 Support Group, Adm. Daniel Callaghan.
  Cruisers: *San Francisco, Portland, Helena, Juneau.*
  Destroyers: *Cushing, Laffey, Sterett, O'Bannon, Barton, Monssen.*
TG 62.4 Support Group, Adm. Norman Scott.
  Cruisers: *Atlanta.*
  Destroyers: *Aaron Ward, Fletcher.*
TG 67.1 Transport Group, Adm. Richmond Turner.
  AKA transports: *Betelgeuse, Libra, Zeilin.*
  Troop Transports: *McCawley, Crescent City, President Adams, President Jackson.*
Task Force 16—Adm. Thomas Kinkaid
  Carriers: USS *Enterprise* (VBD-10, Lt. Cmdr. James Lee; VF-8, Lt. C. Franklin).
  Battleships: *South Dakota, Washington.*
Task Force 63—Land-based Aircraft, Adm. Aubrey Fitch
  Henderson Field, "Buzzard Patrol"
    Marine Air Group 142, Major R. H. Richards.
    132 VBD, Dauntlesses, Maj. Joe Sailer.
    131 TBF, Avengers, Capt. Jens Aggerbeck.
    121 VFS, Wildcats, Capt. Joe Foss.
    67th Army Fighter Group, Capt. Daile Brannon.
  Espiritu Sancto, heavy army air force B-17s.
    11th Bomb Group, Col. LeVerne Saunders.

Ground Units, Guadalcanal
  American Division, Gen. Alex Patch.
  Reinforcement Group, 182, 4th, and 2nd Regiments plus support groups, Gen. Alex Vandegrift.

## Special American Participants

USS *San Francisco*
  Young, Cassin, Captain, commander.
  McCandles, Bruce, Commander, communications officer.
  Shonland, Herbert, Lt. Cmdr., damage control officer.

Ross, Don, Lt. Cmdr., gunnery officer.

Arison, Rae, Cmdr., navigation officer.

USS *Cushing*

Parker, Ed, Lt. Cmdr., commander.

Stokes, Tom, Lt., executive officer.

USS *Fletcher*

Cole, William, Commander.


## Japanese Units and Participants

8th Area Forces, Rabaul, New Britain, Gen. Hitoshi Imamura

17th Army, Rabaul, Gen. Harukuchi Hyakutake

Japanese Combined Fleet, Truk Islands, Adm. Isoroku Yamamoto.

8th Japanese Fleet, Adm. Gunichi Mikawa

Raiding Force II, Adm. Hiroaki Abe

Battleships: *Hiei, Kirishima*.

Cruiser: *Nagara*.

Destroyers: *Amatsukaze, Yukikaze, Akatsuki, Ikazuchi, Inazuma, Teruzuki, Asugumo, Marasame, Yudachi, Harusame, Samidare*.

Main Attack Group, Adm. Nobutake Kondo

Crudiv 4, Adm. Kondo

Cruisers: *Chokai, Kinugasa, Maya*.

Destroyers: *Asashio, Arashio*.

Crudiv 7, Capt. Shoji Nishimura

Cruisers: *Suzuya, Tenryu, Isuzu*.

Destroyers: *Makigumo, Yugumo, Kazagumo, Michishio*.

Reinforcement Group II, Admiral Raizo Tanaka.

Destroyers: *Hayashio, Oyashio, Kagero, Umikaze, Kawakaze, Suzikaze, Takanami, Makinami, Nagami, Amagiri, Mochizuka*.

Transport marus: *Arizona, Kumagawa, Sado, Nagara, Nako, Canberra, Brisbane, Shinanogawa, Hirokawa, Yamaura, Yamatsuki*.

Support Group II, Adm. Gunichi Mikawa.

Carriers: *Junyo, Hiyo*.

Battleships: *Kongo, Buruna*.

11th Air Fleet, Rabaul, New Britain, Adm. Jinichi Kusaka

25th Air Flotilla, Rabaul, Adm. Kusaka
26th Air Flotilla, Buin, Bougainville, Captain Hideo
Shoji.

## Special Japanese Participants

Battleship *Hiei*:
Nashida, Masao, Captain, commander.
Kimura, Susumu, Captain, chief aide.
Sekino, Hideo, Cmdr., gunnery officer.
Yukumo, Horishi, Cmdr., fire control officer.
Destroyer *Amatsukaze*:
Hara, Tameichi, Captain, commander Desron 10.
Matsumoto, Kijuro, Lt., pilot.
Shimizu, Dima, Lt., gunnery officer.
Iwata, Shigeru, W/O, communications officer.
Destroyer *Hayashio*:
Tanaka, Raizo, Admiral, commander.
Yamamoto, Tadashi, Cmdr., communications officer.
Ground Units: Guadalcanal
Ichiki Detachment, Col. Kiyonao Ichiki.
24th Infantry Division, Gen. Kiyotaki Kawaguchi.
38th Hiroshima Division, Gen. Tadayoshi Sano.